"IF A GREAT MUSICIAN
PLAYS GREAT MUSIC BUT NO ONE
HEARS . . . WAS HE REALLY
ANY GOOD?"

ALSO BY GENE WEINGARTEN

Old Dogs

I'm with Stupid (with Gina Barreca)

The Hypochondriac's Guide to Life. And Death.

The Fiddler in the Subway

THE TRUE STORY OF WHAT
HAPPENED WHEN A WORLD-CLASS
VIOLINIST PLAYED FOR HANDOUTS
. . . AND OTHER VIRTUOSO
PERFORMANCES BY AMERICA'S
FOREMOST FEATURE WRITER

GENE WEINGARTEN

SIMON & SCHUSTER PAPERBACKS
NEW YORK   LONDON   TORONTO   SYDNEY

Simon & Schuster Paperbacks
A Division of Simon & Schuster, Inc.
1230 Avenue of the Americas
New York, NY 10020

First Simon & Schuster trade paperback edition July 2010

SIMON & SCHUSTER PAPERBACKS and colophon are registered trademarks of Simon & Schuster, Inc.

For information about special discounts for bulk purchases, please contact Simon & Schuster Special Sales at 1-866-506-1949 or business@simonandschuster.com.

The Simon & Schuster Speakers Bureau can bring authors to your live event. For more information or to book an event, contact the Simon & Schuster Speakers Bureau at 1-866-248-3049 or visit our website at www.simonspeakers.com.

Designed by Davina Mock-Maniscalco

Manufactured in the United States of America

10   9   8   7   6   5   4   3   2   1

Library of Congress Cataloging-in-Publication Data

Weingarten, Gene.
    The fiddler in the subway/Gene Weingarten.
        p.   cm.
    1. American wit and humor. I. Title.
    PN6165.W385 2010
    818'.5407—dc22   2009051668
ISBN 978-1-4391-8159-1
ISBN 978-1-4391-8160-7 (ebook)

Art reprinted by permission of Universal Uclick: Doonesbury © (2004) G. B. Trudeau (pp. 236 top and bottom, and p. 242); Doonesbury © (2006) G. B. Trudeau (pp. 245, 252, and 259). The photograph on p. 158 is courtesy of the author.

Acknowledgments

All the stories in this collection are published by permission of the *Washington Post,* where they first appeared. My gratitude goes beyond this small kindness; I am indebted to the newspaper's publisher and editors for their support of fierce journalism, for their leadership, and, all too many times, for their forbearance.

I want to thank the people who taught me to write, and to apologize for any plagiarism that may have semi-inadvertently weaseled into my words over the years: Edward Albee, Dave Barry, Mike Bassett, Meyer Berger, Homer Bigart, Madeleine Blais, Margaret Wise Brown, Michael Browning, John Dickson Carr, Raymond Chandler, Agatha Christie, Charles Dickens, "Franklin W. Dixon," Arthur Conan Doyle, Will Elder, Piet Hein, Crockett Johnson, Franz Kafka, Tom Lehrer, the *New York Daily News* headline writers from 1958 to 1972, Edgar Allan Poe, Rod Serling, Dr. Seuss, Rex Stout, Bill Watterson, and Ruth S. Weingarten.

Dozens of talented copy editors made my prose presentable; if I try to name them all, I will forget some. Ably standing in for all of them here will be Pat Myers, the world's funniest copy editor and America's greatest backstop. She is the Johnny Bench of journalism.

A newspaper's librarians make its writers seem omniscient. We are not; we just have the best librarians in the business. I thank them all.

A good journalist knows when something you've written stinks; a good friend will actually tell you. These people are both: Tom Scocca, David Von Drehle, and Hank Stuever. On countless occasions they have saved me from myself.

And finally, even though his thumbprint is on nearly every page, this is the only place in the book that you will see the name Tom Shroder. That is exactly as it should be. Tom is an editor; his work, by its nature, is occult. The relationship between a writer and his editor is sacrosanct—as private and privileged as that between doctor and patient, lawyer and client, priest and penitent. Tragically, because of this sacred principle I cannot ethically reveal just how much of this book is Tom Shroder's doing, just how much credit he deserves. Whew.

Contents

The Fiddler
in the
Subway

Introduction

I WAS DRUNK THE night I learned to write. It was the end of a
bad day at work, which was at *The Detroit Free Press,* where
I was a reporter.

This was 1978. I was twenty-seven. For weeks, I'd been
hanging out at the Detroit Wastewater Treatment Plant, the city's
chronically mismanaged sewage facility. What I had seen there,
in a word, stank. There was plenty of sewage but not much treatment. The equipment was obsolete, the bosses were inept, the
workers were poorly trained. Instead of turning raw sewage into
clean water, the plant was scooping it up, pouring it into vats,
performing abracadabra alchemy over it, and then pumping it out
into Lake Erie insufficiently altered. At times it was brownish,
pungent, and unnervingly . . . lumpy.

On the afternoon of the night I would learn to write, I'd finished my reporting and had typed out the first paragraph of the
story. Like many young writers, I considered this an opportunity
to display the breadth of my vocabulary, the depth of my knowledge, and the extent of my importance. I wrote something like
this: "The Detroit Wastewater Treatment facility, long the bane of
environmental regulators, continues to be grievously plagued by a
thicket of problems involving underfunding and mismanagement,
and remains in flagrant violation of federal clean-water standards."

I proudly showed this to my editor, the great Hugh McDiarmid. Had I been describing Hugh at the time, I would have called him "crusty," but today I would avoid both the cliché and the understatement. Calling Hugh "crusty" would be like calling the Nazis "rude." It just doesn't capture the half of it.

Hugh read what I had written, then turned his back on me. "It's fine," he said, returning to his own work.

In reporter-editor patois, "fine" is a word sodden with contempt. It means "adequate." No writer wants to be told his work is "fine." "What's wrong with it?" I asked. Hugh didn't even turn around. "You've been coming back from that place every day, excited about how screwed up it is," he said. "Your anecdotes were funny. You were really pissed off on behalf of the public. Where'd all the passion go?"

I did not take this well. I went home and consoled myself with cheap tequila and eventually fell asleep in my own drool.

At some point during the bleak hours, I got up from my bed, staggered over to my portable typewriter, and banged out a new first paragraph. To this day, I don't remember doing it, but I know I must have because the words were on paper the next morning, and I'd slept the night alone. What I had written, with a few small revisions, became the new top of my story, which would win a national award. This was it:

"Every day, liquid sewage—three million tons of it from starting points across metro Detroit—roars through subterranean channels into a collecting point five miles down the road from the Renaissance Center, on West Jefferson. Then it hits the fan."

That night, I'd learned two lessons. The first is that without passion, you have nothing. The second is that the most important words in your story are the ones you don't write. They're the ones you imply—the ones that you cause to pop into the reader's mind and get her to think "Aha!" That's how you transform her from a passive observer into an ally. And that's when you win.

The meaning of life is that it ends.
—Franz Kafka

Kafka nailed it.
—Me

Not long after learning to write, I stopped doing it. The proximate cause was a desire to have sex on a regular basis with a particular woman, the one I would eventually marry. She happened to live not in Detroit but in New York, and the only good job I could get there was as an editor. There are worse reasons to make major life decisions.

I liked editing and kept at it for the next twenty years, which meant I had to learn to think extremely analytically about narrative writing: You can't tell a professional journalist that what he has done isn't good enough unless you are prepared to explain why. That requires a coherent philosophy. I had to find one.

After reading narrative works I admired and narrative works I didn't, I came to some important conclusions about what distinguished the first group from the second. This led me to adopt something of an eschatological approach to feature writing, which I codified into the Talk. I became famous for the Talk. Writers hated the Talk. I don't blame them.

The script seldom varied: The writer would tell me what his story was going to be about, and then I would explain to him, patiently, why he was wrong. Your story, I would say, is going to be about the meaning of life. This tended to take some people aback, particularly when their subject was something ostensibly small—say, the closing of a local amusement park. Usually, a Socratic dialogue would ensue:

"Well, what is an amusement park about?" I would ask.

"Fun."

"And why do people want to have fun?"

"To take their mind off their worries."

"And what are they worried about?"

You see where this is going. Pretty soon, through one route or another, we'd arrive at Kafka.

My method may have been obnoxious and condescending, but my point was on target: A feature story will never be better than pedestrian unless it can use the subject at hand to address a more universal truth. And, as it happens, big truths usually contain somewhere within them the specter of death. Death informs virtually all of literature. We lust and love so we can feel more alive. We build families so we can be immortal. We crave fame, and do good works, so both will outlive us. The Gods of our choosing promise eternity.

This is the big mystery of life, and any good narrative can be made to grapple with some piece of it, large or small. A writer has to figure out what that piece is before she can begin to report her story. Only then can she know what questions to ask and what things to notice; only then will she see how to test her thesis and how to change it if it is wrong.

That's what nonfiction storytelling is about. It is not enough for you to observe and report: You must also think.

Some lessons I learned by osmosis from the generously gifted writers whose work I stevedored into print over the years at the *Miami Herald* and the *Washington Post*. I learned that for a long narrative to have power, it can't just be delivering information— it needs to create a textured experience, the way a movie does. A writer hasn't the advantage of a mood-setting soundtrack, or actors who can communicate emotion with an expression or a gesture, but he has something of potentially greater impact: the descriptive power of words. Use them with care; arrange them shrewdly. Remember that sentences have cadence and meter and melody—don't let them become a one-note lullaby. Interrupt the long with the short, the simple with the complex, and use them all to build a vivid narrative, a theater of the mind that each reader then edits and personalizes for himself. It's a collaboration, this process. Don't take your new ally for granted. Don't bore her, even for an instant.

When I write now, I consciously structure my stories as though they were movies, with a hill-and-dale topography to keep the reader off-balance but interested. A section with scene and action and presence will usually be followed by a section of reflection and philosophy. Above all, each section will conclude to a purpose: maybe a cliffhanger, or a kick in the gut, or a slap-to-the-forehead revelation. You must get there honestly, so that the moment is earned. I never begin writing a section until I know how it is going to end.

I learned to write humor almost entirely from Dave Barry, whom I hired and then edited for years. Once, I impulsively asked Dave if there was any rhyme or reason to what he did, any writing rules that he followed. The question surprised both of us; he and I were never much for rules or strictures or limits or templates. Eventually, he decided yes, there was actually one modest principle that he'd adopted almost unconsciously: "I try to put the funniest word at the end of the sentence."

He's so right. I stole that principle from him, and have shamelessly made it my own. When asked today whether there are any good rules for writing humor, I say "Always try to put the funniest word at the end of your sentence underpants."

I hate writing. I love having written.

This is probably the most widely quoted line about being an author. It has been attributed to Dorothy Parker, Mark Twain, Eudora Welty, Neil Simon, Gloria Steinem, Joan Didion, Ernest Hemingway, and William Zinsser.

I'm happy to credit them all. And they were all correct, but only because they all did most of their writing in the era of the typewriter. Sadly, the "having written" part is now severely devalued. That's because it is now possible to assemble one's life's work in a single electronic file—as I have just done, for this anthology—and then, with a simple click of a mouse, answer one's own idle, innocent question, such as this one: "Gee, I like the adverb 'measuredly.' *I wonder how many times I've used it?*"

Note to other authors: I do not advise this exercise.

Most of the stories in this anthology were written after 1997. That's when I left my last editing job and returned to writing full-time at the *Washington Post*, filled with precepts I'd crammed into other people's heads, challenged now to do them on my own. I know that writers I had edited highhandedly were watching me, waiting for a pratfall. I'm sure I supplied a few.

Rereading this body of work is humbling: I see lines I wished I'd omitted and I long for the answers to some questions I wished I'd asked. But these are works of journalistic nonfiction, inextricable from the times in which they were written. Aside from correcting a couple of minor factual errors, recrafting a particularly inelegant phrase or two, and rectifying the appalling recurrence of "measuredly," I offer these stories exactly as I wrote them, for better or worse.

Aspiring feature writers often ask me to critique their work, wanting to know if I think they have talent. The manuscripts they enclose range from the hopeless to the promising, from the threadbare to the luxuriant. I always try to be honest without being cruel.

Lately their cover letters have been tinged with anxiety. We are in bewildering times for young people who want to make nonfiction writing their careers. Journalism jobs are scarce, and getting scarcer. I deliver the only solace I can, by telling them what I believe: The art of storytelling is as old as civilization. There will always be a hunger for it. Learn to do it well, and somehow, you will find a way to make it pay.

I tell the most fragile of them that being a good writer mostly means being a good observer and a good thinker, and that, with work, it's possible to triumph over a lack of innate writing skill. I use myself as an example; I believe I did exactly this.

There's one last truth that I don't tell them, because it's needlessly disturbing and would serve no pragmatic purpose. I'll say it now, just once, and be done with it. A real writer is someone for whom writing is a terrible ordeal. That is because he knows, deep down, with an awful clarity, that there are limitless ways to fill a page with words, and that he will never, ever, do it perfectly. On some level, that knowledge haunts him all the time. He will always be juggling words in his head, trying to get them closer to a tantalizing, unreachable ideal.

It's a torment you can't escape. It will reach even into the comfort of a drunken sleep, and it will shake you awake, and send you, heart pumping, to an empty piece of paper.

If you have that, you can be a good writer. Congratulations, I guess.

The Great Zucchini

Asking a writer which of his stories is his favorite is said to be like asking a parent which of his children he loves the most. The question is supposedly an impertinence, an unforgivable diplomatic misstep, an insult to the craft of storytelling and to the art of literature.

What a load of crap. This is my favorite.

January 22, 2006

T HE GREAT ZUCCHINI arrived early, as he is apt to do, and began to make demands, as is his custom. He was too warm, so he wanted the thermostat adjusted. It was. He declared the basement family room adequate for his needs, but there was a problem with the room next door. Something had to be done about it.

The room next door was emblematic of the extraordinary life and times of the Great Zucchini, Washington's preeminent preschool entertainer. The homeowners, Allison and Donald Cox, Jr., are in their late thirties, with two young children—Lauren, who is five, and Donald III, who goes by Trey, and whose third birthday was being celebrated that day.

Tall and handsome, Don is a federal government lawyer.

Short and pretty, Allison is an IT recruiter. Like most successful two-career couples who started a family later in life, the Coxes have resources to lavish on their children. When they bought this spacious Colonial in Bethesda, Maryland, the large area next to the family room was going to be Don's study. But it soon surrendered itself into a playroom—filled, floor to ceiling, with entertainment for the kids. A wall unit became a storage place for dolls, games, and action figures, all neatly partitioned and displayed like heirlooms. The floor is a warren of toys: There is a little girl's vanity and a tea table primly set with cups and saucers. For Trey, there is a ride-on choo-choo train. A fully functional mini moon bounce occupies one capacious corner. In another is a wall-mounted TV.

The Great Zucchini's problem? This room has no door. Its enticing contents were visible from the room where he would be performing, and the Great Zucchini tolerates no distractions. So he asked Allison to hang a bedsheet across the open archway, which meant making pushpin holes in the sheet and in the walls. Good-naturedly, Allison obeyed. Parents almost always do.

When the Great Zucchini arrived that Saturday morning, Don had no idea who he was. Frankly, he didn't look like a great anything. He looked like a house painter, Don thought, with some justification. The Great Zucchini wears no costume. He was in painter's pants, a coffee-stained shirt, and a two-day growth of beard. He toted his beat-up props in beat-up steamer trunks, with ripped faux leather and broken hinges hanging askew.

By the time the show began, more than a dozen kids were assembled on the floor. The Great Zucchini's first official act was to order the birthday boy out of the room, because—a little overwhelmed by the attention—Trey had begun to cry. "We'll retransition him back in," the Great Zucchini reassured Allison as she dutifully, if dubiously, whisked her son away.

At the back of the room, Carter Hertzberg, the father of a

party guest, was watching with frank interest. He'd heard about the Great Zucchini. "Supposedly," he explained dryly, "all the moms stand in the back and watch, because they think he's hot."

Many moms were, indeed, standing in the back. And—in a tousled, boyish, roguish, charmingly dissolute sort of way—the Great Zucchini is, indeed, hot. (Emboldened by a glass or three of party Beaujolais, moms have been known to playfully inquire of the Great Zucchini whether there is any particular reason he merits that nickname.)

At the moment, the Great Zucchini was trying and failing to blow up a balloon, letting it whap him in the face, hard. Then he poured water on his head. Then he produced what appeared to be a soiled diaper, wiped his cheek with it, and wore it like a hat as the kids ewwww-ed. Not to put too fine a point on it, but the Great Zucchini was behaving like a complete idiot.

Trey's aunt saw me taking notes. "You're writing a story about him?" Vicki Cox asked, amused. I confirmed that I was.

"But . . . why?" she asked.

A few feet away, the Great Zucchini was pretending to be afraid of his own hand.

"I mean," Vicki said, "what's the *hook*?"

Now the Great Zucchini was eating toilet paper.

"I mean, are you that desperate?" she asked.

On the floor in front of us, the kids—two-, three- and four-year-olds—were convulsed in laughter. Literally. They were rolling on the carpeted floor, holding their tummies, mouths agape, little teeth jubilantly bared, squealing with abandon. In the vernacular of stand-up, the Great Zucchini was killing. Among his victims was Trey, who, as promised, had indeed been retransitioned into his own party.

The show lasted thirty-five minutes, and when it was over, an initially skeptical Don Cox forked over a check without complaint. The fee was $300. It was the first of four shows the Great

Zucchini would do that Saturday, each at the same price. The following day, there were four more. This was a typical weekend.

Do the math, if you can handle the results. This unmarried, thirty-five-year-old community college dropout makes more than $100,000 a year, with a two-day workweek. Not bad for a complete idiot.

If you want to understand why the Great Zucchini has this kind of success, you need look no further than the stresses of suburban Washington parenting. The attendant brew of love, guilt, and toddler-set social pressures puts an arguably unrealistic value on someone with the skills, and the willingness, to control and delight a roistering roomful of preschoolers for a blessed half-hour.

That's the easy part. Here's the hard part: There are dozens of professional children's entertainers in the Washington area, but only one is as successful and intriguing, and as completely over-the-top preposterous, as the Great Zucchini. And if you want to know why that is—the hook, Vicki, the hook—it's going to take some time.

———

EVEN BEFORE THEY respond to a tickle, most babies will laugh at peekaboo. It's their first "joke." They are reacting to a sequence of events that begins with the presence of a familiar, comforting face. Then, suddenly, the face disappears, and you can read in the baby's expression momentary puzzlement and alarm. When the face suddenly reappears, everything is orderly in the baby's world again. Anxiety is banished, and the baby reacts with her very first laugh.

At its heart, laughter is a tool to triumph over fear. As we grow older, our senses of humor become more demanding and refined, but that basic, hard-wired reflex remains. We need it, because life is scary. Nature is heartless, people can be cruel, and death and suffering are inevitable and arbitrary. We learn to tame our terror by laughing at the absurdity of it all.

This point has been made by experts ranging from Richard Pryor to doctoral candidates writing tedious theses on the onto-logical basis of humor. Any joke, any amusing observation, can be deconstructed to fit. The seemingly benign Henny Youngman one-liner, "Take my wife . . . please!" relies in its heart on an un-derstanding that love can become a straitjacket. By laughing at that recognition, you are rising above it and blunting its power to disturb.

After the peekaboo age, but before the age of such sophisti-cated understanding, dwells the preschooler. His sense of humor is more than infantile but less than truly perceptive. He compre-hends irony but not sarcasm. He lacks knowledge but not feel-ing. The central fact of his world—and the central terror to be overcome—is his own powerlessness. This is where the Great Zucchini works his magic.

The Great Zucchini actually does magic tricks, but they are mostly dime-store novelty gags—false thumbs to hide a hand-kerchief, magic dust that turns water to gel—accompanied by sleight of hand so primitive your average eight-year-old would suss it out in an instant. That's one reason he has fashioned him-self a specialist in ages two to six. He behaves like no adult in these preschoolers' world, making himself the dim-witted victim of every gag. He thinks a banana is a telephone and answers it. He can't find the birthday boy when the birthday boy is standing right behind him. Every kid in the room is smarter than the Great Zucchini; he gives them that power over their anxieties.

The Great Zucchini's real name is Eric Knaus, and the last few analytical paragraphs will come as a surprise to him. Eric is intelligent, but he is almost aggressively reluctant to engage in self-analysis, even about his craft. What he knows is that he in-tuitively understands preschool kids, because he's had a lot of practice. He worked at Washington area preschools and day-care centers for more than a decade.

During a brief stint as a party host at the Discovery Zone in Rockville, Maryland, Eric discovered his ability to entertain as well as babysit. He was making $2 an hour, so tips were vital. And he found that the most substantial tips came when he acted dumb, serving up laughter along with the pizza.

Four years ago, he decided to go solo. It may have been the best decision he ever made. The Great Zucchini's clientele is mostly from affluent neighborhoods—Northwest Washington; Chevy Chase, Bethesda, and Potomac, Maryland; and Great Falls, McLean, and Arlington, Virginia. He's been to homes the size of small cathedrals and to parties where he was only one of several attractions, including cotton-candy and popcorn machines, lawn-size moon bounces, and petting-zoo sheep. Most famously, he did a party at the vice president's residence for a granddaughter of Dick and Lynne Cheney.

I first met the Great Zucchini at a location he chose, a coffee shop in White Flint Mall. "In the beginning, I had almost no clients," he said, "and I would sit at a table like this in a place like this, and if a mom would be walking by with her three-year-old, I would pretend to be talking on my cell phone. I'd say, 'Yeah, I do children's parties geared for three-year-olds!' And a lot of times, the mom would stop, and say . . . 'You do children's parties?'"

When he first started, he found out what other birthday party entertainers were charging—roughly $150 per show—and upped it by $25. That worked; it seemed to give him agency. After a while, his weekends were so crammed with parties— seven or eight, every weekend—he felt overwhelmed. So, applying fundamental principles of economics, he decided to thin his business but not his profits by raising his prices precipitously— from $175 to $300. It turns out that the fundamental principles of economics are no match for the fundamental desperation of suburban parents. He still was doing seven or eight shows a weekend.

Weekdays, he mostly haunts places like this, drinking coffee and tending to his cell phone. It rings a lot. It's ringing right now.

"Hello. Yes. Okay, sure, what date are you looking at?"

He flips open the tattered appointment book that is always with him. He's got dates penciled in as far into the future as October.

"I have nothing on the twelfth, but I can do the thirteenth at eleven o'clock. Okay, good. You've seen my show? Excellent. Sure, I remember Dylan's party. Dylan's got short hair, right? Oh. Well, I remember Dylan anyway. He's got two ears, right? This party is for . . . ? He is turning, what? Six, okay. Your name is . . . ? Okay. And the dad's name?"

He listens, wincing slightly at his own misstep.

"Okay, Dad's not invited. We don't feature Dad. Not a problem!"

RAISING CHILDREN HAS always been stressful, but these days it seems even more so, with single-parent families, two-career time pressures, and a bewildering explosion of diagnosed childhood developmental disabilities. Things are hard, even if you have a nice income and a nice house in a nice neighborhood. In some ways, that can make it even harder.

I first found out about the Great Zucchini through a friend of mine who lives in Northwest Washington. She gave up a high-prestige job to raise her four young children. Because her husband has a successful career, they can swing it, if not entirely comfortably. She doesn't want her name used because she has hired the Great Zucchini three times and, like many of the parents I interviewed for this story, is more than a little conflicted about it.

"It's an insane, indulgent thing to do," she said. "You could just have a party where you all played Pin the Tail on the Donkey or musical chairs or something. But that is just not done in this part of D.C. If you did that, you would be talked about.

"The whole thing has snowballed into levels of craziness, and it's just embarrassing to be a part of it. I would never tell my father about this. He grew up in Arkansas during the Depression. It would physically cause him pain to know what I spent on a child's party, for some guy to put a diaper on his head."

What's indisputable is that the kids love the guy with the diaper on his head. They talk about him all the time. They repeat his dumb jokes. They recognize him on the street.

They see him at their playmates' parties and ask for him at theirs. "The Great Zucchini," said my friend's husband, who deals professionally with Washington's power elite, "is the most famous person my children know."

It is crazy, and a little unseemly, and the Great Zucchini knows that. When he was a kid in Bethesda, he says, his own birthday parties consisted of a cake and touch football with friends in the back yard, and that was just fine.

Not that he's complaining about his good fortune, or bashful about discussing it. The Great Zucchini can elevate self-confidence to amusingly Olympian levels. "Why shouldn't I charge as much an hour as the best lawyer in town?" he asks. "I am the best children's entertainer in town." And: "David Copperfield couldn't keep these kids from running around wild. I can do that." And, when I noted that he relies on many of the same routines, time and again, he said: "When people come to see Springsteen, they don't want new stuff. They want to hear 'Glory Days.'"

His business plan? To become the children's entertainer to the stars, a star in his own right who is flown first-class to Beverly Hills to do parties at $5,000 a pop for Angelina Jolie's kids, or Britney's.

For all his swagger, Eric Knaus is instantly likable and effortlessly charming. He's got a hitch in his smile that says he's not taking himself all that seriously. His hair is moussed into an appealing, spiky mess, like Hobbes's pal, Calvin. He speaks with a gentle, liquid "l" that tends to put children at ease and seems to work with adults, too. And he is just stupendously great with kids, which is not an inconsiderable factor for a single mom looking for a mate, or a married mom with a single-mom friend whom she'd like to set up. It happens. Eric once had a romance with a single mother he met at a party, but he isn't entirely sure he'd do it again. When they broke up, the child was inconsolable.

Eric is aware that some of his party-time demands can seem obnoxious, but he insists they are reasonable. Very short people, he explains, have very short attention spans, which is why he is notorious for shushing parents who insist on talking during his show, even to the point of ordering them from the room. As he puts it, with characteristic grandiloquence: "I have the power. I've actually said, 'Do you want me to refund your money and leave?'" No parent has ever chosen that option, not with a roomful of kids sprawled on the carpet, giggly and expectant.

This has led to the occasional testy moment, particularly with one mother not long ago who not only balked at covering a picture window with a sheet but insisted on giving her child some macaroni during a show, in defiance of the Great Zucchini's inviolable no-eating rule. ("A choking hazard," he said. "He was hungry," she said.) She not only got a dressing down from the Great Zucchini at the party but a scolding letter afterward. "My husband threw it away," she said. "He didn't show it to me, because he knew it would really upset me."

This mom happens to be a high-profile attorney with a big-name law firm. Though the Web contains quotes from her on important public policy matters, you won't find her name in this story about a children's entertainer. She, too, insisted on anonymity. Some subjects are just too personally perilous. This lawyer-mother thoroughly dislikes the Great Zucchini and used a potentially litigable word to describe him.

So, is she sorry she hired him?

Pause.

"I have to say, he did a great job with the kids."

Both anonymous moms I talked to mentioned something curious. They were surprised that the Great Zucchini required payment in full, up front, the day the party was booked. He actually drove over, that day, to pick up their checks.

It was odd, they said—almost as if, for all his financial success, the Great Zucchini has cash-flow problems.

From the moment I met him, there were things that puzzled me about the Great Zucchini. Unless I drove him, for example, he relied on cabs to get to all of his gigs. He'd recently totaled his car, he explained, and hadn't gotten around to buying a new one. Besides, he said, he found cabs less restrictive.

Also, the Great Zucchini didn't seem to live anywhere. He had an address in Bethesda, but he would always want to meet at one Starbucks or another. Every time I proposed coming to his house some morning, he was staying elsewhere overnight. He seemed to crash everywhere but home.

His act was never fancy, but in recent months it had lost whatever frills it once had. On his Web site, the Great Zucchini is pictured at the White House Easter Egg Roll, where he once performed in a fancy black vest with cartoon smiley faces on it. He used to wear that vest to all his performances but lost it some time ago and has no plans to replace it.

He is more than a little disorganized. He lost a glowing-thumb trick, then found it, but it was broken, and he never got a new one. At one point, he lost his cell phone. When we were together, he often commandeered mine. Many of his magic props seem to be weathered to the point of decrepitude. His dirty diaper is years old. His magic bag with a false panel—a "change bag," in magicians' terms—is soiled and ripped. The once-orange sponge balls he palms for an illusion are brown with use. And there's that persistent, just-rolled-out-of-bed stubble. He didn't always have that.

Some parents I talked to were worried that the Great Zucchini might be rotting on the vine. Their guess was substance abuse, or something even darker.

This was understandable, but wrong. His demons turned out to be of a different species, more benign, perhaps, but also more interesting.

———

HAVE YOU EVER tried to peel a zucchini? It's not like a potato. The skin is pretty thick. You don't get it all with the first swipe.

Eric and I were in Arlington, at a fifth birthday party for a boy named Charlie. It was the first time the mother, Sarah Moore, had hired the Great Zucchini, and she had no complaints. He was everything she'd been told he'd be, she said, as she surveyed her postparty, preprandial dining room, aswarm with giddy kids.

"He's a big draw. You know, we wouldn't have gotten half this turnout with a moon bounce," Sarah said, completely seriously.

On our way to the party, Eric and I had been talking football, and I had said I thought the New York Giants would win their next game. He agreed but said they wouldn't beat the spread. I'd found that a little odd, and on our way back from the party I took a stab.

"You're a gambler," I said.

"I need a cigarette," he said.

We stopped for cigarettes. He took a long drag and smiled. It was as though he'd been waiting for this release for weeks.

"Look, I'm not Mister Rogers, okay?"

Eric definitely has cash-flow problems. They stem from the

fact that, for the last several years, the Great Zucchini has been in debt to bookies.

"I remember the first bet I ever made," he said. "I went to buy a voice-mail system for my phone, and was talking sports with the guy at the desk, and he asked if I bet with anybody. I made my first bet that day."

What followed, he said, was years of gambling, sometimes thousands of dollars a week, invariably more money than he could afford. He once went to Las Vegas on a Super Bowl Sunday and lost $100 before the game even began. He'd bet on the coin toss. Then he lost some more. Once, he went to Atlantic City, won more than $2,400, and then proceeded to lose it all, down to his last penny. He didn't have money for tolls on the way home and had to beg the tollbooth attendants for mercy.

When the phone rings, it's generally a mom or dad. But he always checks the number warily before answering, because sometimes it's a creditor. Court records show he has a $1,500 income-tax lien against him in Anne Arundel County, a debt he said he didn't even know about until I told him.

Anyway, he said, the worst is behind him. He decided some time ago that it's a no-win deal with sports bookies. "You get in a hole, and you can never get out," he said. He has stopped using bookies.

Good, I said.

Recently, he said, he's been doing most of his betting in off-shore sports casinos, over the phone.

Eric believes that his gambling helped end the best romantic relationship he ever had—one that might have led to marriage. This was a beautiful, funny, intelligent woman who, he said, chose him over a far more illustrious suitor, pro football quarterback Gus Frerotte. But in the end, by ignoring her needs, Eric chose gambling over her. "Gambling almost becomes your mistress," he said. "It grabs hold of your soul."

He knows he has a problem, he said, and he is planning on getting professional help. Lately, though, he said he's been making some progress on his own. "I've slowed down a lot," he said. "Let me tell you what I did on Sunday. I used to lay down two or three hundred on four or five different games. Well, I only bet a hundred dollars the whole day, which is a huge step up."

A few minutes passed. We talked about women, and how both of us love them. We talked about addictions, and how both of us have had them. And then, to cement our newfound openness, Eric proposed that, in a week or so, he and I take a road trip. To Atlantic City.

ERIC'S PERSONAL FRIENDSHIPS are strong and enduring. His closest friends are his oldest friends. Nights out are filled with drinking, bragging, and testosterone-laced one-upmanship. With a reporter present on two different Friday nights, it all turned into good-natured savagery, a pile-on, with Eric at the bottom of the pile.

Mike Conte, a seventh-grade math teacher, asked me if I'd seen Eric's apartment yet. Funny you mention it, I said, giving Eric a glance, but no.

"Listen to this," Mike said. "The guy gets an apartment, a big apartment, and all he has to put in it is a couch and a coffee table, right? That's all he's got in the whole place, right? So, then he gets some more money, and what do you think he buys next?"

Mike paused for dramatic effect.

"A bed, you think? No. An air hockey table."

Eric raised a hand and called out to the bartender. "Could I have a little dignity and self-esteem in a glass, please?"

On these nights, Eric tends to stick to Miller Lite. He has parties the next morning, and though he has missed, forgotten, and mislaid many other things in his life, he says he's never re-neged on a date with a roomful of expectant four-year-olds.

K. B. Bae, a financial adviser for Legg Mason who has been Eric's friend since childhood, told of the time the two of them were at a strip club, and Eric was taken with a certain dancer, who was both pretty and personable: "She seems to be taking a liking to him, talking to him between dances, and he's tipping like an idiot, not understanding what's going on. The next day, he says to me, 'Let's go back to that place.' Same thing happens. The third day, Eric reaches into his pocket, and he's got this glam photo of himself, and on the back he's written this really deep stuff, 'Is this chance, fate or love?' that sort of thing. And she's dancing naked onstage, right? And he goes up and tips her with the picture. She reads the back of it, and after that, she's no-where to be found, dude!"

Everyone laughed.

"When he goes into a house, his attitude is 'You're lucky to have me.' When I go into a house, my attitude is 'I'm happy to have the job.'"

This is Broccoli the Clown, né Jake Stern, who at fifty-seven has been a children's entertainer in the Washington area for twenty-seven years. He is one of the best. It was only recently that Jake saw a show by the Great Zucchini, when he met Eric to sell him some of his old magic props. Broccoli the Clown has seen a great many characters in his career, but nothing prepared him for the disheveled package of strut and gumption that is the Great Zucchini.

"At first, I was pissed. I was sitting there kicking myself. I have full clown gear and expensive equipment, and he's got this change bag with a broken handle and a bedsheet with jelly stains on it, and he's making more money than I am."

After a while, Broccoli the Clown realized he was focusing on the wrong thing. It wasn't about the props or the costumes.

"He's got an incredible rapport with the children. I've known guys in this business who are stiff as a board. To them, it's a job, and they're bitter. They hate what they do, and they can't relate to the children. This guy relates amazingly to kids. He understands and enjoys them."

The Great Zucchini doesn't know how to juggle. But he does a bit where he claims to be a great juggler, and then fails dreadfully, the balls bouncing every which way. The kids crack up. Jake Stern, on the other hand, teaches juggling. But after seeing Eric, he began to modify his act. Now he sometimes lets the balls bonk him in the head.

"If you want to call me the poor man's Great Zucchini," says Jake, "I don't mind. I really don't. Listen, I look into his eyes, and he's a good guy. I look into his eyes, and there's almost . . ."

Broccoli the Clown hesitates.

". . . there's something almost innocent there."

———————

ON THE TURNPIKE en route to Atlantic City, I was doing 80 mph when I whipped past a state trooper. He followed me into the next rest stop, lights flashing.

As we waited for the trooper to check my license, Eric said quietly, "You know, if I had been driving, I would have been in real trouble."

I smiled, relieved. "I know," I said. "Your court date is November twenty-first."

"How do you know that?"

"I ran your police records," I said.

For a moment, there was dead silence. Then: "So you didn't buy that I just really like to talk to cabdrivers, huh?"

The cop may have been 20 feet behind us, but I suspect he

wondered why two guys he'd just pulled over for speeding were busting a gut laughing.

———————

THE GREAT ZUCCHINI hadn't been driving because his license was suspended for nonpayment of parking tickets—well over $2,000 in tickets that he'd simply tossed in the glove box. After the license suspension, he still drove for a while, furtively. ("Do you have any idea how careful a driver you become when you're on a suspended license?") Twice he was stopped by the police. The second cop checked his record, found a bench warrant for his arrest, and hauled him in, despite Eric's desperate last-ditch plea to perform a free party for the guy's kid. It was in the police station, with his car impounded, that the Great Zucchini decided maybe he really ought to start taking cabs.

Eric's misadventures with traffic tickets are symptomatic of larger problems involving his inability to conduct life as a reasonably mature, moderately organized, marginally integrated member of polite society.

Take his apartment . . . please.

I did get to see it, finally. On the morning of the day I was to arrive, Eric awoke to discover he had no electricity. So he quickly had to get cash and run to the utility company. He knew exactly what to do because it had happened many times before. That's his tickler system: When the lights go out, it's time to pay the bill.

As I entered the apartment, to the left was a spare bedroom. It was empty, except for a single broken chair. Down the hall was the living room, with that couch and that air hockey table, which was covered with junk, clothes, cigarette butts, and coins. ("You want to play? I can clean it off.") Coins and junk also littered the floor, along with two or three industrial-size Hefty bags filled with Eric's soiled clothing he'd brought back from a summer camp that he'd helped staff, three months earlier. The closets were completely empty. There were no clean clothes.

The kitchen was almost tidy, due to lack of use. There was a fancy knife set and a top-of-the-line microwave, neither of which, Eric said, has ever been deployed. There was also a gleaming, never-used chrome blender and a high-end Cuisinart coffeemaker that was put into play exactly once, when a woman who slept over wanted a cuppa in the morning. Most of these appliances were purchased in a frenzy of optimism when Eric moved in almost a year ago. ("You know how when you get a new place, it's all exciting, and you say, Mmm, I'm gonna get me a blender and make smoothies!")

The cupboards were bare. The only edible thing I saw was a 76-ounce box of raisin bran, the size of a small suitcase.

The bedroom was similar to the living room, down to the Hefty bags, except there was actually something in the closet. Not clothing, though. A shoebox.

It doesn't belong on the closet floor, Eric knows that. He was going to bring it to the French Quarter of New Orleans, but that's out now. He's thinking maybe the bluffs of Big Sur. He just hasn't gotten around to it. It's been three years now, so another few weeks or months or years won't really matter one way or another. It holds his father's ashes.

ERIC DOESN'T KNOW why he is the way he is. He knows he's perfectly ridiculous, and that his disability—or whatever it is—is out of control. We were about an hour outside Atlantic City, discussing his life.

"I make more than a hundred thousand dollars a year," he said, "and I literally have no idea where any of it goes." He is simply lacking, he said, whatever mechanism most people have for dealing with the mundanities of life. His personal finances resemble his apartment: total chaos. He keeps no records. He knows he's not entirely square with the Internal Revenue Service but hasn't a clue how much he owes. He's taking steps to negotiate a payment plan.

But it's not just about money, I said.

No, no, he agreed. It's not just about money. It's about a fundamental inability to cope.

"Some people promise themselves that maybe one day they'll sky-dive, to prove to themselves they can do it," he said. "I'll promise myself that maybe one day I'll clean my house."

The devolution of the Great Zucchini's act over the last few years is not because his life has been spiraling any further out of control than it's ever been. It's just that he started his business with some discipline, but when it became clear his career wouldn't suffer because of inattention to detail, inattention to detail seamlessly followed.

I've known other men who approach Eric's level of dysfunction, including myself. I'm saved by the fact that I've been able to hang on to a competent wife. That doesn't seem to be an immediate option for Eric. He's frightened of commitment, he says, because he is terrified of making the wrong choice. The divorce of his parents, and divorces he's seen among his friends and his clients, make him particularly scared. It's odd, because he's not really afraid of much else. He's not even particularly scared of death.

Why not?

"Life is a crapshoot," he said. When you understand and accept that, he said, it eliminates fear. Plus, there's something else.

"When I was seven years old," he said, "I was walking in the street with my grandmother, and I got kissed on the cheek by an angel."

I laughed. He did not. He meant it. He said he felt the kiss, knew instantly what it was, and believes that this angel has been watching over his life ever since. He has survived serious car accidents, he said, and as a child recovered from two broken arms that doctors said, by all rights, should have turned into rag doll appendages. He believes he is protected. It's a healthy attitude for living, perhaps, but maybe not for gambling.

Our plan for this trip was to stay a few hours in Atlantic City and go home. Eric had told me he'd bring $200 in cash and see what happened. But he wound up bringing $500. If things were going good, he said, he just might gamble into the night.

An overnight? But you didn't even bring a toothbrush or a change of clothes, I said.

"Won't need 'em," he said, if things go good.

Half an hour away, he phoned a friend and left a message: "Gettin' near Atlantic City. Gonna roll some bones."

He saw me looking at him.

"Okay, I'm seriously geeking out," he said, laughing.

Five minutes later, he made another call, and left another message.

"Gonna be rollin' some bones, baby."

––––––––––

WE ARE ROLLING bones.

Because he likes the company of people, Eric's favorite game is craps. Craps is not a solitary pursuit, like blackjack or slots. You are throwing dice, and other people around the table are betting on your throws. If you are hot, you can gain a lot of close friends.

At the moment, Eric is white-hot, and the table is going rip-roaring crazy.

Laying down bets of $10 and $20, Eric is up a couple of hundred. Others at the table are hitchhiking on his luck, including a large woman with a large tumbler of wine. Right before every roll of the dice, for luck, she hollers the same thing at the top of her lungs, a corruption of a Kanye West lyric. "I ain't messin' with no gold digger," she bellows, "but I ain't messin' with no broke nigga!" Appalled, the pit boss implores her to stop. When she refuses, he backs off. At a casino, you don't monkey with mojo.

With each cast of the dice, the large woman's sister, who is even larger, is standing behind Eric, pounding his shoulders, yelling, "Lady Luck! Lady Luck!"

Eric is up to $350 and climbing.

The women keep yelling their inane mantras, Eric keeps rolling, everyone keeps winning. The noise becomes deafening. People from other tables migrate over to get part of the action.

We are in Bally's, which is pretty indistinguishable from any other Atlantic City casino—which is to say, it is an illusion. The rooms are brocaded and chandeliered, the croupiers tuxedoed, the waitresses sequined, all to establish an atmosphere of genteel, aristocratic gaming, but it's all in service of banal desperation. The patrons tend toward the taut and the hollow-eyed, the pale and the pit-stained, dressed less for Monte Carlo than for Monty's Steak 'n' Ribs. Eric is in a Maryland Terps polo shirt, and the large ladies are in drugstore pink, and most everyone, as always, will go home a loser.

But while you're winning, anything seems possible. Eric is at the moment a heroic character, a romantic lead, a suave Bogart or Bond, rolling sixes and nines and never a losing seven, and the cheering continues. The classy illusion holds right up until the moment that the bellowing woman falls silent, sways, hiccups, and vomits all over the table.

———

IT'S NOW JUST after midnight. We'd arrived at seven, and Eric shows no sign of tiring. He's lost some money at blackjack but is making it back on a craps table, again. Beside him is a sweet, funny, attractive woman named Mollie, in a low-cut black blouse and white pants with a big belt. Mollie's maybe thirty, a businesswoman from Texas. She'd arrived with friends whom she seems to have jettisoned.

Eric is hot.

"You want to see a five?" He teases the table, which has bet heavily on five. "Is five what you want, a five?" He rolls a five. The table erupts in cheers.

"I'm a magician," he says to Mollie. "I don't know if you knew that."

"It's showing," she says. She is leaning against the table, hip-shot, dangling a sandal, watching his every move.

Eric is generous with his winnings, every once in a while tossing a few chips to the croupier, tipping waitresses magnani-mously. He has switched from rum-and-Cokes to coffee, to keep alert, but he still tips $5 or more. That's a signature of his: At coffee shops, Eric will sometimes leave $20 on a $5 tab. He says he does it to make the day of someone who is not accustomed to generosity.

By 1:30 A.M., he's up more than $600, and still rolling strong. "I'm going to call it a night," Mollie says. She shakes Eric's hand and leaves for her room, his business card in her pocket. Then she comes back, looks at the table and Eric. She thought she might have forgotten something, but she guessed not. She leaves again, for good.

"This is the hottest roll I've been on all night," Eric tells me. "When it's over, they are definitely going to give me an ovation."

A few minutes later he finally craps out. There is some polite applause, and someone else grabs the dice.

I tell him: "You could have hooked up with Mollie."

"What? No way," he says.

"Eric, at one point there, she was giving you a back rub."

"Well, yeah."

"You had her."

"You think, really?"

"Yeah."

He smiles sheepishly, goes back to the table.

I went to bed. I found Eric again at 7 A.M. at another casino. He hadn't slept. He was up $1,100 but wasn't ready to leave.

The next three hours were ugly. The craps tables had cooled off ("The felt was too old, the table was hard"), and he had a couple of bad outings with steely-eyed dealers at the blackjack tables. ("Those women were cruel.") Eric finally quit at 10:30 A.M. His all-nighter had left him with a profit of $200, roughly his fee for twenty minutes of children's party entertainment. He wasn't disappointed. Life is a crapshoot, after all.

On the ride home, there was one image I could not get out of my head.

The Great Zucchini's tattered loose-leaf appointment book is filled with the names and dates of his scheduled parties, months and months into the future. He keeps no backup—no other notes, nothing on a computer disk, nothing anywhere. If he were to lose that book, he'd have no idea where he was supposed to be, or when. For months of weekends, preschool children would be waiting expectantly in homes across greater Washington, and the Great Zucchini would simply never show.

Eric understands the importance of that book. Without it, the Great Zucchini would cease to exist, and all that would be left would be Eric Knaus. And so he carries it with him everywhere. He won't leave it in a car, in case the car is stolen. When he goes out of his house, if he absolutely must leave the book behind, he hides it in a special place no burglar would think to look.

The sight that I could not get out of my head was the Great Zucchini hunched over the craps table, lost in that flagrant illusion, flinging dice with his right hand, his left hand pressing that book hard to his chest, white-knuckled, like a man holding on for dear life.

———————

LAUREN COX, FIVE, on why she likes the Great Zucchini, whom she saw at her little brother's third birthday party: "Because when the snake came out, and it didn't stop coming out? And when there was nothing in that box, and then there was jelly? He's for boys. Boys are funny and dumb, but they like trucks and trains, and I don't, and I'm not having the Great Zucchini. I'm having a party somewhere else in Virginia that's girly."

The Great Zucchini, on why he likes little kids: "Because they are totally innocent and totally nonjudgmental, but they will say whatever they think, and that's beautiful."

ERIC'S MOTHER, JANE Knaus, is a small, cultured, soft-spoken woman of sixty. We met at yet another Starbucks, to discuss the enigma that is her son. I said I was trying to understand him.

"I don't know if I understand him," she said, smiling. "Actually, I don't know where he came from."

Literally, he came from Jane Cohen and Rodger Knaus, beat-era liberal intellectuals who met at Berkeley in 1963. They split to Sweden in disgust in 1968, with $2,000 between them, after Hubert Humphrey got nominated for president over Eugene McCarthy. There, they had their only child. They were back in the United States by Eric's second birthday.

Now Jane is creative services director at Montgomery College. Rodger was a Ph.D. in mathematics whose pioneering work in early software design is still celebrated. What Jane means about Eric's dubious ancestry is that, temperamentally, from the earliest age, he fit neither parent.

Jane was a fine artist. Rodger was a scientist. "Our work required solitude," Jane said. They were eggheads, and loners. Eric was neither.

"In grade school," Jane said, "I would ask the teacher how Eric was doing in math, and the teacher would say, 'Eric likes to show off his muscles and flirt with the girls.' And I would ask, 'But how is he doing in math?' and the teacher would say, 'Eric likes to show off his muscles and flirt with the girls.'"

The most significant fact in Eric's upbringing, Jane said, was when she and her husband separated. Eric was thirteen. The divorce became final two years later, and the whole thing was obviously deeply painful. At fourteen, Eric was living with his mom in an apartment with cockroaches; Eric wouldn't let her kill them. "Cockroaches have families, too," he would say.

"Who still thinks like that at fourteen?" she said, smiling sadly.

Divorce is traumatic for any child, I said. But Eric had told me the divorce wasn't that big a deal, that he'd loved and respected his father, and stayed close to him. Was that right?

Jane hesitated. At the end of Rodger's life, yes, the two men were close, she said. Eric actually quit his job when his father lay dying of a brain tumor, she said, to spend his final months beside him at the hospice. At Rodger's funeral, she said, Eric delivered an impromptu tribute so moving and heartfelt and self-deprecatory that it helped heal the wounds.

Wounds?

Jane took a sip of tea.

Rodger had been born prematurely, she said, with some attendant physical difficulties. He was blind in one eye, and had a palsied leg. He was not good-looking, like Eric, or affable, like Eric, or always surrounded by friends, like Eric. He drove himself to overcome his handicaps, but at a significant emotional cost. He had an incendiary temper, particularly if his peace and quiet was threatened by Eric, a rambunctious kid. When Eric's pals would come over, Rodger would lie and say Eric wasn't home, and literally slam the door in the faces of flabbergasted ten-year-olds. He would storm and rant at Eric, call him names, break objects in rage.

His violence was only to objects?

"There was physical violence to Eric. It's why I left Rodger. As Eric got older, and bigger, I knew he wasn't going to take it anymore. And I feared something terrible was going to happen, that one of them was really, really going to hurt the other. It got scary. I was a mother, and I had no choice. I had to leave, to protect my cub."

Jane never remarried, and loved her husband—"a difficult, cantankerous, challenging, funny, impossible, brilliant man"—until the day he died.

Jane said she has no doubts that Eric's mistreatment at the hands of his father influenced his life, though she isn't sure exactly how. She knows he's never fully accepted adulthood, growing up both guileless and naïve—still in many ways a child, for better or worse.

"Actually, he doesn't see the bifurcation. He probably feels five-year-olds should be able to vote. He's very, very protective of children."

Jane Knaus took another sip of her tea, which must have been cold. We'd been talking for well over an hour.

"Did Eric ever mention what happened to the people across the hall?"

No, I said.

And then she told me what happened to the people across the hall.

———

WHEN I PICKED Eric up for his court appearance on his license suspension, he was dressed in a nice pair of pants and a shirt still crisp from the package. He'd taken a cab to Filene's just that morning to buy both of them, because he hadn't a clean outfit in his house. He also bought a tie but wasn't wearing it.

Eric never learned to tie a necktie. I had to make the knot on myself, then loop it over his head.

The court appearance proved anticlimactic. Eric's lawyer—a dad for whom he'd done parties—negotiated a continuance.

Afterward, Eric and I stopped for hot chocolate in Rockville. One customer recognized both of us. She seemed particularly delighted to finally meet the Great Zucchini. Then we stopped for lunch. Over tacos, I asked Eric about what happened to the people across the hall.

"I don't really remember it," he said. "I told you, I don't remember anything before fourth grade."

"Fourth grade is age nine. You were thirteen," I said.

"The thing about fourth grade is I had a tyrant of a teacher, and my dad told her to stop picking on me, and that is why my fifth-grade teacher was important to me, and I started liking school, which is why . . ."

"What about the family across the hall, Eric?"

"I just don't remember it. I was watching a football game, maybe the Super Bowl. That's all I remember."

Not the Super Bowl. The New York Giants were playing the St. Louis Cardinals on Monday night, October 24, 1983, and midway through the first quarter, there was a sound of a scuffle, and then shots from the apartment across the hall.

Eric knew that apartment. On at least two occasions, he had babysat for the eighteen-month-old boy there, a child named Laurence. It was Eric's first babysitting gig, in a life that would, ultimately, be all about babysitting.

"I don't really remember him. He was just a baby. A lot of babies have passed through this head. All babies look the same."

"You've told me you can tell, just from looking, what sort of personality a six-month-old will have."

"I just don't remember. What I remember of my childhood was running through the sewers of Bethesda with K.B., and popping up out of manholes. We used to . . ."

"Eric . . ."

"I know you want this to be important, but it just isn't."

"I've never seen you upset before. Why are you getting upset?"

"I'm not getting upset."

The woman who lived in the apartment across the hall was a dark-haired beauty named Paula Adams. Five years earlier, Paula Adams had been a chief lieutenant of the Reverend Jim Jones, the brilliant, messianic madman who led 900 followers to a mass suicide in the jungles of Guyana. Adams survived the holocaust in Jonestown and fled to the United States with her lover, the man whose government influence had given her safe haven. His name was Laurence Mann, and he had been the Guyanese ambassador to the United States.

They had a child here, but their relationship—no doubt haunted by the horror—was deeply troubled. No one knows exactly what caused it, but at nine-thirty on that Monday night, Mann forced his way into the apartment, shot Paula in the head, shot the baby in the head, and then turned the gun on himself. None survived.

"How can you not remember it, Eric?"

"It's easy for someone who is thirty-five to not remember someone he babysat for when he was twelve."

"Thirteen. Your mother says you were really attached to that little boy. She said you were devastated to realize that a child can be unsafe in his own home. She said you never really got over it. Those were her words."

"Look, what do you want me to say? You want me to say I remember? Okay, I remember. I'm pissed because that mom still owes me nine dollars for babysitting, okay?"

We both laughed. Okay, Eric. Good one. No more questions.

ONCE, WHEN ERIC was leaving a restaurant, he saw a man disciplining his two-year-old son. The kid had done something of which the father disapproved, so the father poked the boy in the face with a knuckle, so hard it left a mark. Eric says he made a scene, telling the parents he would call the cops if he ever saw anything like that again. He's stopped parents in the street to inform them that, at three, a child is too old for a pacifier. Once, when a four-year-old at a party seemed painfully timid, Eric told the mom to stop letting the child sleep in her bed. "How did you know he does that?" the mother asked. Eric just knew.

"At that age," he explained, "a child can't do much by himself. Making it through the night alone is a big accomplishment. You have to give him that victory."

In the two months I'd gotten to know him, I'd seen several slightly awkward encounters between Eric and a parent, but not one such moment between Eric and a child. It's tempting to imagine him as Holden Caulfield imagined himself, protector of children's souls, poised beside the field of rye at the edge of a cliff, catching them before they plummet to their spiritual deaths. But this man with the guardian angel on his shoulder; who forfeits love for gambling but looks to find it in a strip club; who can't tie a tie or remember to pay a bill; who makes a tidy living but doesn't know where the money goes; who can't recall things that deliver him emotional pain; who solemnly prays to God in the bathroom before every performance for the strength and wisdom to make the four-year-olds giggle—this guy has not yet surrendered himself, as Holden reluctantly did, to adulthood. He may never. Maybe it's that he's seen the alternative and wants no part of it.

Maybe he's Peter Pan. He's even got some magic dust, until he loses it.

"If Eric ever grows up," Jane Knaus had told me, "his career might be over."

———————

WE ARE IN the Great Falls home of Melanie and Denny Sisson, where eight children and their parents are gathering for a show. A few minutes earlier, Eric had asked me to pull my car up to the side of another one, so we were hidden from the house while he finished a cigarette.

The Sissons jokingly call their house a "bowling alley" because of the open space. It's more than 6,000 square feet of atria, solaria, and balustrade, a beautiful home that is a testament to Denny's successful business as a landscape architect, which is itself a testament to the opulence of Great Falls real estate. It all dovetails nicely.

Things don't always work out so perfectly, though, even in Great Falls. The birthday girl is the Sissons' five-year-old, Phoebe, and her guests are mostly kids from her special-needs class. Like Phoebe, these are children with developmental disabilities of varying degrees. They're a handful and a half.

A former elementary school teacher, Melanie chose Eric after seeing him perform elsewhere. She concluded he is "a true artist" who could entertain a roomful of kids equally well "in Great Falls or in the Sudan."

Eric didn't know these were going to be mostly kids with special needs, but it becomes apparent right away. They're beautiful children, and seem plenty smart, but they're all over the floor, with nanosecond attention spans. One mother with tired eyes and a wary bearing hovers at her son's elbow the whole time.

The show starts, and within seconds, Eric's got them. Instinctively, he's streamlining his act, making his gags last half as long as usual. He takes a drink of water, calling it, in a goofy, sonorous voice, "WA-WA." For some reason, this sends the kids into hysterics, so he repeats it. Hysterics, again. He does it a third time, and now they're doubled over, gasping for air. Eric looks out at the parents, shrugs, winks, and says, "I'll just keep doin' this all afternoon, okay?" The parents laugh, maybe for the first time in a while.

For thirty-five minutes, Eric handles the crowd, improvising deftly as he goes. When one boy walks up excitedly and slugs him in the leg, he takes no notice. When another grabs a prop, Eric turns it into a joke. When he is done, he has actually worked up a sweat. Some parents applaud.

A little girl in pink walks right up to him and extends a fore-finger, straight up in the air. It's puzzling. Eric meets her eyes. Something indefinable passes between them, something only they understand, and Eric reaches out, seizes that little finger in his big fist, and gives it a shake. The girl breaks into a grin. Then she hugs the most fabulous person she's ever known in her whole life, the Great Zucchini.

––––––––––

Postscript: Eric Knaus feared this story would end his career. It didn't. He had underestimated the willingness of parents to forgive the personal flaws of a man who loved their children, and whom their children loved. The Great Zucchini has more business than ever.

The First Father

On the first few pages of My Life, *his 2004 auto-biography, Bill Clinton recalls his astonishment on reading this story in the* Washington Post *just a few months after taking office.*

I knew I had discovered an explosive and potentially humiliating fact about the president, something even he had not known. I decided to present it in as dignified a context as possible.

Didn't matter. Judging from letters received, half the readers (liberals) were outraged because they thought I had no business embarrassing the new president this way. The other half (conservatives) were outraged because they thought I had buried the scandalous news in an overabundance of tact.

June 20, 1993

THE CAR PASSED them fast, not crazy fast but fast like a stranger who did not know the local roads, with their quick turns and occasional slick patches of gravel. Roscoe Gist remembers thinking exactly that, must be a stranger, and noticing a young man's face behind the wheel.

Two minutes later he saw the car again. It churned his stomach. The big Buick sedan was upside down on the shoulder, its headlights pillowing out into an alfalfa field, its radio blaring corny country music into the black of night.

It was May 17, 1946, an overcast Saturday night on Missouri's Highway 60 halfway between Morehouse and Sikeston. Gist and his wife, Bernice, were returning from the movies. Ronald, the newborn, was asleep in the back seat.

Gist surveyed the macabre scene. The driver was nowhere. The car doors were closed, but the window was wide open. With dread, Gist inspected the brackish drainage ditch next to the car; the water couldn't have been more than 3 feet deep, but an injured man could roll into that muck and drown. In the dark, Gist hunkered down, rolled up a sleeve and raked the channel with his hand, feeling uneasily for cold flesh or wet cloth. Nothing but cattails.

By now a crowd was gathering, and someone went for the police. Roscoe took Bernice home to nurse the baby, but then he drove back, frankly curious. And so he was there an hour later when someone in uniform yelled "Hey" and dragged the drowned man from the ditch. He was belly down a full 25 yards from his car, far away from where Gist had searched—a well-dressed, sandy-haired fellow with no apparent injuries. But what Gist could not take his eyes off was the young corpse's hand, balled into a fist, clutching a clump of dry grass and weeds.

"It was like he had tried to pull hisself out of the water, but didn't have the strength. You're just kind of stopped, you see something like that."

It can be bewildering how quickly time passes, how you turn around and suddenly you are retired in Oklahoma, and Ronald the baby has four kids from two marriages and is living on a houseboat in San Diego, and now someone is on the telephone asking about the man in the ditch and damned if you don't remember it like it was the day before yesterday.

"Where'd you get my name from, anyhow?"

From the accident report.

"But . . . why?"

He didn't know. No reason he should know, when you think about it. And so, forty-seven years later, Roscoe Gist is told the identity of the man in the ditch. For a very long time, he says nothing at all.

Finally: "You know, I heard something."

While he was squatting down there in the dark on the side of the road beside the overturned car, he says, he heard a kind of a gurgle and a splash, but it was so feeble and far away he figured it was a frog. Yet that's exactly the spot from which the body was recovered. It haunts him still.

"I might could've saved his life."

Life is filled with might could'ves. Roscoe Gist might could've followed the sound of the frog, and he might've dragged W. J. Blythe out of the ditch in time, and Bill Clinton might've had a real dad instead of a drunken stepfather who walloped his mother and forced him to grow up fast and focused. And Clinton might not have been so oppressively aware of the possibility of sudden death at any age that he might not have hurried up and become the youngest governor in America, and president of the United States at forty-six. Or he might could've anyway.

So far, the story of the Man in the Ditch has been treated as a minor prologue to the inspiring public biography of the Man from Hope. What little has been published is almost caricature: William Jefferson Blythe was a handsome traveling salesman from Texas who met pretty nurse Virginia Cassidy in a Louisiana hospital in 1942. Their eyes locked across the emergency room, and it was love at first sight. They married; he went off to war, then returned home and perished on the highway a few months later at age twenty-eight.

He was traveling to Hope, Arkansas, from Chicago to bring

his pregnant wife back north to start a new life. The baby became president.

It's all the truth, but it is not all of the truth.

Reporters following the Clinton campaign through the South last year heard tantalizing rumors of a shiftless drifter who resembled not so much a mythic American hero but the traveling salesman of bawdy humor, a footloose ladies' man who left a trail of broken hearts across the south-central United States, and maybe a baby or two. Nothing was written; it was just talk.

Talk is unreliable. Sometimes it is true. Sometimes it is hooey. Sometimes it is a thick embroidery of both.

If the Bill Clinton story is about the American Dream, no less so is the story of his father, W. J. Blythe, a rag-poor farmer's son who grew up at a time and in a place when the American Dream nearly strangled in the dust. It was an era of unimaginable desperation; if you weren't careful, you could drown in your own despair. People sometimes did things not because they made sense but because nothing else made much sense either.

Bill Clinton was surely shaped by the challenging circumstances of his youth, and by the imprint of a strong-willed mother. But every parent leaves a mark, even if the child never knew him. The president of the United States has his father's genes, a legacy as apparent as his nose and as elusive as his nature.

———

IN THE MIDDLE of the Mojave Desert, in a sun-caked valley ringed by snowcapped mountains, an old woman with an exquisite face comes to the door. You apologize for arriving unannounced, explaining that you were afraid that if you called ahead she would not have agreed to see you. You say you want to talk about private matters that are more than a half century old. You want to ask her about W. J. Blythe, her first husband. You want to know if he is the father of her only son, which would mean that her son is the half-brother of the president of the United States. A brother no one knows about, not even the president's mother.

The woman puts down the quilt she is sewing, with pretty pink hearts, and asks you politely if you would mind repeating what you just said. You do, and she smiles and says, okay, she supposes it can't hurt now.

EVERY FAMILY HAS its secrets, its old scandals, seldom-entered rooms with hidden recesses. This is true of the Blythes, an ordinary family that—with the spectacular prominence of one of its members—suddenly becomes a public curiosity. Who was Bill Clinton's father? Where did he come from?

The Texas branch of the Blythes has passed down a tale of how the family moved to Sherman, Texas, from Tippah County, Mississippi, in 1909. They came in a covered wagon, it is said, and as they lumbered through Arkansas in the gathering dusk they became aware of furtive shapes in the distance.

Indians.

And so they pulled the horses up short, and the men stood guard, talking robustly, brandishing their weaponry while the women and children huddled inside. In this fashion they spent the next ten hours, braced awake by their own terror, peering into the darkness, waiting for the attack. At dawn, with reddened eyes and raw nerves, they studied the shadows to discover that the lurking Indians were nothing but a field of tree stumps.

The Texas Blythes love that story, because it evidences how uncertain were the lives of their forebears. A farmer had as many children as he could, and he had them as quickly as he could because you needed extra hands and you never knew how many children would survive. And so Willie Blythe—Bill Clinton's grandfather—married young. It was 1906. He was twenty-four and his bride, Lou Birchie Ayers, was all of thirteen, and they started up a family right away. Clifford was first, then Raymond, who was nicknamed "Doc" and died at nineteen of "yellow jaundice," then Pauline, then Earnest, then Maureen, then W.J., then Cora Lucille, the crippled girl, then Vera, and finally Glenn, the baby. Nine children, eighteen years from first to last, by which time mother Lou Birchie, at 4 feet 11, weighed 200 pounds.

W.J., the fourth son, was born in 1918, and he was named exactly that way—just two initials—to distinguish him from his father, William Jefferson Blythe. W.J. did not officially become William Jefferson Blythe until years later, when his birth certificate had to be re-created after a lynch mob dynamited and burned to the ground the Grayson County Courthouse and all its vital records. The vigilantes were trying to flush out a black man jailed there on charges of raping a white woman. He was mutilated, hanged from a tree, his body burned. It was 1930; it was one of the last lynchings in America.

"In later years, one of the main lynchers' mothers became a good friend of our family. That's how things were."

This is Vera Ramey, one of two of the Blythe children still alive. The other, Pauline, is eighty-three and her memory fades in and out. But Ramey is sixty-nine and her recollections of her favorite brother, W.J., remain as vivid today, she says, as they were when he was imprisoning her in an inner tube and hurling her, happily squealing in protest, into the pond.

Ramey does not consider herself an emotional person, but she cannot watch Bill Clinton on television without choking up. She sees in the president the unmistakable imprint of his father: the eyes, the high forehead, the large but slender hands, the pleasantly plebeian nose. "I wish I could look without bawling, but I can't," she says.

No death of a loved one is easy to bear; for Vera Ramey, a seamstress in Denison, Texas, the death of W.J. was very nearly disabling. She was a young woman when her brother had his accident, but she recalls the time as one recalls a tragedy from which complete recovery is impossible.

"I have a good husband and I love my kids and hug 'em every time I can, but I don't believe I have ever been as close to anyone as I was to W.J. I think my husband would tell you that."

Ramey describes her early childhood as hardscrabble but almost idyllic. There was no money on the farm, but plenty of food. They lived in a nice house, a lot of poor people getting along fine.

W.J. was a tall, friendly kid who loved an old flop-eared hound dog, and figured out a way to catch and keep squirrels as household pets. There were 40 acres of pastureland, cotton to be harvested, cows to be milked, chickens to be fed, and the two-room White Rock school was a saunter down the road. There was an old wooden root cellar to which the children were banished when a twister was sighted; the kids huddled down there in the dark on an old bed, next to their mama's preserves and tinned meats, their father outside on a chair, leaning against the house, balefully scanning the horizon. There was a swaybacked old mule that five children could ride at once. There was the old cow barn, which had a 6-foot hayloft from which the kids would leap.

The barn is still there, out on Preston Road off Route 691, midway between Denison and Sherman. It is a rotting firetrap of bowed gray oaken board and rusted hinge, leaning precariously. The current owners have left it standing because they fear that if they try to tear it down it will collapse on them. In front of the barn stands the farmhouse in which the president's father and his eight brothers and sisters grew up. Outside, two chairs ooze their stuffing onto the ground.

Your first thought is, there must be some mistake.

In a pink housecoat, Lucille Waw invites you into a small living room dominated by an enormous color TV. Yes, she says, this is the old Blythe place. She's lived there since '36. The house is dismayingly tiny, just three medium-size rooms and a kitchen.

There's no upstairs, no downstairs. The rooms were even smaller, back then; her husband added on.

"How they lived, I do not know," said Waw. "I've wondered. Lord, I've wondered. Nine children they had. The walls were canvas and paper, it crumbled when you touched it. They didn't have a closet, didn't have a cabinet. Didn't have running water. Didn't have electricity."

Waw says she's heard that one of the Blythe boys was a cousin of the father of the president of the United States.

Actually, she is told, he was the father of the president.

"The president's father lived here?" she says dubiously.

To UNDERSTAND WHAT happened to the Blythe family, what flattened them, you need only leaf through the scrapbook of old photographs kept by Ann Blythe Grigsby, Earnest's daughter, who still lives in Denison. She has Blythe family pictures going back to the turn of the century.

The oldest are a Joadian gallery of weather-beaten faces, grizzled men and hardy women in baggy clothes, smiling gamely beside barns and silos and livestock and children. Among these is a photo taken in Sherman in 1921 or '22. Father Willie Blythe, dressed in a Stetson and a dark suit and looking like a lean country preacher, is proudly holding an infant, Cora Lucille, as the older children grin at the camera—all except three-year-old W.J., sullen in a prissy sailor suit. A big, young family squinting hopefully into the sun.

Then there is another picture, taken just a decade later, of Willie Blythe on his front porch. He has become an old man. He is unshaven, hollow-cheeked, someone ready to give up the fight. His sallow face is creased with pain.

In 1930, Willie Blythe contracted colon cancer, and it took five bad years to kill him. These were years when country banks failed and even hale American farmers lost their homesteads to debt. The small Blythe farm, with its patriarch shivering in a bed in the back room, didn't stand much of a chance.

They tried. Much of the burden fell on W.J., at fifteen the oldest unmarried son. W.J. took a job at Ashburn's dairy down the road, bringing home milk and butter and eggs and a meager paycheck that he handed over to his mother.

W.J.'s bed was in the living room, but he was hardly ever in it. "He would go to work in the afternoons after school at two or two-thirty, and work till ten o'clock," Ramey recalls. "Then he'd sleep till three A.M., when he would milk our cows, wash them down, carry the milk to the dairy. Four hours of sleep a night was enough for him." After eighth grade, he quit school altogether.

By late 1934, Willie Blythe was near death. Vera was eleven; she recalls how convulsions would seize her father and rattle his body.

"I would take my crippled sister and run out of the house. W.J. and my mother held him down. They'd have to give him morphine by mouth and wait for it to take effect."

After fifteen minutes of this, W.J. would come out of the house, smiling, and tell the girls everything was okay now.

"He was always smiling," says Ramey. "Things that would be disturbing to other people would just make him laugh. I think he felt that was one way of keeping the rest of us happy."

In February 1935, Willie Blythe succumbed. An undertaker came to the house to embalm him, and then he was to be taken to the cemetery. But a storm rolled in, and the roads froze and became impassable. And so for more than a week, the cold body of Willie Blythe lay in the family's living room.

"I never went into that room alone again," Ramey said, "unless Mama or W.J. was with me. Never.

"I was a daddy's girl. And when my daddy died, I think W.J. just kind of took over. He used to come and hug my neck. I guess

I was afraid he was going to leave us like the other brothers did, and he said, 'Puddin', I will always be there for you,' and he was. He never called me by my name. He called me Puddin'."

In the Blythe family, there is some uncertainty over just what happened to the farm. By 1936, with Willie dead, it is clear that Lou Birchie was having trouble meeting her mortgage payments. Ramey and other family members recall that she somehow disposed of the property to avoid foreclosure; that some money came out of it, that it wasn't total disaster.

But in the Grayson County Courthouse, in Deeds Book 387, p. 203, there is no ambiguity about what happened.

In January 1934, with the farm failing along with Willie Blythe's health, Lou and Willie had secured a loan from the Federal Farm Mortgage Corporation, an emergency lending organization created by the New Deal.

But by June two years later the new widow was two payments delinquent, and the bank foreclosed. The language is brutally precise: ". . . unable to pay said installments and unable to protect any equity which the undersigned has . . ." With a few dozen dollars due on a promissory note of $3,500, Lou Birchie lost the farm.

The family moved into an upstairs apartment on Houston Street in downtown Sherman. At forty-three, W.J.'s mother became a hotel chambermaid.

And at eighteen, W.J. resolved two things about his life: He would not become a farmer, and he would become a millionaire.

By 1938, he was working out of Oklahoma for an auto parts distributor, on the road all the time. By all accounts, he was a persuasive salesman. He came off as forthright and friendly, a man without pretension. Everyone liked him.

"I think that's why he was such a good salesman," says Ramey. "He never saw a stranger."

And here is where the few sketchy public accounts of W.J.

Blythe's life kick in. He traveled all over the middle South, selling shock absorbers and oil filters and such to auto dealerships. In 1942, while bringing a woman friend to a hospital emergency room in Shreveport, Louisiana, he met Virginia Cassidy, a student nurse with mischievous eyes, generous lips, and a personality as outgoing as his. They courted, he was drafted, and they married just before he left for Europe. He served in North Africa and Italy and was discharged in December 1945.

In the months afterward, living with Virginia in Arkansas, he talked almost not at all about the war. Ann Grigsby remembers sending her uncle a letter when he was in Italy, asking him to mail her some leaves for a school project she was working on. "Sorry, there are no leaves on the trees," he wrote back. "They're all shot off."

That was about as close as he ever came to discussing what he'd seen in the war. When W.J.'s mother had a stroke in early 1946, Virginia traveled to Texas to help nurse her, creating a reservoir of goodwill with the Blythe family that remains strong to this day. Vera Ramey remembers how the attending doctor predicted that her mother would survive, but Virginia the nurse looked doubtfully at the pallor of the older woman's feet and gravely warned the family that she was done for. And she was. She died the next day. W.J. insisted on paying the funeral expenses, Ramey recalls. He had a little money, and it was important to him.

Both W.J.'s mother and his father had died young, at fifty-two. The whole family was acutely aware of this, but only W.J. made a joke of it. He talked about hurrying up and starting a family real quick, because who knows how long you'll be breathing? He wanted lots of kids.

In May 1946, with Virginia pregnant and staying with her family in Hope, W.J. secured a job with a Chicago auto parts company. The couple had chosen a house, and he was driving home to get her when he passed Roscoe Gist on the road, moving, as was his custom, a little too fast.

And the story could end there, except it can't. There was another side to W. J. Blythe that was as much a part of what he was as were his ingratiating temperament, his devotion to his family, his prodigious appetite for hard work, and his determination to transcend the heartbreaking poverty into which he was born. Just like those things, his other side was a product of the times in which he lived.

SHERMAN, TEXAS, IN the 1930s was something of a frontier town, but Madill, Oklahoma, some forty miles away, was even more so. Madill was the place where Texas folks drove when they had public business to transact but didn't want too many questions asked.

And so it is that in the Marshall County Courthouse in Madill is an old marriage license, dated December 1935, under a handwritten notation, "Don't publish." It registers the marriage of W. J. Blythe to one Virginia Adele Gash. Bride and groom are listed as being eighteen years old.

Behind the story, another story.

"There was a child," confirms Vera Ramey.

She says she vowed to talk about this only if someone else brought it up—and only to correct what she believes is a terrible misperception and clear her beloved brother's name.

As Ramey remembers it, Adele Gash was the daughter of a Sherman saloonkeeper who got pregnant, and W.J. married her. She stayed in town a few months, even living briefly with the Blythes, but then left for Dallas. That was no secret in town, she says.

The secret, Ramey says, was that W.J. was not the father.

She says she recalls lying awake at night as a thirteen-year-old, listening to her mother and young W.J. talking heatedly. The father of the child, she says, was another member of the family, a married man whose identity she does not wish to disclose. She says Lou Birchie asked her son to claim paternity and marry the girl, to prevent not only a scandal, but a divorce within the family. W.J. protested, but did it, Ramey says.

The baby, a boy, was born in a hospital in Sherman, Ramey says, and after the mother moved away, W.J. came to her and said, "Don't worry, Puddin', it wasn't mine anyway." The mother and child moved to California somewhere, and have not been heard from in a long, long time. That's the story as Ramey swears she remembers it.

APPLE VALLEY, CALIFORNIA, is a cozy oasis in the western Mojave Desert. The wooden sign above the door of the simple stucco ranch house says THE COFFELT'S. Adele Gash Coffelt looks like someone's favored grandma. Though seventy-five, she seems fifteen years younger, and her handiwork is all over the house: a fruit pie cooling on the kitchen table, handsome quilts on the couch, elaborate Christmas stockings that she sews for her grandchildren. On the wall in a hallway is a photograph of her only child, Henry Leon, born in Sherman, Texas, more than fifty years ago. He is a pleasant-looking man with a high forehead and a plebeian nose.

Is he W. J. Blythe's son?

"Yes."

Adele Coffelt says she knew W.J. from the time they were both children, that they were good friends and that she married him at seventeen. He was seventeen, too. They lied about their age, which is why they went to Madill.

She was definitely not pregnant, she says. No truth to that at all. It may be that she and W.J. were keeping too close company and that her father wanted them to marry to avoid scandal. That could be true, she says. But she was not pregnant.

Exactly why did they marry?

"Well, I wasn't madly in love with him, or anything like that."

She sits back on the sofa and says she doubts anyone could really understand who did not live through those times.

"All I wanted," she says, "was a home."

Adele's mother died when she was six years old. Her father owned a bar and a domino hall, which he believed was not a suitable environment to raise a girl. And so Adele and her younger sister, Faye, spent their childhood raised by aunts and other relatives.

When she and W.J. were seventeen, an opportunity arose. W.J. was in line for a job at the dairy that would have given him meager living quarters on the company grounds. A home! And so they got married. Just like that.

"Young and dumb is what we were."

The job and the apartment never came through, and Adele moved in with the Blythes in that tiny house on Preston Road. Adele says she liked W.J.—"he was a clean, pleasant, decent person"—and might have stayed with him for a long time if they'd just had some privacy.

She and W.J. shared a bedroom with Earnest Blythe and his wife, Ola Maye.

"I don't require a whole lot. I never wanted to be rich, but I never lived with so little," Adele Coffelt says. "We were poor, but they were poorer than we were."

She says the Blythes treated her well, and she liked and respected all of them, but that she felt as though she was a terrible burden on a family that could weather no additional burdens.

After a few months, Adele went to visit an aunt in Dallas. W.J. was supposed to come for her in a few days. Instead, she says, a package arrived in the mail. It was all of her clothing.

"That's how it ended, right there." Adele Coffelt is smiling. "I stayed in Dallas." She got a divorce the following year.

None of which explains the baby.

Coffelt says that after her divorce, she returned to Sherman several times and would spend time with W.J. It was on one of these trips, she says, that her son was conceived. She stayed in Sherman to give birth.

When she is told that someone in the family said W.J. was not the father, she is thunderstruck.

"It wasn't anybody but W.J." Pause. "Why would anyone say that?"

She is told why, and for the first time her formidable composure deserts her.

"If I am not telling the truth, may God strike me dead."

The public records support her version of events. The certificate recording her marriage to W.J. is dated December 1935. The divorce petition, on file in Dallas, is dated one year later. And Henry Leon's birth certificate, on file in Austin, is dated January 17, 1938. It lists W. J. Blythe as the father.

"I'm not proud of everything I did in my life," Adele Coffelt says, "but I am not sorry, either." In fact, she is deeply grateful to W.J. for giving her a child. In 1939, just before her second marriage—a happy one to the police chief of Brawley, California, that would last more than thirty years, until his death—she was involved in a serious auto accident that shattered her pelvis. She could never bear children again.

"People without children," she says, "are miserable."

When her baby was a few months old, she says, W.J. came to visit her in California. He was traveling for his company. He hugged her, held Leon, "and was as nice as he ever was." He left that night, and it was the last time she ever saw him.

There is one more thing.

"W.J. also married my sister."

What?

"It was a fling thing," she says. "Didn't last long."

In 1940 or '41, Coffelt says she got a distressed phone call out of the blue from her younger sister, Faye. "She was back East somewhere, and she wanted to know if she could come to live with me. She had married W.J. and it wasn't going to work."

Why not?

"She did not say and I did not ask. I did not care to know."

But—

"When someone needs help, you give it to them. You don't ask questions."

Why did they get married? Was she pregnant?

"No, some other gal was pregnant. . . . The reason he married her was to keep from having to marry a girl who was pregnant. That's what my sister told me."

(Faye is ill and unable to sit for an interview. But Ola Maye Blythe Hazelwood, Earnest's widow, later confirms that, yes, she recalls something about W.J. coming back to marry Faye. And, yes, there was some trouble with another girl who was pregnant.)

There is a TV in the Coffelts' living room, and at this moment Bill Clinton's face flashes on the screen.

"Doesn't mean anything to me that he is W.J.'s son," Adele says. "He doesn't look that much like W.J. But I wish him well. He'll always be welcome in this house, you tell him that if you talk to him."

A big smile.

"But I didn't vote for him."

———

IT IS SAID that people are shaped the most not by what they want, but by what they fear. Perhaps W. J. Blythe—who watched his father die screaming and his mother lose the family home—so feared death and destitution that he became a man of relentless good cheer, with a ferocious appetite for life-affirming things, sometimes at the expense of good sense and good judgment. But even those people who had cause to dislike him could not find it in themselves to do so. He must have been a wonderful salesman. When he met and married Virginia Cassidy, he took a new name, shedding the initials with which he grew up. For the first time in his life, he became Bill Blythe, the only name his new wife ever knew him by, and it was as Bill Blythe that he was to start a family. It may well be that the change represented something of a turning point, that W.J. was prepared at last to settle down and take responsibility for himself.

It's a theory, as good as any, half a century later.

For four months, Bill Clinton's mother declined repeatedly to discuss her first husband for this article. Finally reached by telephone last week and asked about Bill Blythe's other life, she said it was all news to her. Blythe never told her about his marriage to Adele Gash, or his marriage to Faye Gash, or any other marriages or children he may have had along the way. She also said W.J.'s family never told her, either, even after his death.

"I'm seventy years old," said Virginia Kelley, "and things sometimes slip my mind. But as far as I can remember, no one ever told me."

What does she think of it?

There is the briefest of pauses.

"I don't know what to think," she said. "I loved him very much. He was a wonderful person to me. For his own reasons, he did not mention it to me."

If he had, would it have bothered her?

"I'm sure it would have bothered me." Might she not have married him? Might she never have had a child with him?

"It's hypothetical what I would have done about it."

Life is full of might could'ves.

LIKE MANY OF Clinton's relatives, Vera Ramey was invited to the inaugural events in January. She attended the big gala, and saw Michael Jackson and Chuck Berry, but she wasn't really enjoying herself. All the while she was fighting a hollow feeling she could not quite puzzle out.

Afterward, without telling anyone, not even her husband, she got in her car and drove three hours to Hope, Arkansas, to the Rose Hill Cemetery, where a footstone marks the grave of William Jefferson Blythe, born February 27, 1918, died May 17, 1946.

For four hours, she talked to her big brother about the family. Mostly, she talked about what had become of his baby boy. Just in case he didn't know.

Feeling much better, she drove back home.

ADELE COFFELT DID not discover that the father of her son was also the father of Bill Clinton until a relative sent her a clipping from *People* magazine, during the presidential campaign, mentioning the name William Blythe. And so, of course, her son did not find out about his famous half-brother until then either.

Henry Leon Ritzenthaler—he changed his name from Blythe when his mother's second husband adopted him—is fifty-five. He lives in Paradise, California, with his wife, Judith, a hairdresser. He has two children. The former owner of a janitorial service, Ritzenthaler was forced to retire some time ago because of ill health. He has a heart condition.

Late in the campaign, he and Judith wrote to Bill Clinton, care of the Governor's Mansion in Little Rock. Ritzenthaler says he introduced himself, included a copy of his birth certificate, and requested any information the governor could give them about the Blythe family's health history.

"I don't want any money out of this or anything," Ritzenthaler said. "All I would like to do is meet the man. I would be honored to get to know him a little. To find out after fifty-five years that I've got a brother eight years younger than I am, well, that's kind of nice."

Not to mention that he is the president of the United States?

"It's very nice."

Ritzenthaler says he never heard back from Clinton or his office, but that he doesn't take it personally.

"In the business he is in, I'm sure he was busy and under a lot of pressure. I would just consider it an honor and a privilege to get a phone call or a letter from the man, saying, 'Hey, I know you're alive.'"

The Ghost of
the Hardy Boys

What does it mean that the literature that most influenced my love of writing turns out to be some of the worst bilge ever published?

This is a story about the soul of writing. I started working on it with a chip on my shoulder; I ended it with a lump in my throat.

August 9, 1998

I RECENTLY REDISCOVERED MY youth. It made me sneeze.

It lay unremembered at the top of a tall bookcase: fifteen vintage Hardy Boys novels by Franklin W. Dixon. In getting them down, I took a faceful of dust and beetle carapaces.

I carried the books to my favorite rocking chair, beside my favorite lamp, and reverently broke them open to revisit the literature that had inspired in me a lifelong love of language. The pages were as thick as a shirt collar and ochered with age. They smelled the way old books smell, faintly perfumed, quaintly mysterious, like the lining of Great-Grandma's alligator handbag out in the steamer trunk. I began to read.

Pretty soon a new smell entered the room.

The Hardy Boys stank.

When a group of literati last month published a list of the hundred greatest English-language novels of the twentieth century, lionizing *Ulysses* and *The Great Gatsby* and *The Sun Also Rises*, I was privately disappointed they had not included *The Missing Chums*. I remembered *The Missing Chums* as the pinnacle of human achievement, a meticulously crafted work of American fiction in which Frank and Joe Hardy, the sons of famed sleuth Fenton Hardy, braved choppy seas and grizzled thugs to rescue their kidnapped friends. I had first read it in a backyard hammock strung between sycamore trees during the summer of my twelfth year.

Now, through my bifocals, I again confronted *The Missing Chums*. Here is how it begins:

> "You certainly ought to have a dandy trip."
>
> "I'll say we will, Frank! We sure wish you could come along!"
>
> Frank Hardy grinned ruefully and shook his head. . . .
>
> "Just think of it!" said Chet Morton, the other speaker. "A whole week motorboating along the coast. We're the lucky boys, eh, Biff?"
>
> "You bet we're lucky!"
>
> "It won't be the same without the Hardy Boys," returned Chet.

Dispiritedly, I leafed through other volumes. They all read the same. The dialogue is as wooden as an Eberhard Faber, the characters as thin as a sneer, the plots as forced as a laugh at the boss's joke, the style as overwrought as this sentence. Adjectives are flogged to within an inch of their lives: "Frank was electrified with astonishment." Drama is milked dry, until the teat is sore and bleeding: "The Hardy boys were tense with a realization of their peril." Seventeen words seldom suffice when seventy-one will do: "Mrs. Hardy viewed their passion for detective work with considerable apprehension, preferring that they plan to go to a university and direct their energies toward entering one of the professions; but the success of the lads had been so marked in the cases on which they had been engaged that she had by now almost resigned herself to seeing them destined for careers as private detectives when they should grow older."

Physical descriptions are so perfunctory that the characters practically disappear. In fifteen volumes, we learn little more than this about sixteen-year-old Frank: He is dark-haired. And this about fifteen-year-old Joe: He is blond.

These may be the worst books ever written.

I felt betrayed. Or, as Franklin W. Dixon might have said: I thought to myself, "Golly," assailed as I was in that moment by a dismayingly uncomfortable feeling that I had been jolted with an unfairness that was profoundly extreme.

Thomas Wolfe warned: You can't go home again.

But shouldn't you be able to saunter past the old neighborhood without throwing up?

The Hardy Boys are still published—all the old titles and dozens of new ones. They sell by the millions, still troweling gluey prose into the brains of America's preadolescent boys.

It is too late for me, but what of them?

I felt I had to do something. But what?

Writing is an exercise in power. You wield the words, shape events. You are God. You can make anything happen. You are bound by no laws but your own.

And so I decided to find Franklin W. Dixon. And kill him.

———

DRAT. HE'S ALREADY dead.

In one sense, Franklin W. Dixon never existed. Franklin

W. Dixon was a "house name," owned by a company called the Stratemeyer Syndicate, which created and published the original Hardy Boys. From 1927 through 1946, each Hardy Boys book was secretly written by a man named Leslie McFarlane. I found myself, quite literally, chasing a ghost.

I caught up with him on the telephone, in the person of the ghostwriter's daughter, Norah Perez of Youngstown, New York. Perez is an accomplished novelist. Her father died in 1977.

Recently, Perez leafed through some old Hardy Boys books. "I was almost shocked," she said with a laugh. "I thought, Omigod. They are not great."

So her father was a hack?

"My father," she said, "was a literate, sophisticated, erudite man."

He was?

He loved Dickens, she said. "He was a great Joycean."

He was?

"He corresponded with F. Scott Fitzgerald. He had aspirations to be that kind of writer."

She seemed uncertain where to go with this. Finally: "He hated the Hardy Boys."

It turns out the story of the Hardy Boys—call it their Final Chapter—isn't about the worst writer who ever lived, not by a long shot. It is about a good writer who wrote some bad books, and if you wonder why that happened, as I did, then you are likely not very old and not very wise. Sometimes homely things are done for the best reasons in the world, and thus achieve a beauty of their own.

———

LESLIE MCFARLANE KEPT voluminous diaries. His family has them. He wrote in fountain pen, in elegant strokes that squirreled up a little when he was touched by despair or drink. In these diaries, "The Hardy Boys" is seldom mentioned by name, as though he cannot bear to speak it aloud. He calls the books "the juveniles." At the time, McFarlane was living in northern Ontario with a wife and infant children, attempting to make a living as a freelance fiction writer.

November 12, 1932: "Not a nickel in the world and nothing in sight. Am simply desperate with anxiety. . . . What's to become of us this winter? I don't know. It looks black."

January 23, 1933: "Worked at the juvenile book. The plot is so ridiculous that I am constantly held up trying to work a little logic into it. Even fairy tales should be logical."

January 26, 1933: "Whacked away at the accursed book."

June 9, 1933: "Tried to get at the juvenile again today but the ghastly job appalls me."

January 26, 1934: "Stratemeyer sent along the advance so I was able to pay part of the grocery bill and get a load of dry wood."

Finally: "Stratemeyer wants me to do another book. . . . I always said I would never do another of the cursed things but the offer always comes when we need cash. I said I would do it but asked for more than $85, a disgraceful price for 45,000 words."

He got no raise.

He did the book.

And another. And another. And another. And another. And another. And another.

"WRITING IS EASY," said the author Gene Fowler. "All you do is stare at a blank sheet of paper until drops of blood form on your forehead."

Writing, particularly fiction writing, is an act of quiet terror. You are alone all at once with your genius and your ineptitude, and your errors are as public as possible. To be a writer of fiction requires extreme self-discipline and extreme self-confidence, and many of the people drawn to writing have neither. It can be a recipe for dismal failure. Writing is also, financially, a crapshoot. Always has been. Sometimes, good writers starve. Sometimes, dreadful writers succeed. John Grisham's sentences thud and crepitate all over the page, and he has become a literary tycoon. Edgar Allan Poe nearly starved. Mostly, you become a writer not because you want to get rich or famous, but because you have to write; because there is something inside that must come out. When a baby is to be born, she is born.

Leslie McFarlane, a 5-foot-4 Irishman with mischievous eyes, grew up in a northern Ontario mining town and never got past high school. He had to write. He knew it from childhood. He served his apprenticeship at a succession of small, gritty daily newspapers. At his first, the *Cobalt (Ont.) Nugget*, he received his first lesson in journalism from grizzled news editor Dan Cushing: "Spell the names right. Get the addresses right. Don't use the word 'very' in a sentence."

Thus schooled, McFarlane was off to be a reporter.

As Cushing might say, the kid had something.

Once, at the *Sudbury Star*, he covered a fire that consumed the town he grew up in:

> A leering tornado of flame from the southwest roared down through a half mile of underbrush upon the town of Haileybury basking sleepily in the September sunlight on the shore of Lake Temiskaming early Wednesday afternoon, ate its way across the railway tracks and then, fanned by a 60-mile-an-hour gale, ripped its way to the water's edge, scattering the town's 4,000 inhabitants before its terrific blast.

Later, as an old man, in his memoirs, McFarlane would recall this fire. His prose had matured considerably:

Paul Cobbold had been the local weatherman. Every morning, for years, I had watched him emerge from a doorway like some quaint figure in a mechanical clock, to read his instruments and jot down the figures in his little notebook. My mother said she had last seen him there in the smoke and wind when the fire was beginning to ravage the town. Paul and his frail little wife were victims of the fire. Next door another Englishman, the gloomy, taciturn Mr. Elphik, whom no one knew very well, was a charred skeleton in the garden of the home he had refused to leave.

But small-town newspapering seldom sees excitement like that. Mostly, it sees fender-benders and sewage hearings and the petty maneuverings of beady-eyed local politics. After a time, McFarlane was bored. He dreamed of writing fiction. He began noodling at his desk, after deadline. Once he sent off a short story to the magazine *Smart Set*, edited by the great H. L. Mencken. It was about a young man who one day runs into his long-lost sister. Reunion by coincidence is an ancient device, as old as Shakespeare. But McFarlane added a wicked twist: They meet in a whorehouse.

Unfortunately, McFarlane had never been to a whorehouse. He may well have been a virgin. The most gifted of writers—the giants of literature—can bring to their work a maturity of thought and an understanding of human nature that transcends their callowness. T. S. Eliot wrote "The Love Song of J. Alfred Prufrock"—perhaps the greatest exposition ever on the anguish of growing old—at the age of twenty-six. There are few Eliots, and McFarlane was surely not one of them. Mencken rejected the manuscript. Sent it back with a one-word notation: "Naive—HLM."

McFarlane would keep this note for fifty years.

He became desperate to hone his fiction skills, but he had no time. He was newspapering in Canada and then in Springfield, Massachusetts, for fifteen hours at a stretch.

One day he answered an ad from the Stratemeyer Syndicate, a fabulously successful enterprise that wrote children's books through a conveyor-belt production process. The New York syndicate made the strangest offer: Would McFarlane like to write books for youths based on plot outlines Stratemeyer would supply? He would be paid by the book, and have no copyright to the material. In fact, he could never reveal his authorship, under penalty of returning his payments. The company shipped him samples of some books about a character named Dave Fearless— dreadful, thickheaded novels with implausible plots and preposterous narrative.

McFarlane cheerfully agreed. Years later, in his memoirs, he would observe: "To write a chapter of a book without having to worry about character, action or plot would call for little more than the ability to hit the keys of a typewriter. . . . They were straightforward, cheap paperbacks for a public that would neither read nor relish anything better. . . . And besides, I would be under no obligation to read the stuff. I would merely have to write it."

This was the cockiness of youth; the swagger of a young man with big plans and no horizons. He could quit his newspaper job, devote all his time to fiction. And so he did.

The first Hardy Boys novel, *The Tower Treasure*, was published in 1927. It begins with the boys on motorcycles, riding side by side, speeding along a shore road, having a conversation:

> "After the help we gave Dad on that forgery case, I guess he'll begin to think we could be detectives when we grow up."
>
> "Why shouldn't we? Isn't he one of the most famous detectives in the country? And aren't we his sons?"

Just how they could be having this ludicrous discussion over the roar of two motorcycles is never quite explained.

The fact is, McFarlane whipped off this passage in minutes, and it was just dandy with the syndicate.

It was dandy with him, too. The Hardy Boys were to be a brief, inconsequential meal ticket. They would take a few days apiece; he would expend no intellectual energy on them, and he would use the pay to underwrite more serious work. He would launch a family and a writing career, and in time be recognized as a man of letters.

Briefly, things went swell. And then came 1929. A bad time to be a writer without a steady paycheck.

"We had no car. We had no coal. My mother always had food on the table, but sometimes it was spaghetti with tomato juice on it."

This is Brian McFarlane, Leslie McFarlane's son. Brian McFarlane would grow up to be a hockey player, and later, a sports broadcaster and prolific writer of books about hockey. He is a member of the Canadian Hockey Hall of Fame.

In his father's diary, there is an entry from the early 1930s. He took baby Brian for a walk, but had to return. Brian's only shoes had fallen apart. Another entry: He had to mail out a manuscript, but he had no money, so he borrowed 10 cents from Brian's piggy bank. Another entry: "We are hoping for some money in time to go to the dance Friday night. It is humiliating to be so hard up."

McFarlane was writing good fiction, but few places were buying. He had only one steady patron, a syndicate that was paying him peanuts to write according to a formula it supplied.

There were children's books at the time written with eloquence—Laura Ingalls Wilder's *Little House on the Prairie*, for example—but the Stratemeyer editors weren't interested in that, certainly not willing to pay enough to achieve it. They wanted simple and dumb.

In the early volumes, McFarlane gamely tried invention. As a foil for the ingenious Hardy Boys, he created two stumblebum local police officers, Chief Collig and Deputy Smuff, who dithered and blundered and misinterpreted clue after clue. It was a technique used by detective writers from Conan Doyle to Christie. But the Stratemeyer Syndicate was not amused. This was fostering a disrespect for authority, it said. McFarlane was ordered, in subsequent volumes, to give the cops a brain.

The message was clear. These were not McFarlane's books. They belonged to men named Edward Stratemeyer, who wanted bilge, and Franklin W. Dixon, who did not exist.

Around this time, McFarlane received a letter from Stratemeyer, reminding him that he might never disclose to anyone his role as ghostwriter of the Hardy Boys. McFarlane was actually relieved. He had been contemplating writing a letter of his own, asking that they never disclose his identity, either.

Nineteen thirty-one. Nineteen thirty-two. Nineteen thirty-three. Norah was born. Now there were three children, and no coal, and precious little food.

The Ghost was chained to his creation.

THE BEST TEACHER I ever had taught tenth-grade English. He made books breathe and tremble. When he gave us an essay exam, he would write the question on the blackboard, and then sit down at his desk, infuriatingly, and wait. For ten minutes, he would not distribute any paper. It forced us to think before we wrote.

He disdained Cliffs Notes and Monarch Notes, those crib-sheet synopses you could buy for a few bucks. They were intellectually bankrupt, he said. Tools of inferior minds.

He looked like a tormented artist. He had a hunted air about him. He dressed well, but often in the same suit, and sometimes it wanted a pressing. He was a talented, driven young man earning a small public school paycheck.

As final exams approached, I found myself swamped with no time to read. We were studying *Gulliver's Travels*. Guiltily, I bought the Monarch Notes. They were written, it turned out, by my teacher.

Sometimes, you do what you have to do.

To see Leslie McFarlane's talent, you need only read *The Ghost of the Hardy Boys*, his autobiography published by Methuen Press in 1976, shortly before his death. It sold only a few thousand copies.

The Ghost of the Hardy Boys is an elegant book, full of charm and pathos and whimsy. The writing is restrained, the characterizations deep and rich, the humor nuanced.

McFarlane reveals that he was a poor student who barely survived high school math. He passed, he writes dryly, only "by a process of elimination, like a tapeworm."

He fell in love with newspapers as a boy when he walked into the offices of the *Daily Haileyburian*: "Every place of employment has its own odor of sanctity. At the sawmill you sniffed fresh pine boards and the wet bark of trees. . . . The movie theater had its own special fragrance of celluloid and collodion and the blond cashier's eau de lilac. But the composing room of the Haileyburian was rich with the smell of Ink!"

His favorite editor was a curmudgeon named Beckett. One day, Beckett tried to stamp out a burning wastebasket, and got his foot caught. McFarlane writes:

> Laughing uproariously, Beckett lunged around the office with one leg of his pants on fire, trying to kick himself free. Every kick sent blazing papers in all directions. The society editor screamed and bent over to pick up one of the papers. If you have never

seen a blonde society editor kicked in the ass by a flaming wastebasket, you have missed one of the rare experiences of journalism.

And, finally, Leslie McFarlane wrote of the Depression:

There was so much that was demeaning about the Depression, such wreckage of hopes, plans, careers and human pride . . . if a family became penniless, there was merely relief in dribs and drabs of food and fuel, grudgingly dispensed by a municipality that couldn't collect its taxes. And there was an old stigma attached to these bounties, the stigma of failure. Proud people would starve before they would let their plight become known.

———————

I ENVISIONED THE young Leslie McFarlane, a fine writer, hunched over his typewriter, babies at his feet, desperate for the money to buy the coal to stoke the furnace to survive another day, haunted by fear, humiliated by his failure, guilty over his gall at subjecting the people he loved to the reckless dream he chased, banging out another idiotic novel for a plutocrat who abused him.

If you are a bad writer, then writing poorly must be no big deal.

But if you are a good writer, writing poorly must be hell. You must die a little with every word.

———————

FROM THE DIARIES, Saturday, December 27, 1931: "Did some more work on the juvenile. . . . It is dull stuff. . . . I will make a New Year's resolution never to do another if I can help it."

As he hacked away, year after year, anonymously becoming

one of the most widely published writers in history, McFarlane held on to his dignity. He maintained a correspondence with great writers of his day, offering his opinions robustly. Norah Perez has a copy of a handwritten letter written to her father in 1938 by F. Scott Fitzgerald. It was responding to a letter from McFarlane in which he apparently had savaged *Tender Is the Night*. Fitzgerald thanked McFarlane for his honesty:

> One of the ghastly aspects of my gloom was a horrible feeling that I wasn't being read. And I'd rather have a sharp criticism of my pet child Tender Is the Night such as yours was, than the feeling of pouring out endless words to fall upon few ears. I rather think I am done as a writer—maybe not, of course. The fact that I can still write a vivid metaphor or solve a technical problem with some suavity wouldn't be an indicator one way or another.

Fitzgerald was as skillful, and as rewarded, as any writer of his time. He died two years later, deeply doubting his talents.

For five years after the Depression hit, during the worst years of doubt and shame, Leslie McFarlane hit the bottle. Drink is the bane of the writer at war with himself, and it nearly destroyed this one. His wife, Amy, a woman of uncommon strength, threatened to leave him.

This is not a chapter of his life that McFarlane has chosen to chronicle in his memoirs. His son, Brian, reveals it. His father, he says, was endangering his life and his family.

A writer can be the most selfish person on Earth—demanding silence, expecting adulation, shamelessly mining the privacy of those around him for literary material. McFarlane did all that. He was no hero. But at his center lay something heroically unselfish. It showed up in the Hardy Boys—not on the pages themselves, but in the simple fact that he was writing them at all. McFarlane was willing to demean himself and, as he saw it, to betray his craft, in order to put food on the table.

And now he faced the loss of his family. The end was in sight, and he knew it.

So McFarlane took the page out of the typewriter, crumpled it up, and wrote a new end. Good writers know when to do that.

He left home for a few weeks and went to a clinic in Hamilton, Ontario. Got himself straight. And never was drunk again.

McFarlane finally unchained himself from the Hardy Boys in 1946; the syndicate didn't care. It found another hungry writer to continue the series. To date, there are more than one hundred Hardy Boys mysteries, and they are still going strong. In 1959, many of the old Hardy Boys books were redone, streamlined, modernized, sterilized. McFarlane was never consulted, but he didn't mind. Nor did he feel ripped off by their fantastic success. A deal is a deal, he always said. He agreed to it, so he couldn't complain.

McFarlane found a new niche. Briefly, he was fiction editor of *Maclean's* magazine. He produced acclaimed documentary films, wrote an excellent hockey novel (*McGonigle Scores!*) and TV scripts for *Bonanza* and *The United States Steel Hour*. He never made a hell of a lot of money, but he made a living, and he did it the way he wanted.

Always, he encouraged his children to write, and Norah Perez credits her father's love and support for her successful career.

"In your writings," he wrote her in a letter in 1973, "don't ever give way to feelings of inadequacy or doubts. . . ."

In another letter: "It occurs to me that Shakespeare must have been the happiest man who ever lived. Imagine being able to set down really marvelous lines every day of one's writing life and being able to say: 'There now. That, by God, is really good.'"

Shortly before he died in 1977 of complications from diabetes, he spoke with Norah. He had been hallucinating, and when he came out of it, he was afraid. Not of death, but of history. He told her he feared he would be remembered only for the accursed Hardy Boys.

———————

WELL, HERE THEY are. The accursed Hardy Boys. Volumes 1 through 21. The official Canon.

I read them again, for the first time.

Yes, the writing is pedestrian. Words are misused and over-used. Teenagers speak in a language so dated it likely never existed. "What the dickens!?!" says Frank. "That fellow is certainly a queer stick," says Joe. Between pages 9 and 17 in *Hunting for Hidden Gold*, a storm "redoubles" its "fury" four times. Clichés abound. Hearts pound with excitement. People breathe sighs of relief.

I can see McFarlane at the typewriter, numbed stupid by the strictures under which he wrote.

Still, I couldn't help but notice that virtually nowhere in these books does one find the word "very."

And in some odd way, I found myself reluctantly captivated by these idiotic coincidence-driven plots. They do move along nicely. Every chapter ends with a cliffhanger. McFarlane made you turn the page.

And as you turn, you notice something else. After page upon page of dreary writing, there is an all-too-brief moment in which the writer seems suddenly engaged. You stumble onto a passage of unmistakable quality. It often occurs at the appearance of Gertrude, the Hardy Boys' cantankerous maiden aunt. McFarlane liked Gertrude. Here she is described as "an elderly, crotchety lady of certain temper and uncertain years." That's nice.

And here, from *The Missing Chums*, is Gertrude's debut: "Frank rushed to the window in time to see Aunt Gertrude, attired in voluminous garments of a fashion dating back at least a decade, laboriously emerging from the taxicab. She was a large woman with a strident voice, and the Hardy boys could hear her vigorously disputing the amount of the fare. This was a matter of principle with Aunt Gertrude, who always argued with taxi drivers as a matter of course, it being her firm conviction that they were unanimously in a conspiracy to overcharge her and defraud her."

If you are a good writer, you cannot hide it forever, no matter how hard you try. It's like trying to stifle a sneeze.

Gertrude enters the house and learns that Frank and Joe are planning on going out on their boat to search for Biff and Chet, who are missing. She lectures the Hardy Boys' mother:

> "I suppose they were out on a boat trip, too. I knew it! And now they're lost. That's what happens when you let children go out in boats. They get lost. Or drowned. And now you would let these two youngsters go out in a boat, too. And I suppose in a few days some of their chums would have to go out in a boat to look for them. They'd get lost, too. And then some more little boys would go out to look for them. And they'd get lost. By the end of the summer there wouldn't be a boy left in Bayport. Not that it would be much of a loss."

There, now. That, by God, is really good.

Roger and Me

I came up with the idea for this essay in the mid-1980s, but I did not write it. It had to be published on a specific day that was years away.

I am chronically disorganized. I keep no calendar. My memory is terrible, and in this case it didn't kick in until the last moment. I wound up writing this in one hour, on deadline.

October 1, 1995

DURING THE AUTUMN of 1961, I was in Sal's every two weeks or so. Haircuts were short and required maintenance. They all cost the same, a buck seventy-five. They all *were* the same. In the South Bronx in 1961, every man and boy walked the streets looking like Howdy Doody.

In Sal's, I was not permitted to speak. I was nine years old, and the floor belonged to men my father's age, men who arrived in topcoats and fedoras. As they got their hair cut, they smoked cigars with the bands still on. Sal's smelled of Hav-a-Tampas and witch hazel and sour grapes.

All they talked about in that fall of 1961 was the disgraceful thing that was happening day after day a mile or two down the road, in Yankee Stadium. A kid with a sneer on his lip and fear in his eyes was closing in on a record that was thirty-four years old. Damn record was older than he was.

It was the Babe's record. A nobody, chasing Babe Ruth. Like he coulda carried the Babe's jockstrap. Like the pitchers today wasn't all cream puffs. Like there was anyone in the Bigs who could throw like Feller anymore.

Every last one of these men, it seemed, had watched the Babe hit his sixtieth home run. They all had been at the Stadium to see it, thirty-four years before.

Sal was Italian. He talked like Chico Marx. His Jewish customers talked like Jackie Mason. His Irish customers talked like leprechauns. These men shared nothing in their lives, but on this issue of Roger Maris's inadequacy, they were in agreement.

Thirty-four years. A record lasts that long, it's supposed to last forever. It's not supposed to be broken by some putz. By some donkey. By some goombah.

To me, thirty-four years seemed like another epoch, so remote it was unreal. I knew it only from pictures in old baseball books. Uniforms fit like pajamas. Gloves were small and lumpy, as though they were made of modeling clay. The players had bad teeth and stubble.

In the fall of 1961, I was a Roger Maris fan, but in Sal's Barber Shop I kept my mouth shut.

I understand now that it was not Maris that these men hated, but the thirty-four years. Time was crowding them. You look up, and pretty soon thirty-four years are gone, and the Babe is dead, and what does that make you, going to the same barbershop for the same haircut? With every home run Roger Maris hit, the men in the barbershop suffered a loss. They were grieving for themselves.

On the day that Maris pulled a 2-1 fastball into the right-field bleachers, I was in my back yard, listening to a staticky transistor radio, not quite sure what had happened until Red Barber repeated it twice. I remember running in circles, drunk on the moment, until I collapsed.

The next day was my tenth birthday. I would get a birthday party, and for my party I would get a haircut. For once, I couldn't wait.

These days, when I take my son to the hairstylist, no one talks sports. No one talks at all. The place is too big and too impersonal. Not like in my day.

My son is eleven. He humors me, but the truth is he doesn't care much for baseball. He's into Nintendo.

"Into" Nintendo. Listen to me.

I still root for the Yankees, though it's not the same anymore. Players are mercenaries who hop from club to club. You find yourself rooting for a uniform now, not a team. I'll still watch the games, sometimes. Sometimes, I'll be smoking a cigar.

Roger Maris is dead now. When I hear someone say he was a bum, a one-year wonder, it gets me pretty burned. I saw the man play. In person. At the Stadium. He played with heart. His arm was a howitzer.

When was the last time you saw a right fielder throw two men out at home in the same game?

When was the last time you saw someone hit sixty-one home runs in a season?

I'll tell you when, kid.

Thirty-four years ago, today.

The Armpit of America

I am a smartass. The malady was diagnosed at an early age and appears to be incurable. And so, when a quick Web search discovered that dozens of different cities and towns have been at times contemptuously described as "the Armpit of America," I knew instantly that this was a problem that needed to be rectified. So I set out to find, and officially designate, the One True Armpit.

What happened between my reporting the story and writing the story was something no smartass could anticipate or preempt: the 11th of September, 2001. The country was united in sorrow, and suddenly, the snotty story I intended to write became unthinkable.

I told my editor that I thought we should kill it, but he refused to let the smartass off the hook. Go back to the Armpit, he ordered, and find its heart.

December 2, 2001

MY LITTLE PUDDLE jumper begins its descent into Elko, a charmless city of 20,000 in the northern Nevada desert. Eighteen seats, all filled. This is not because

Elko is a hot tourist attraction; it is because almost everyone else onboard belongs to a mariachi band. These guys have identical shiny blue suits and shiny blue shirts and shiny blue ties and shiny blue-black hair, like Rex Morgan in the comics, and they seem embarrassed to have accepted a gig in a place as tacky as Elko.

Compared with my final destination, Elko is Florence during the Italian Renaissance.

When I tell the Elko rental car agent where I am headed, she laughs. Elkonians, who proudly sponsor a yearly civic event called the Man-Mule Race, consider their neighbor seventy miles west to be an absolute clodhoppy riot.

"Don't sneeze," snorts the rental car woman, "or you'll miss it."

Yeah, I know. I'd been to Battle Mountain five weeks before, to see if it was dreadful enough to be anointed, officially, "the Armpit of America." I was exorbitantly convinced.

That first visit was in late August. This second one is in early October. In the interim, Everything Changed. With the nation united in mourning and at war, with the Stars and Stripes aflutter in places large and small, slick and hicky, the idea of poking fun at any one part of us became a great deal less funny. The *Zeitgeist* had shifted. Snide was out.

I had to go back, to rethink things.

The road to Battle Mountain is flatter than any cliché—even pancakes have a certain doughy topology. On this route, there is nothing. No curves. No trees. It is desert, but it is lacking any desert-type beauty. No cacti. No tumbleweeds. None of those spooky cow skulls. The only flora consists of nondescript scrub that resembles acre upon acre of toilet brushes buried to the hilt.

You know you have arrived at Battle Mountain because the town has marked its identity on a nearby hill in enormous letters fashioned from whitewashed rock.

I have returned to this place to find in it not America's armpit, but America's heart. I am here to mine the good in it, to tell the world that Battle Mountain doesn't stink. That is my new challenge.

I hang a right off the highway at the base of the hill, which proudly proclaims, in giant letters:

BM

Man. This is not going to be easy.

Take a small town, remove any trace of history, character, or charm. Allow nothing with any redeeming qualities within city limits—this includes food, motel beds, service personnel. Then place this pathetic assemblage of ghastly buildings and nasty people on a freeway in the midst of a harsh, uninviting wilderness, far enough from the nearest city to be inconvenient, but not so far for it to develop a character of its own. You now have created Battle Mountain, Nevada.

The letter was signed by Seattle resident Peter Hartikka, one of 220 people who mailed in their nominations for the nation's foulest place. I had invited these letters in my humor column after discovering on the Web a dismayingly indiscriminate use of the term "Armpit of America." Hundreds of people were describing dozens of locations they happened to dislike. It seemed an unacceptable anarchy of scorn.

The nominations were, literally, all over the map. There were predictable urban cesspools (East St. Louis, Illinois; Elizabeth, New Jersey). There were places of idiotic purpose (Branson, Missouri; Las Vegas, Nevada). There were places of legendary lack of class (Buffalo, New York; Fargo, North Dakota).

The winnowing proved easy. Several nominees bit the dust because they are proximate to someplace immeasurably better. Gary, Indiana, and Camden, New Jersey, two of the nation's least appealing locales, won reprieves because of their nearness to Chicago and Philadelphia. The armpit must smother. It can permit no escape.

Likewise, many promising candidates succumbed to personal knowledge or basic research. Terre Haute, Indiana, a bland and sullen city popular with the KKK, offers too many cultural opportunities to make the cut. Wilkes-Barre, Pennsylvania, may be awful, but next-door neighbor Scranton is awfuller, and Scranton has a certain likable pugnacity that comes from knowing you are famously crummy and not giving two hoots. The otherwise leprous Bridgeport, Connecticut, was spared because it produced my wife. (The winnowing was not entirely without bias.)

Butte, Montana, may have surrendered its soul and much of its natural beauty to rapacious mining interests, and its citizenry may be congenitally inhospitable, and the city may resemble a suppurating chancre sore and smell like the sulfurous Stygian River of Woe, but . . . actually, there is no but about Butte. Research confirmed its foulness and it might well have become the Armpit had it not been blown out by the competition.

There is a maxim in journalism that some stories are just too good to check out. What that means is that the juiciest of tips, when subjected to research, tend to desiccate and crumble. I feared this with Battle Mountain, but after two days of research, I was ablubber in juice.

The town began as a lie. Prospector George Tannihill christened it in 1866 as a mining district, saying he chose the name to commemorate the fierce battle he and twenty-three settlers led by a Captain Pierson had heroically won against marauding Indians there in 1857. Nevada historians have since poked a few holes in this story: There appears never to have been a Captain

Pierson, or twenty-three settlers, or any attacking Indians, or a battle, or pioneer heroism, or, for that matter, a mountain. (There does appear to have been a year 1857.)

According to David Toll's *Complete Nevada Traveler,* the Battle Mountain area has two famous alumni. The first is W. J. Forbes, the Mencken of the Southwest. His was a brilliant if quixotic journalistic march across California, Nevada, and Utah, culminating in the creation of a Battle Mountain newspaper named *Measure for Measure* in 1873. Unfortunately, it was designed to appeal to people who liked to read and knew how to think. When it failed, Forbes spiraled into depression and drink. As summarized half a century later by Carson City journalist Sam Davis: "A friend found [Forbes] stiff and cold across his shabby bed. He had fought a fight against all odds all his life, was one of the brightest geniuses the coast had ever seen, but he . . . lived in communities where his mental brightness was more envied than appreciated."

Battle Mountain, where genius comes to die.

But no Battle Mountaineer past or present reached the level of fame attained by Civil War General James H. Ledlie, who retired to the area after the war, and even has a railroad siding named after him. Ledlie's name actually found its way onto the lips of a president of the United States, and in a startling superlative. Ulysses S. Grant himself called General Ledlie "the greatest coward of the Civil War."

A notorious gambler and drooling drunk, Ledlie had been in command of a division of Union soldiers in 1864 when a group of Pennsylvania coal miners boldly dug a tunnel underneath Confederate lines protecting Petersburg, Virginia, packed it with explosives, and blew it up. Ledlie's troops were to have stormed the confused enemy, but the general was soused in his bunker and refused to come out. His men mounted the attack in leaderless disarray and were slaughtered like rabbits.

Battle Mountain was built as a mining town, and still survives as one, but just barely. Gold prices have lately been low, and the local mines have been cutting back. The population has recently sunk to just under 4,000. Without money from mining, there isn't much to recommend it. Even God discourages visitors: In the summer, Battle Mountain temperatures hit 100 by day and plummet to 45 at night. Winters typically see a month or more at subzero.

It is valuable to research a town through published material; it is far more valuable to talk to people who know it well. I found that the surest way to get a spirited defense of a place was by phoning a reporter who works there. Journalists may be notorious for their negativity, but when the *Washington Post* calls to say it is thinking of identifying as the Armpit of America the city or town in which your career is unspooling, negativity often yields nicely to sputtering indignation. At least, that was the way it usually worked.

I telephoned Lorrie Baumann, editor of the *Battle Mountain Bugle*, and told her my idea.

"The Armpit of America?" she said.

"That's sort of the, um, concept."

Silence.

"Sounds about right," she said.

But it's a such a big country, I said, with so many crappy places. How could I be sure this was the 'pit?

Lorrie's response was as dry as a desert full of toilet brushes.

"I think a quick drive around downtown will answer any questions that might be lingering in your mind."

I ordered up a plane ticket.

Still, I had one more call. The tough one. I couldn't very well arrive unannounced. Sharlene "Shar" Peterson is the executive director of the Battle Mountain Chamber of Commerce. She told me a little about the town, and then I told her what I was proposing to do.

She laughed, then didn't say much of anything for a bit.

The Battle Mountain Chamber of Commerce was thinking. Shar?

"Well, I mean, who wants to be called an armpit? But, you know . . ."

I sensed where she was going. I wanted to kiss her.

". . . This could be an asset. We're just a dying, ugly little mining town without a real identity. It could be an opportunity."

Is this a great country, or what?

"Listen," Shar said, a trace of concern creeping into her voice, "I have to tell you we now have a Super 8 Motel and a McDonald's. I hope that doesn't knock us out of the running."

AND SO I went. It was my first trip, the one where cynicism was still allowed.

Signs are designed to convey information, and the signage of Battle Mountain speaks with eloquence. I'm not just talking about the big, thundering messages, like the enormous BM. Humbler signs have their stories to tell, too.

Downtown Battle Mountain boasts three principal business establishments, each with its own marquee, each a triumph of misinformation. The most elaborate sign adorns the Owl Club; it is a huge neon triptych featuring a smiling hoot owl proudly serving up a tray of piping hot food, a cow dourly contemplating the words CHOICE STEAKS, and a big, blocky, authoritative FAMILY DINING.

The Owl Club serves no food. It's a bar. Its restaurant is closed.

Two doors down is the Nevada Hotel, where several placards inside, yellowed with age and indifference, caution against "obcene" language. Outside, the Nevada Hotel's marquee is 20 feet high and transforms nightly into the defiantly gap-toothed NEVADA HO EL.

It is not a hotel. It's mostly a bar and restaurant. There are rooms, but they have no TVs and no phones and they don't rent them out.

But my favorite sign is the one down the block, at Donna's Diner. If there exists in America a more eloquent testament to the Jughead shrug, a better paean to intellectual lassitude and inertia, I demand to see it. At some point in the past, evidently, Donna's Diner ordered itself up a fancy illuminated sign. And the sign came, and the letters came, and the time came to put the letters on the sign, and wuh-oh. Not enough room.

Now, there are several ways to deal with such a situation. You can order yourself up a bigger sign, or you can buy some smaller letters, or you can do what Donna's Diner did, which is this: DONNA' DINER.

According to *The Complete Nevada Traveler,* Donna's Diner is "a local treasure." I headed there dubiously, because in my first half-hour in town I had not observed much in the way of riches. I'd seen age, but no quaintness. I'd seen buildings, but no architecture. There was a coin-operated community car wash, but no community park. There was a store that sells only fireworks, but none that sells only clothing. There was a brothel, but no ice-cream parlor. There were at least seven saloons, but no movie theater.

(There were entertainment opportunities. A flyer advertised an event at the upcoming county fair, where a cow is led over a grid of numbered squares, and you bet on the numbers, and you win if the cow poops on your number.)

Sensing there must be more to Battle Mountain—a hidden sophistication behind its bucktoothed rustic front—I bellied up to an oilcloth-covered table at Donna's and signaled for service. I picked up a humor book that sits on every table and opened to a list of "Things That Will Not Impress City Women." One was "Leaving the hanky from your nosebleed stuffed up there when you go dancing."

I told owner Jerry Williams I was trying to get a feel for the soul of the place, and I wondered if he could be a sort of ambassador for Battle Mountain and tell me what there was to do.

"Do?"

"Right."

"In Battle Mountain?"

"Yes."

"Absolutely nothing."

Eventually, as I ate Donna's specialty sandwich—fried, breaded frozen shrimp on toast with green pepper and a slice of cheese the color of a traffic cone—Jerry opined that the two things people do are what people do in every city in Nevada, which is drink and gamble.

I am not a particularly knowledgeable gambler, but I have an image of what a casino is, thanks to James Bond. Casinos contain tuxedoed cads and rotters with slender mustaches, and ladies in sequined gowns that hug their behinds. There are dice tables, and blackjack tables, and roulette wheels, and games so complex and exotic they can only be played by persons from Zurich.

In Battle Mountain, casinos are basically drunks at slot machines. They play with the intensity and excitement of people sorting socks at a Laundromat.

At the Nevada Hotel bar, there is a video poker machine at every bar stool. I was playing and losing, and drinking a beer. Beside me, mechanic Mel Langer was playing and losing, and drinking a beer. Mel is a mechanic. He said the people here are nice and friendly, but there isn't much to do.

Bartender Helen Lumpkin agreed. It's worst for the kids, she said, because they find excitement in the wrong places: "Fifteen-year-old girls with bellies out to here." Mel looked around conspiratorially and lowered his voice.

"When I moved here seven years ago from California, the odd thing was, the thing I noticed, and I'm not being negative . . ."

He took a drink.

". . . I am just saying, without being faultfinding, don't get me wrong, what I noticed was the obesity of the women. Have you noticed that?"

Gallantly, I said I had not.

"Well, the men work in the mines day and night and there's nothing to do for the women except eat."

One thing to do is bird huntin'. There is nothing quite as delicious, or as beautiful, as ducks in the wild, with splendiferous iridescent greens and blues and broad chests of rich mahogany. Alas, there aren't that many ducks around Battle Mountain. Battle Mountain bird hunters tend to settle for something called a chukar, a bird with the peculiar habit of running up hills and flying down. Chukars don't make good eating, but locals are pretty proud of them just the same.

Helen has one in a glass showcase behind the bar. She showed it to me.

"So that's the famous chukar I've been hearing about," I said.

It's a scrawny little flapdoodly thing with mottled feathers and a hooked beak.

"Yep, that's the chukar."

It looks like a cross between a chicken and a pigeon, with the least fortunate features of each. It is the color of dirt.

"So there it is, then."

"There it is."

As you enter Battle Mountain, a large billboard promises two things: FINE DINING and A GOOD NIGHT'S REST. Having despaired of finding the first, I aspired to the second at the famous Owl Club, where rooms are only $29 because the place doesn't go in for fancy big-city amenities like a coffeemaker in the room, or an iron, or a shoe-buffing cloth, or shampoo, or a clock, or a telephone, or spotless carpeting.

I sank into bed for my promised good night's sleep, which I admit, in all candor, was delivered exactly as advertised, the solemn covenant between Battle Mountain and its guests remaining intact right up until 4:21 A.M. when the Union Pacific rumbled and roared and clanged and whistled its way through downtown, about 200 feet away.

Breakfast was pretty good flapjacks at the counter at the Nevada Hotel, where I had come to discover for myself the niceness and hospitality that I'd been hearing tell of.

I soon found myself surrounded by guys who plainly did not like who I was or what I was doing there. Hubert Sharp, a short, square man with a short, square haircut, has been living in Battle Mountain for twenty years, and he informed me he would not live in Washington, D.C., "if you gave me title to the whole place." When I asked why, Hubert said something about the citizenry of Washington that was so offensive, it occurred to me he might have kin in Terre Haute.

Hubert and his pals Bill Elquist and Tom Beebe meet here some mornings, a sort of rump parliament of Battle Mountain. Tom used to be the sheriff. Bill, who owns a backhoe and does odd jobs, is one of three Lander County commissioners; the commissioners run the town, which has no mayor.

Pretty soon the door opened and a big guy named Max walked in and occupied a stool. Max is a pooh-bah. As the town's justice of the peace, he presides over all criminal and civil matters. I told him who I was and why I was there, and he grunted noncommittally and picked up a fly swatter.

"Max, what's your last name?" I asked, pen in hand.

A fly alighted on the counter.

"I'm not going to tell you."

"But you're the judge. You're a public official. You have to tell me."

Whap! The fly escaped.

"No, I don't," said Judge Max.

His name is Max Bunch. I learned that from Lorrie Baumann, the editor of the *Battle Mountain Bugle*. Lorrie knows everything. She does everything: Takes pictures, writes stories, edits stories. With her knowledge of the town, she has few illusions.

Nevada, she said, attracts people who have trouble fitting in anywhere else, and of those misfits, the ones who have trouble fitting in in Nevada go to small towns like Battle Mountain.

"For the folks who like it here," she said, "it's mostly a matter of not being able to imagine anything else."

When I'd asked Battle Mountaineers what they most wish they had, a startling number mentioned a Wal-Mart. The closest one is in Winnemucca, fifty-two miles away. No one mentioned what I would have mentioned, which is anything bespeaking age, history, or architecture. The town once had a nice old train station. They tore it down.

In Battle Mountain, entropy reigns; architectural context is nonexistent. One of the prettier wooden houses, with two levels and a porch, is 40 feet from the twenty-four-hour car wash, serve-yourself, $1. Corrugated aluminum and aluminum siding seem to be the building material of choice. There are a lot of trailers. One had a smaller trailer in the back yard.

"When I first came here a couple of years ago," Lorrie said, "Battle Mountain was in the middle of constructing a new jail. Well, when it opened, one of the county officials was speaking, and he said it's great we have a wonderful new jail but it's a pity that it is the nicest building in town."

I had one more question, and I was almost embarrassed to ask it: How could she bring herself to live here?

"I don't."

Lorrie Baumann lives in Winnemucca. That was the deal under which she took the job editing the *Battle Mountain Bugle*: that they didn't make her live in Battle Mountain.

Shar Peterson is a slim, attractive, intense woman with striking hair that appears to have been styled by a Van de Graaff generator. The executive director of the Battle Mountain Chamber of Commerce is always smiling, and she was smiling at this very moment, but I knew she wasn't glad to see me. After our first phone conversation, Shar had talked to some of the town mothers and fathers, who apparently had not shared her vision about the terrific publicity potential of this armpit thing. As Shar put it, "Some people are taking it as a negative."

Shar had apparently been strongly encouraged to dissuade me from my mission, to argue the case against the armpit. Once enthusiastic collaborators, we were, at the moment, potential antagonists.

I sat down. Laid my cards on the table.

"Shar," I said, "this is not a handsome town."

"We understand that," she said, her smile defiantly unbroken.

Shar was doing her level best to show me the highlights of Battle Mountain. It was not easy. It was, in fact, a grim little exercise in desperation salesmanship.

Heading out on Route 305, Shar pointed out several distant hills in the Shoshone mountain range.

"That looked better before the fires."

And:

"Usually, in different weather, that's a nice view of the valley."

And:

"The people aren't exactly xenophobic. You just have to earn their trust."

We saw several distant peaks with bald smears caused by mining. "They'll look normal afterwards. They'll just be a little less high."

Shar wanted to show me some of the nicer houses, but they

were scattered around, so to get to them we had to pass homes that looked like the sort of place Snuffy Smith's wife, Loweezy, is forever brooming out.

Shar came here many years ago, when her husband got a good job in a local mine. He still has it, and so she is still here. She loves it, she said. She said it three times.

I said nothing. We passed one of the more expensive homes. It features a rather startling facade of faux boulders that sort of look like stone, the way cardboard sort of looks like oak.

"I have two choices," Shar said at last. "To make myself miserable or to learn to love where I am. Do you know what I mean?"

I did.

"Okay, maybe we're an armpit," Shar said. "If so, we're shaven, and clean, and sweet-smelling because out here in the desert, we're arid, extra dry."

The woman is very good.

DOUG MILLS OWNS Battle Mountain's Mills Pharmacy, which was the only place in town I could find a "Battle Mountain" T-shirt for sale. It had a cartoon of a mining car filled with nuggets of something oddly brown that are either shining or stinking, depending on how you interpret the lines radiating from it. Doug is a major civic booster; he has a pet project he thinks can help turn the town's fortunes around.

Out at the airstrip are a few vintage airplanes. They just need a little restoration, Doug figures, and they could become the centerpiece of a Battle Mountain museum. His concept is something called "Planes, Trains, and Automobiles," celebrating Battle Mountain's storied history involving all three transportation modes.

Trains, I understood. Battle Mountain was built by the railroads. What about planes?

Amelia Earhart, he said, once stopped here to refuel during a solo transcontinental autogiro flight.

Okaaaay. And automobiles?

Doug studied his shoes.

The town of Carlin, he said, which is real nearby, "was the home of the first Datsun dealership in Nevada."

I let this marinate in the silence.

"Well," Doug said, "you got to go with what you got."

HANG A LEFT at Battle Mountain's only sort-of traffic light (it blinks red twenty-four hours a day), cross the railroad tracks, follow the big red arrows, and you're at Donna's Battle Mountain Ranch. An enormous parking lot accommodates eighteen-wheelers, which tend to park outside for about twenty minutes at a time with the engines running. Donna's Battle Mountain Ranch, open twenty-four hours a day, Visa and MasterCard accepted, ATM on the premises, is probably the most successful retail business in town.

One hundred dollars an hour, three girls on call, take your pick: the one who is a little skinny, the one who is a little big, or the one who is a little old. They all seem nice and friendly and accommodating. It's all perfectly legal.

I was here only because I was ordered to come. When I asked Gene Sullivan, one of the three county commissioners, where I should go in town, he'd nodded solemnly in the direction of the railroad tracks. "Whorehouse," he said.

I figured he must have had his reasons. Probably he knew that the management would express its gratitude to the town that sustains it, and respect for the locals who are open enough to expose their vulnerability in the timeless transaction of the hungry heart.

The locals are louts and creeps, said Paula Navar, day manager, who tends bar beneath a painting of a voluptuous nude.

"They raise hell," she said. Most of the clients at Donna's Ranch are transients, drivers en route from one place to another. Paula said they're swell.

"They're gentlemen. It's the locals, when they come in, who cause the most trouble. They just don't know any better. With them it's 'whore' this and 'whore' that. Listen, I know whores. I've worked with whores. These ladies are not whores."

A middle-aged redhead with big glasses, Paula said she loves her job and loves and respects her bosses, if not the town.

Paula considers herself an outcast in Battle Mountain—an attractive single mother, perennially under suspicion by Battle Mountain wives as a potential home wrecker. She finds this funny.

"I don't want their husbands. I don't want to be married to Billy Bob."

Evening was approaching and it was almost time to leave, but I had one more place to visit. The literature about Battle Mountain said the sunsets are spectacular, if viewed from the prime sunset-viewing spot. So I went. I was alone, at the top of a hill, Battle Mountain behind me, squinting westward as the Earth wheeled and the sun began to sink behind the Shoshones.

The clouds were like shredded gauze, and slowly they glowed a resplendent, fiery orange against the baby-blue sky, outlined like the beard of a disapproving Celtic god. It all seemed beautiful and humbling, out there at the famous sunset-viewing site, above the NO DUMPING sign riddled with buckshot, beside the placard authorizing acceptance of "municipal solid waste," "construction and demolition debris," "tires," "dead animals," "medical waste," and "non-friable asbestos," out there alone with nothing but my thoughts and a disquieting fragrance carried on the west wind, out there at the dump.

———————

ALAS, THE EARTH kept wheeling. September 11 came and went, and everything you have just read became impossible to publish. Which is why I have returned, with a new mission. A rescue mission.

Seattle photographer Brian Smale arrived the day before me and began shooting on his own. He knew this was about the Armpit of America, but no one had told him about the new mission. So, when we finally meet up, Brian Smale is all smiles.

"This is easy!" he says. "This is like fishing with poison!"

Oh, man.

Karen Davis is the owner and chief hairstylist of Stewart's Styling Salon, a full-service beauty parlor that also sells china figurines, candles, clocks, leather jackets, celebrity posters, and underpants.

"It's a small town," says Karen, "so you have to diversify or you'll never make it." She is forty-two, a Kate Winslet type, and she grew up in Battle Mountain and raised her children here. She is smart, sophisticated, the kind of woman who could succeed anywhere, but who has chosen to succeed here. I have decided she is to be my first triumphal interview in the Battle Mountain Reclamation Project.

So, it's a pretty okay place, then?

"There a lot of good people here," she says, measuredly. "There's a lot to be said for living in the wide-open desert. People who can't see the beauty here are lacking something in themselves."

So, it's a *great* place, then?

Karen says it can be a little difficult for people like her and her husband, who don't drink or gamble and who like culture and fine dining and nice clothes. But, she quickly adds, there's plenty to do when you're raising kids, because you are involved in their school activities.

Her kids are almost grown up, now?

"Yes."

And?

"And I want out of here so bad I could scream."

IT IS NOT coincidence that I have returned to this place during the week of October 1–6. This is to be Battle Mountain's finest hour. The town has been chosen to host an international event, the world championship human-powered vehicle race, in which competitors attempt to set a land-speed record on recumbent bicycles. The trials take place every night near dusk, out on Highway 305, just outside of town.

There are only a few dozen spectators, but it's a spectacular sight. The bikes are sleek. They look like bullets, encased in plastic aerodynamic shells, and they reach speeds of almost 80 mph, whizzing nearly soundlessly across the finish line, faster than you could ever imagine an engineless vehicle moving.

Afterward, I collar Matt Weaver, the bike racer surfer dude from California who started the event several years ago, and asked him what factor, or combination of factors, led him to choose, of all places on Earth, Battle Mountain.

Basically, Weaver explains, building up enormous speed on a bike requires a very long stretch of straight road, almost six miles. But it has to be more than straight. It has to be straight and flat, with virtually no gradient. So he got in his car, with sophisticated measuring instruments on the seat beside him, driving thousands of miles looking for a high enough level of flatness, on a flatness meter.

"So, I'm, like, wow, I'm never gonna find this, six miles of road flat enough," he says, "and then suddenly, I am on this stretch, and it says it's level one, and then level two, and then level three, and I'd never seen a level three, and then four, and five, and ding ding ding!"

So he chose Battle Mountain because it had a boring road?

"Very, very, *very* boring!" Matt corrects. But that's not all, he says. It had to be a road that could be closed down easily for the races, he says, so it couldn't be in a place that's used a lot.

So it had to be a very, very, *very* boring road in a very, very, *very* boring place?

"Exactly!"

The reclamation project is not going well at all. In a funk, I find myself shambling over to the most depressing place in town, the cemetery, where I notice something odd. The most recent headstone I can find is from 1988. Have Battle Mountaineers stopped dying? Is boredom some sort of elixir?

It makes no sense. I begin to explore, and finally, I literally stumble over the truth. It's a stone marker level with the ground. All the newer graves have no tombstones. They're easy to miss from a distance.

Here's one with two festive helium balloons tethered to it, dancing in the wind. It's the final resting place of Robert Nevarez, died 1999. There's a handwritten note tucked into his bucket of plastic flowers, and I consider reading it, but I haven't the heart.

The balloons say HAPPY 18TH BIRTHDAY!

Which is when I realize I've been going about this all wrong. This isn't about architecture, roads, weather, cultural opportunities, or ugly little birds.

It's amazing what you can discover when you start to look in the right places.

From today's classifieds in the *Battle Mountain Bugle:* "Several photos and negatives found in Turner Lane. They are miscellaneous shots of people fishing, and a school photo of an eighth-grader named Charlee. To pick them up, please . . ."

I think: Who on Earth would take the sort of time and effort to take out an ad for something so trivial? Not anybody where I come from. We're not boring enough.

On this day, Battle Mountain is transformed. It is homecoming weekend, when the undefeated Battle Mountain Longhorns are taking on the hated Mustangs from Lovelock High, in Pershing County. Nearly every store window is soaped up with pro-Longhorn or anti-Mustang slogans.

And suddenly, I remember something. Back when Shar was squiring me around town, she brought me to see Tom Reichert, the head of Lander County building and planning and economic development. Tom was one of those people who didn't really cotton to this whole armpit idea. He was polite, but prickly.

I dig through my notes.

"This is a very family-oriented place," he'd told me. "The number-one adult entertainment in Battle Mountain is attending youth sports events. I guess it is embarrassing that we're so lacking in things to do, we have to concentrate on our kids."

Now, I'd talked to kids, asked them about growing up here, and mostly I got rolled eyes and vows to bomb out of there at the earliest possible moment. Still, I have to say, a whole lot of kids seem to have spent a whole lot of time soaping the heck out of this town for homecoming.

OVER AT THE Civic Center auditorium, high-schoolers are putting on a talent show. There are maybe thirty rows of seats, maybe twenty seats across. And in a town too small to support two fast-food restaurants, every seat is filled, moms and dads and little brothers and sisters, crammed in the aisles and spilling out into the vestibule, craning to see and straining to hear, over an insufficient PA system, a high school girl lip-syncing Michael Jackson's "Billie Jean."

Afterward, everyone—kids, parents, teachers—repairs to the high school grounds, for the homecoming bonfire. There aren't many trees in these parts, so Battle Mountain High makes do with a giant mound of wooden forklift pallets donated by local businesses.

When ignited with gasoline, these frames make a better than passable bonfire, the flames licking 50 feet into the night sky, against the cheesy backdrop of high-rise signs for the McDonald's and Super 8 Motel, the pyre disbursing heat devils that dance on the grass like little tornadoes. Chipper, fresh-faced teenage girls in cheerleader costumes, girls no bigger than Labrador retrievers, are high-stepping and kicking and chanting in voices that squeak, "We are the mighty, mighty Longhorns," and even littler girls on the side are imitating their varsity big sisters, and the high school band is playing a spiritedly terrible "Born to Be Wild," and parents are whooping and cheering, passing cameras back and forth to remember this forever.

The bonfire throws a lot of heat. You really feel it. It stings your eyes, and reddens your face.

IT'S ALL ABOUT the football game, of course. The Longhorns have a shot at the state championship, but first they must destroy Lovelock. One cheerleader, Natalee Ormond, sixteen, in full costume, has an arm in a sling. What's a broken arm? This is homecoming; you play hurt.

The game has started, but I am watching the grandstands, not quite believing my eyes, and doing some math, and not quite believing my numbers. I count 670 people here, plus the players, which amounts to approximately one-fifth the entire population of Battle Mountain. In the city of Washington, that would be like 115,000 people showing up for a high school game between the Ballou Knights and the Woodson Warriors.

The game is too close for comfort—Battle Mountain is leading 17–14 in the fourth quarter—when the Longhorns have to punt from their 40. A bad snap. Gasps from the crowd. Longhorn punter Nick Sandru is forced to tuck the ball and run. He cuts right, shakes a tackler, sheds another, and races 60 yards for the touchdown, and the game.

The crowd explodes. Out of the corner of my eye, I see a figure in jeans and a polo shirt racing down the sideline, jubilantly trailing the play, arms pumping the air. This is not a coach or a trainer. This is someone who got so beautifully caught up in the joy of this moment that all professional skepticism and cynicism have evaporated here in Battle Mountain, the place she doesn't want to live.

This is Lorrie Baumann, the hard-bitten newspaper editor.

THE SHIRT THAT Rose Carricaburu is wearing has a photograph of the flag-raising at Iwo Jima, and beneath it, it says, "If you want to burn the flag, why don't you ask one of these guys for a match?" Rose owns this place, Rosa's Cantina, out across the railroad tracks, near the whorehouse.

A month after September 11, you can see plenty of American flags in town, though the pall that hangs over Washington and New York is not evident here. Osama bin Laden is unlikely to be targeting Battle Mountain. The can behind the bar is taking donations, but not for disaster relief. "We Love You, Sherry," it says. Sherry is the owner of a nearby bar, and she has a bum ticker, and they are raising money to maybe get her a new one.

Rose is collecting for a business rival?

"There are no rivals in Battle Mountain," she says.

A weathered-looking guy sidles over. He is James Hopper, who owns H&H Exploration. "There's a flag flying on my trackhoe," he says. "The terrorists, what they've done? They've screwed up! They vaporized those poor people in New York, and they brought the whole nation together. The way I see it, little town USA is just like Big Town USA. We all have hearts, and we all bleed."

He extends a hand.

"The way I see it," Hopper says, "you're my friend. Right?"

Oh, man.

BRIAN THE PHOTOGRAPHER and I are cruising the streets, one last tour through town, and I am explaining to him my dilemma. I don't want to officially declare Battle Mountain the Armpit of America, and the townspeople don't want me to, and I don't have to, and, truth to tell, maybe it isn't. Sure, it's got some jerky people, but it has some fine people, too. Maybe it's not the armpit. Maybe there simply is no such body part now.

On the other hand, Shar Peterson was right. Back there on the phone, before all this began, she was dead-on right. You don't have to be an economist, or a sociologist, or an architect, or a land-use planner, to understand that this place is in trouble. It's got almost nothing going for it.

In America in the twenty-first century, you need something. You need an identity. A personality. You need to be someplace someone's heard of. You need to be able to pass a word-association test. ("L.A." "Movies!" "Detroit." "Cars!")

There's no answer for "Battle Mountain." Yet.

That's my dilemma. Do I hurt them in order to help them?

Lord, give me a sign.

Brian sees it first. He stops the car, and looks up at the sky, and points. My jaw drops.

God may indeed work in mysterious ways. But one thing, surely, is no mystery: He uses available material. When He visits destruction upon the tropics, He doesn't send a blizzard, He summons the power of the warm seas and the tropical winds.

In Battle Mountain, He writes in flickering neon.

Above us looms the highest structure in town, the giant sign on stilts 40 feet above the gas station, an enormous red and yellow SHELL.

The S is burned out.

SO HERE IT is, for better or worse.

Having objectively examined the evidence, which is clear and convincing, and having reached its conclusion beyond a reasonable doubt, the *Washington Post* hereby confers upon the town of Battle Mountain, Nevada, the title of Armpit of America, with all the privileges and responsibilities therein.

I FIND MYSELF returning again and again to something Tom Reichert said to me. Tom is the economic development guy who didn't like the armpit idea one little bit. He argued and argued, and finally said, with some defiance: "Well, if you're going to make us the armpit, fine. You do it. Maybe we can work up some sponsorships. Maybe Secret antiperspirant will buy new uniforms for the girls softball team."

That, Tom, is exactly the idea.

And it would be just the beginning.

I can't make this happen. I've just handed you a tool. The rest is up to the image-makers—people like you. And Shar, who better than anyone understands the possibilities. And Lorrie, who cares way more than she lets on. And Doug Mills, who might consider changing the wording on the Battle Mountain T-shirts he sells at his pharmacy, if you get my drift.

A renaissance for Battle Mountain? The way I see it, this is America, we're all in it together, and anything is possible. All it will take is a little sweat.

Postscript: They did it.

First came the billboards on Interstate 80, bragging about the town's new axillary distinction. One read

BATTLE MOUNTAIN—VOTED THE ARMPIT OF AMERICA BY THE WASHINGTON POST. MAKE US YOUR PIT STOP!

Next came the Festival in the Pit, an annual town fair and carnival, sponsored by Old Spice, that drew visitors from all over the state.

Eventually, the financial anxiety caused by the recession of 2008 turned Battle Mountain's gold mines into . . . gold mines. Property values soared, jobs flowered and the New York Times gave the Armpit a shave, declaring it, at least for the moment, America's boomtown.

My Father's Vision,
Part I

*My father, Philip Weingarten, was born on the day,
almost to the minute, that Archduke Franz Ferdi-
nand was assassinated, triggering the first World War.
I used to joke with my father that he might be the
reincarnation of the pompous, colorful, kangaroo-
hunting aristocrat with the preposterous mustache
and the ostrich-plumed pith helmet. As penance for
his prior arrogance and ostentation, I told him, he'd
been consigned to live this next life as a meek Jewish
accountant in the Bronx.*

December 29, 2002

MY FATHER WAS waiting for me downstairs, punctual
as always, smiling as usual. But when he got into the
car—we were headed to my house for dinner—he
said, "I have a problem."

I am not sure I'd ever heard him use that phrase before. At
eighty-eight, my father is half deaf, three-quarters blind, and 100
percent "fine." He has no problems whatsoever. He would not

consider it a problem if, at dinner, his nose fell off into the soup. "I've still got face holes," he would say. "I'm fine."

So he had my attention, and he kept it.

"I'm seeing things that aren't there."

"What sorts of things?"

"People. People with big teeth."

I pulled out into traffic.

"When do you see them?"

"All the time. I'm seeing them now."

"How do you know they're not real?"

"Well, if they were real, you wouldn't be running them over."

Ah.

And suddenly, I *knew*.

"Do they look like cartoons?" I asked, as matter-of-factly as I could.

"Yes."

"Are they dressed any special way?"

For the love of God, don't say in military outfits.

"Some are wearing uniforms. Khakis. They have chevrons on the sleeves."

Several years ago, while doing research for a quasi-medical humor book I was writing, I happened upon the description of a real neurological condition so rare, and so preposterous, that even some neurologists haven't heard of it. Peduncular hallucinosis occurs when perfectly sane people begin to see small, unthreatening cartoon characters, often in military attire. It is usually caused by a stroke or a tumor deep in the brain. Historically, the diagnosis has been confirmed at, ah, autopsy.

There might be 500 people in the United States who either have this condition or know enough about it to recognize its symptoms, and, near as I could tell, two of them were in my car.

"Do you see anything else? Animals?"

"Only donkeys."

(I feel it necessary to assure you that this is all completely true.)

My father has always been a meek man—given to understatement, reluctant to assert himself, content to let others set agendas. And yet he is also the most practical and centered person I have ever known, blessed with a peace of mind I envy. Because worry is counterproductive, he simply banished it from his life. When I dropped out of college with three credits to go, and proceeded instead to infiltrate a teenage street gang with some vague notion of writing about it, it was my father who persuaded my mother to get her head out of the oven. He said I probably knew what I was doing, and, to my mother's astonishment (and mine), he was right.

Throughout my adult life, my father has remained—even now, in his fragile winter—a bedrock of patience and reassurance upon which can be balanced the most fanciful of ambitions. On this unyielding ground, no plan I ever made ever seemed rickety or unsafe. I've never feared risk.

"How long have you been seeing these things?"

"Two days now."

"Why didn't you tell me sooner?"

Silence.

"You thought you were losing your mind."

"That might have bothered me a little, yes."

We dined that night on false cheer. Afterward, as I was walking him to the car, my father froze in his tracks. He wouldn't budge. I felt his arm trembling.

"There's a hole in front of me," he said. "A deep pit."

I assured him it was level ground, but he would not move. My wife came out and gently took his other elbow. Trust us, she said. So my father closed his eyes, took a breath, and stepped out into the abyss.

The next day we went for a brain scan. No tumor, no stroke.

My father doesn't have peduncular hallucinosis; his is a simi-lar condition—equally bizarre, but not as rare and not as dire—that sometimes afflicts people who lose their eyesight late in life. The hallucinations are identical.

"You can't see, and your brain is getting bored," the doctor told my father, "so it's filling in the blanks."

That brain of his—still as sharp as yours or mine—is doing a splendid job, churning out images his ruined eyes can no lon-ger provide. Colors are brighter, movements are more distinct, and the details he sees—wedding rings, epaulets, facial expres-sions—are precisely the things that long ago disappeared for him into a blur.

And the people! I suspect it reflects well upon the human species that when our brains are freed to create a world of their own design, they deliver happy mischief. His cartoon characters resemble the work of R. Crumb, my father said, and the Kat-zenjammer Kids, and Tom Toles's chubby little bureaucrats, and Goofy the dog. Buckteeth everywhere. (They don't say anything, but if they did, it would probably be some variation of "gawrsh.")

"Could be worse," said my father.

How?

"They could be frightening."

True enough. In the world of cartoons, pain is funny, and no one ever dies.

He was studying something on the floor. I asked what it was.

"A person."

What's he doing?

"Floating down to the ground, using an umbrella."

Sometimes the hallucinations go away, the doctor had told me, and sometimes they don't. Mostly, people simply learn to navigate this strange new world.

"You know, Pop, these people might be with you for a while."

"I know," he said.

We were walking to the car.

"So I'll move around them. Or wait for them to move a little. I'll be fine."

There is a small pivot point, I think, where meekness and courage are indistinguishable.

"What are you seeing right now?"

"RFK Stadium."

"Where?"

"There."

It was a man, walking a dog.

My father shrugged, smiled. He sees what he sees.

We drove in silence for a bit.

"Now I'm seeing cardboard signs on the side of the road. With Hebrew letters."

"What do they say?"

He looked at me like I was crazy. "You know I can't read Hebrew."

Of course, of course. What was I thinking? My father is eighty-eight, and he can't read Hebrew, and he is not losing his mind, and he is not dying, and RFK Stadium is on a small street corner in Bethesda, Maryland, where it will likely remain for some time.

Everything was fine, just fine.

We rode off together, unafraid.

Snowbound

When I was an editor, I once issued a challenge to five writers: Hammer a nail into a phone book, then go write a great profile about whomever the nail stopped at. The idea was to test the old maxim that in the hands of a skilled journalist, absolutely anything can be a story. My five writers did splendidly; they proved it correct.

That was the basic principle behind "Snowbound." I'd been on a plane, leafing through the maps in the in-flight magazine, when I saw the silly-sounding name "Savoonga." It was a flyspeck island off the coast of Alaska, in the Bering Sea, not far from Siberia. It was nowhere. It would be populated by nobodies. When my plane landed I called my editor and proposed that he send me there the following week, still in the dead of winter, with no preparation at all. Not even a minute of research.

"Why?" he asked.

"Just let me do it. It'll be funny," I said.

He did. It wasn't.

May 1, 2005

Let's say you were looking for a vacation destination in winter. And also, that you were out of your mind. You might pull out a map of Alaska, locate Anchorage, and then let your eyes roam north and west, across mountain ranges, through millions of acres of wilderness, until you ran out of dirt. You would be in Nome. Nome: the last outpost, Babylon on the Bering, famously dissolute, said to be home to the desperate, the disillusioned, the hollow-eyed, the surrendered, the exiles, the castaways, the cutthroats, the half dead and the fully juiced. Nome, the end of the Earth.

Only it isn't the end of the Earth. You can see that, right on the map. To get to the end of the Earth from Nome you would have to hop a small plane and head 130 miles out into the Bering Sea, where you would land on an island so remote that it is closer to Russia than to the U.S. mainland. To the people of Siberia, this island is the middle of nowhere. On it, according to the map, is a village named Savoonga.

Savoonga. Va-voom. Bunga-bunga. Funny, no?

I thought so, too, when I first saw it. It gave me an idea for a funny story. In the dead of winter, I would pack up and blindly head to Savoonga, unannounced and unprepared. No research at all, no planning beyond the booking of a room, if there was one to be had.

The whole thing was an inside joke, one with a swagger. It is a journalist's conceit that a good reporter can find a great story anywhere—in any life, however humble, and in any place, however unwelcoming.

That is how photographer Michael Williamson and I came to be in a small commuter plane in late February, squinting out onto a landscape as forbidding, and as starkly beautiful, as anything we'd ever seen. Land was indistinguishable from sea—the white subarctic vista, lit to iridescence by a midafternoon sun, was flat and frozen straight to the horizon. The first clue that we were over an island was when the village materialized below us. It looked as negligible as a boot print in the snow, the grimy, nubby tread left by galoshes. The nubs were one-story buildings, a few dozen of them, and that was it.

I'm back now, trying to make sense of what we saw, trying to figure out how to tell it. It's all still with me, except for the swagger.

──────────

LET'S PUT TO rest one cliché. You *can* sell refrigerators to Eskimos.

The people of Savoonga are Yupiks, the westernmost of the Eskimo tribes, closer to Siberians than American Eskimos in their appearance, and their customs, and their distinctive, liquidly sibilant native language. And, yes, they all have refrigerators. In the winter, food gets freezer burn if left out in the elements. Eskimos need refrigerators to keep their food warm.

I was still unpacking in the small lodge we had rented (two refrigerators!), wondering how to find a funny story line that somehow would capture the otherworldliness of where we were. At that moment, there was a knock on the door. An Eskimo named Larry walked in and produced from beneath his parka, swaddled in a towel, two treasures to sell. They were bones of formidable size, polished to an impressive shine. Each was roughly the dimensions of the handle of a lumberjack's ax. I asked what they were.

"Walrus dicks," he said.

So far, so good.

──────────

THERMOMETER READINGS MEAN little to Savoongans, because in this treeless island village, wind is a constant irritant; on that first day, we were informed, it was "30." That meant minus-5, adjusted by wind chill to minus-30. In Savoonga, in winter, the "minus" is a given.

There is no real way to prepare, physically or mentally, for 30 below. You can dress as warmly as you think appropriate, with long johns and woolen socks and layers of fleece and a sturdy parka and a ski cap, and then you step out into it and you realize that, in the words of Roy Scheider in *Jaws*, you need a bigger boat. When we'd first landed, Michael and I left the plane for two minutes to photograph the unloading of cargo, then we scurried back aboard. With barely a word to each other, but exchanging stupefied glances, we slipped on full-face balaclavas and thick gloves and eye goggles and a second layer of hat.

And soon we were actually walking in it, heading out to explore the village. Thirty below is opportunistic. If you leave a slit between chin and Adam's apple, 30 below works its way in and moves down and around in a darting shiver, like the icy hands of a pickpocket. To take photographs, Michael had to remove his goggles, freezing his eyebrows, as he put it, "in a permanent state of astonishment." Your first lesson, then, is to expose nothing.

Savoonga is home to about 700 people. The inexpensive frame houses have no numbers, the few streets have no names. In the winter, the town rests on 5 feet or more of packed snow, and the only transportation is by snowmobiles, which roar about day and night.

Trudging through town, we found a grocery store, a K-12 school, a small City Hall, a small Christian chapel, a medical clinic, a firehouse, and finally a post office, at which we briefly stopped. Outside it, scratched into a wooden wall, was a welter of remarkably sedate graffiti. Even though this was obviously the handiwork of the young—pop lyrics and so forth—there was barely any profanity. Most writing was a simple assertion of self, followed by the same plaint, repeated in almost identical words, flat, mild, and disturbing.

Here's one: "I was being bored here. 11/13/04. 7:41 A.M."

Also: "I miss Nicholas."

Also: "I miss Ernie."

Also: "I miss Don."

When we returned to our lodge, we had company. Visitors to Savoonga are an event, or, more specifically, an opportunity. A woman named Bessie, toting a baby, offered to sell us a whale tooth. A man had a small carving of a seal made out of walrus tusk. Would-be vendors arrived and departed serially, a minute or two apart. Polite and self-effacing, each person nodded placidly when we declined, then shuffled off; there was no hard sell, no hard-luck story, just resignation.

One visitor had no wares at all. We thought for a moment that he was looking for a handout, but it turned out he just wanted to talk. He appeared to be about sixty-five, a small, leather-skinned man with a stooped bearing, weary eyes, and an apologetic manner. His deeply fissured face bore a Fu Manchu mustache that framed a toothless mouth. The voice belied it all—it was soft, cultured, almost professorial.

He told us his name, which was Dean Kulowiyi, and his age, which was forty-two. If he saw our surprise, he didn't show it.

Born here but educated on the mainland, Dean said he lives in Savoonga because he is stuck here without the means to leave. "I'm a poor man," he said. Partially disabled from a construction accident, he said he survives mostly by hunting and fishing for his food. The Savoongans call this "subsistence living," which in this village is not a lament but a matter of pride, at least to the elders. Still, Dean said, the old way of life is buckling under ferocious assault from modernity. Teens are questioning the ways of their forebears, he said, losing respect for their authority, staying mostly idle, and taking to drink and drugs.

Even the ancient Savoongan art of ivory carving, Dean said, is slowly being lost. He himself learned it at age seven, beside the bench of his grandfather. He seemed proud of this, so we told him we would love to take a look at any carvings he had. But he had none to show—not on his person, not in his home, nowhere on the island. Ivory carving is painstaking work, he said: A single, substantial piece can take months or even years. He must sell everything immediately to survive, he said. Life can be hand to mouth in Savoonga.

Dean brightened: We could see some of his work, he said, if we ventured to Washington, D.C., in the Lower 48, and found a place called the Smithsonian Institution. Had we heard of it?

———

DEAN KULOWIYI, IT would turn out, is one of the world's elite ivory artists. His pieces have sold for thousands, and some have been marketed at Smithsonian gift shops. He inspires imitators, such as our next visitor, a handsome young man named Jason Iya.

Jason arrived as Dean was leaving. "We're cousins on our mother's side, and maybe a little on our father's," Jason said, and both laughed. There are only about twenty Eskimo surnames in Savoonga, as we would discover, and it is hard to find two island natives who are not in some way related.

Jason, twenty-two, is one of a few young, skilled carvers on the island. He showed us a foot-tall, long-necked cormorant he had made, lovely and delicate, sweeping up from a stone base. He was selling it for $200; we'd seen far more primitively rendered pieces in the Anchorage airport for four times the amount. In fact, Jason said, he'd been living near Anchorage, carving and selling his work until a half-year earlier, when he had to come home to help his family.

Help them with what? I asked.

Jason fiddled with his cormorant. He had a downy mustache and sad eyes, and he sat in an eloquent slouch.

"My brother died," he said.

"I'm sorry," I said.

"Everyone on Savoonga named Iya got together to make his casket and cross."

"How did he die?"

Jason studied his boots.

"He got murdered."

He began repacking his carving in bubble wrap.

"How?"

"He was stabbed."

It was pulling teeth. We were both embarrassed. The first lesson in Savoonga: Expose nothing.

"Did they catch the murderer?"

"It was his wife that did it."

A long silence.

"They were under the influence of alcohol."

AT THE SMALL airport in Nome, we had seen posters warning that it is a serious crime to be caught smuggling alcoholic beverages of any kind to St. Lawrence Island, which is home to Savoonga and Gambell, its sister village forty miles away. The island is dry and has been for some time, part of a desperate effort to control a problem that has gotten painfully out of hand.

Savoongans are only a few generations removed from a near–Stone Age existence. Details from the distant past are murky, but in the late 1870s much of the population of the island was wiped out in a holocaust of complex origins thought to involve illness, climate changes, and behavioral factors. What is indisputable is that the commercial whalers of that era brought some modern ways to the island, along with disease and alcohol. Genetically, in both cases, the natives had no defenses.

Dean Kulowiyi had mentioned a scene he said is repeated all over Savoonga: two young people sharing a smuggled bottle, then getting into a fistfight over the last swallow. Jason Iya said the concept of social drinking is unknown; young people in particular simply drink to pass out.

Alcoholism and depression. It's an old, sad story familiar to Native Americans, whether Eskimos in Alaska or Navajos in Arizona. In Savoonga, for reasons we would come to understand, the phenomenon seems to be intensified.

Jason told us he likes Savoonga, respects the tribal ways of his people, enjoys hunting for seal, whale, and walrus. (As indigenous people with a subsistence lifestyle, Eskimos who are Alaskan natives are permitted to take otherwise protected species.) Jason agreed with Dean, though, that too many of the young people seem spoiled, rootless, and without ambition, content to sponge off their parents. Despair, Jason said, is a constant companion. Bad things keep happening, such as not long ago, when one of his friends from high school, a young woman, fatally shot herself in the head with a .300 magnum. That sort of thing was unusual, though, he said.

Good, I said.

Girls, he explained, will more often hang themselves.

SUICIDE HAS REACHED epidemic proportions among the young people of Savoonga. They have been taking their lives in violent ways and in breathtaking, heartbreaking numbers for some time now, and there is little agreement in the village on precisely why, or precisely how to stop it.

Savoonga is run collegially by a loose, three-part government: a tribal council, a native corporation that owns the island—all Eskimo residents are shareholders—and a civil authority, headed by Mayor Jane Kava. I found the mayor at her desk in City Hall. A sturdy, pleasant woman, she has been here twenty-eight years and said she wouldn't live anywhere else. When I asked her why, she said that it is wholesome: "You don't have to worry about crime. You don't have to worry about your kids."

But, I asked, what about the suicides?

Yes, she acknowledged, that has been a serious problem for people under thirty.

How many have there been?

Lately? She counted in her head. Four in the past year. But those are just the ones that succeeded. Lately, she said, there have been as many as six unsuccessful attempts in a single month among people from ages thirteen to eighteen.

This is in a place with a total population of 700.

The village is dealing with the problem, Mayor Kava said. Two months earlier, Savoonga hosted a federally funded wellness conference for teenagers, with specialists flying in from the mainland. The mayor believes the main culprit is access to drugs.

"What's really hurting," she said, "is marijuana. It's getting to younger and younger kids."

All in all, though, the mayor said cheerfully, Savoonga is doing well. The people may be poor—unemployment is above 30 percent—but the government is working to make things better: There is satellite TV now. And in the past two or three years, she said, the village got running water and in-home sewage, so citizens are no longer dealing with smelly "honey buckets."

The village store is a modern grocery, shelves stocked with goods at eye-popping prices. A Tombstone frozen pizza, $7 at a Washington Safeway, was $13.95. Bean dip in a cat-food-size can, $5. Many of the perishables were well past their expiration dates.

There we found Parson Noongwook, 41, wearing a "Native Pride" baseball cap. He told us he liked it in Savoonga just fine. He loves to hunt, is proud of being an Eskimo, has everything he wants. Michael asked him to pose for a picture. He said sure, if we would give him $50. We thought he was kidding. He was not. No picture.

This sort of scene would play out more than once. Later in the day, an older woman would berate us, whipping a scolding finger: "You earn a lot of money on this, you should give us some! I need false teeth, but I can't afford to go to Nome for them!" This turned out to be Gloria Kulowiyi, Dean's mother. She, too, is an expert carver as well as a seamstress; I would find her work for sale on an Alaskan native art Web site. A small Gloria Kulowiyi ivory hair barrette, sold online, costs $162.

There was something puzzling going on, involving money. The people of Savoonga were being mostly friendly—polite and accommodating, if reserved—except on this topic, where several seemed almost belligerent.

Back at our lodge, not far from the airport, we were bearing witness, day after day, to Savoonga's dispiriting balance of trade. Incoming: boxes of tuna fish and soup and Spam and overly old dairy products at exploitive prices, along with the occasional smuggled poisonous bottle of booze. Outgoing: not much, except for the occasional piece of native culture—elegant art, painstakingly crafted from the wealth of the land, sold in desperation, whenever it is ready, for whatever they can get.

EVERY DAY, AT noon, a procession of old people assembles in the basement of City Hall, where volunteers feed them lunch; it is part of a government program for seniors, but it is administered with extraordinary dignity by a society that reveres its elders. The old men arranged themselves in a row, like the Last Supper, and ate mostly in silence; the women gathered more communally, facing one another and chatting. The teenage server remained quiet and deferential. The setting was banal, the cutlery was plastic, the stemware was Styrofoam, but the feel was almost holy.

From Harriet Penayah, an elder with a snow-white shock of hair, we heard what by now was becoming a familiar complaint:

The kids are raising hell, she said, using drugs and alcohol, not respecting their parents, and losing their native language.

One of the cooks called me over. Adora Kingeekuk Noongwook did not want to challenge an elder. But she told me, quietly, that the problems are not the kids' fault. The kids need skate parks, she said. Then she looked at me and stopped. I was not writing it down. I started writing it down.

"They need bowling alleys. Skate parks. Swimming pools. They need recreation. You tell that to Washington."

I promised her I would. She was not smiling.

MIKE KIMBER IS the assistant principal of the Hogarth Kingeekuk School. He is one of twenty non-Eskimos in Savoonga. Almost all of them work at the school and live in an apartment compound on the school grounds.

At fifty-five, Mike remains enthusiastically dedicated to his job. You can find him working early in the morning, when the pupils arrive, and late at night, for after-school activities, and on his lunch hour, when he teaches basic reading skills to cute little kids. He's a downstater from Royal Oak, Michigan, who came to Savoonga ten years ago and has no intention of leaving anytime soon. He loves the children and he loves his work. In particular, he loves the land, for its archaeology—you can find woolly mammoth bones just a mile outside of town—and for its physical beauty, and even for the physical challenges it presents.

Mike swiveled to his computer and punched up pages of photos he took in the summer, when the mantle of snow is gone and the temperature sometimes reaches 60 above. The most compelling are of the graveyard, out near the airport; it is a surreal scene, either spooky or spectacular, depending on your point of view. Most coffins are only partially buried in the permafrost; that's as deep as a spade can go. That means that many of the plywood caskets are exposed to the air. In time, they collapse in on themselves. You can see bones and skulls among the crosses.

Savoonga gives no quarter; it is merciless even to the dead.

Savoonga is so physically inhospitable it practically orders you to leave. Those who don't are descendants of those who didn't, and they are among the hardiest people in the world. Perversely, Mike said, that makes them vulnerable. Their stoicism, he said, is legendary, their pride intense. They don't often complain. They don't always seek help when they need it. Many resent offers of help. Take a people who bottle up emotion, he said, introduce them to excessive amounts of alcohol, and bad things can happen.

Jason Iya had said much the same thing. His brother—who had threatened suicide in the past, before his wife finished the job—had never discussed the nature of his personal problems at length, Jason said. Neither did Jason's high school classmate, right up until the gunshot to her head. "People here don't communicate," Jason said. "They're too shy or too scared."

Here is what I had noticed: Most Savoongans were walking around with their faces exposed in weather so cold we needed ski masks and goggles. Their skin is impervious, often frostbitten to insensitivity. To survive here, part of you must deaden.

In Savoonga at the start of the twenty-first century, a disheartening drama seems to be playing out as two generations of Eskimo people fitfully try to define their place in the world. Elders watch helplessly as their culture weakens, assaulted on every level by unstoppable forces—some of which are as simple, and as heartless, as nature. As the climate changes, the walrus, seal, and whale meat, upon which their culture has subsisted for so long, is becoming harder to find and harvest, requiring longer and more hazardous forays over the ice. Alternatives in cans and frozen TV dinners are available at the grocery.

Meanwhile, their children are beguiled by TV, and tormented

by it. It is affecting the very tapestry of family life; long evening family conversations, an important part of Yupik culture and history, are being supplanted by the tube, which seems to interest only the young.

"TV," Mike Kimber said, "is giving the young people a twisted idea of what life is, creating desires they can't possibly realistically satisfy. They are cheated by false hopes. They're frustrated."

Yet, physical escape is difficult. People do leave Savoonga, sometimes through the military, sometimes through marriage, sometimes in other ways. But not all have the money, or will, to relocate. The last time a student made it out of the high school to an accredited college on the mainland, the assistant principal said, was twelve years ago. And she returned within two years. The culture shock was too intense. Moving out from a reservation in the Lower 48 is one thing—moving away from a society as insular as this is quite another.

The kids' attendance in school is spotty, Mike said, their performance subpar, their home life, at times, utterly desperate. "Some children," he said, "will live in a house with fifteen people. I had one who came to school exhausted. He said, 'My uncle was up late, so he took my mattress.' There were fifteen people in the house and five mattresses, and so the kid had missed his shift. When that happens, you can't wake them in class. You can shake them, and they won't wake up."

And the adults? For many, their entire lives, their families' histories, and their sense of self-worth are invested in a celebration of abilities and attributes that are less and less significant in a changing world.

"It used to be," said Mike, "that a person here was judged by his skills. He was considered valuable if he could hunt, if he provided meat for the elders and meat for his family, if he could guide his people to a better hunting camp. But that's less necessary now."

To the older Savoongans, it seems, every move toward modernity is, by its nature, a repudiation of the past and of everything they are. A hunting and trading economy has been replaced by one that runs on cash. Money from state oil revenue, and other government subsidies that are intended to help—food stamps, housing and energy subsidies, and such—has the effect of keeping the community in a listless stasis: getting by in a threadbare fashion.

Government programs can backfire, too. The school used to offer half an hour a day instruction in Siberian Yupik, the native language. It no longer does. The rigorous course requirements of the federal No Child Left Behind policy, Mike explained, simply leave no more hours in the day to teach it. The school does what it can, sometimes in small but significant ways; photos of the town's elders line the corridors, as a sort of cultural Hall of Fame. Elementary school essays, posted on the walls, retell the story of a walrus hunt.

Savoongans have enough to live on, barely, considering their expenses. And some of their expenses are costly in other ways as well. Cigarettes are $7 and $8 a pack, and practically everyone seems to be smoking. (Even some grade-schoolers have the habit, Mike said ruefully, and indulge in an alarming fashion. Some will furtively chew tobacco in class, and swallow the juice.)

Mike asked me if I knew what the going rate was, in Savoonga, for a smuggled fifth of booze. I did. Both Dean and Jason had told me: $300.

"That's right," he said. "And a joint is $30."

The island is swimming in both kinds of contraband.

I asked: How can they possibly afford it?

"Priorities," he said sadly.

SAVOONGA IN WINTER has a certain kind of desolate beauty, but Mike and others told us that it was a pity we couldn't see it in the summer, when plants are in bloom, the sea is a spectacular vista, and the wildlife can be gorgeous. I'd looked at some Web sites, seen some pretty pictures, but only one fact registered, for its metaphorical horror. In summer, the island is teeming with one kind of rodent: lemmings.

One night, Michael the photographer and I were walking on the edge of the village, along the seashore. It was 50 below. We happened upon two dogs—small, spotted husky mixes—tethered to poles in the snow. Dogs in Savoonga stay outside, in all weather.

The first pooch was barking at us, tugging at its rope, asserting its territorial rights. But the other was collapsed on the ground, shivering in a tight ball, without the energy even to clear his face of snow. He had settled beside a flimsy shard of sealskin jutting up from the ground, because it was the only available shelter from the wind. It wasn't working.

This fella didn't move when I approached, and offered no resistance when I bent to pet him. He seemed about a year old, with soft, gentle eyes. He let my gloved hand smooth his fur and wipe his face a little.

Up close I could hear him whimpering. It was a shallow, forlorn bleat, only muzzle-deep, as though he hadn't the breath for more.

"This dog is dying," I shouted to Michael over the wind.

We looked around. There was a house nearby, with lights on and furnace roaring. Maybe they know all about the dog, Michael said. Maybe he's sick and they're letting him die.

We should do something, I said.

I looked at Michael. He looked at me. We both looked at the shivering animal, and then the house.

"Are you going to walk over there," Michael said grimly, stowing his gear, "and tell some Eskimo he doesn't know how to care for his dog?"

He started off, toward our lodge.

I stayed a second, and then followed him, not looking back.

BEFORE THIS TRIP, Michael and I had worried we would not be able to handle the weather, that it would break us. But we were handling the weather fine. That wasn't what was breaking us.

At the moment we most needed to find warmth in Savoonga, we did.

As in most of the houses we'd seen, the floors in Floyd Kingeekuk's home are linoleum, the furnishings modest, the decor a controlled riot of clutter (in a society that must bear with an irregular supply of provisions, not much gets thrown out). Also, the inside temperature is stifling, which seems to be the Savoongans' nose-thumb to the elements.

But, the ambience! On the walls of the living room were a gargantuan American flag and a signed photo of two generations of presidents Bush, thanking Floyd for his support. Also, snapshots of Floyd's kids and grandkids, pasted into seashells. Also, a talking Big Mouth Billy Bass. In Savoonga, fads, too, are somewhat past their expiration date.

Floyd is seventy-one, wiry and compact and aggressively hard of hearing. Across the room was his daughter, Adeline Pungowiyi, and her two-year-old niece, Lucy. Lucy was not only adorable but was being adored, as Adeline lovingly brushed her hair into a topknot. There aren't enough houses for all the people, and many families are extended, often eccentrically.

Floyd is a carver; he and his wife, Amelia, make dolls. She had none to show us—they sell for thousands when she finishes them, which is not very often. But she has a scrapbook, and in looking through it you can forget you are looking at inanimate objects. The faces and hands are crafted from ivory, realistic down to the veins in the hands. The hair is made from the skin of unborn seals. The coat is walrus intestine. It is a pride of the Eskimos that every part of every slaughtered animal is used for something.

Floyd learned to carve from his father, who was also a fine artist. But his father would produce pieces on demand from the mainland, and much of it was utilitarian kitsch: napkin rings, pickle forks. When money is in short supply, the practical still trumps the artistic. Dean Kulowiyi had told us that he once produced a few silly, whimsical carvings of turtles eating mushrooms. Mainlanders liked them, so he gave them a name, and, for a while, one of the world's foremost ivory artists was spending a lot of time carving "tundra turtles."

When Floyd told us he still shoots some hoops down at the school gym, we envisioned a klatch of indomitable wrinklies playing a spirited game of H-O-R-S-E. So we were not prepared for what we found when we visited the gym the next night.

The school keeps it open at night, as a sort of free-for-all playground. The floor was filled with older kids. The Savoonga school is big on basketball, and the seventeen- and eighteen-year-olds were practicing for a regional tournament. And right with them was Floyd, seventy-one, huffing, puffing, sweating, running full court, draining the occasional fifteen-foot jumper. He plays a sneaky defense, too.

It was an exhilarating scene—no generational divide on that basketball court. But aside from Mike Kimber, Floyd was pretty much the only adult in the place. Kids of all ages were scrambling in the grandstands, unsupervised. Savoonga's adults were elsewhere. We found them where some kids had sullenly predicted we'd find them—across town, at the firehouse.

The lights were on, and about two dozen snowmobiles were parked outside. Every few minutes, one or two more arrived and one or two departed. Michael tried to walk in but thought the better of it when a smiling-but-insistent patron warned him that

if he brought that camera inside, he'd become "polar bear bait."
So I went in alone.

The firehouse resembled a firetrap. Dozens of people were
sitting at tables jammed wall to wall. Some had impromptu
card games going. Someone was calling numbers. It was Bingo
Night.

But the real action seemed to be happening up front, where
people were shuffling forward, passively queuing up to buy instant lottery tickets; some had $20 in their hands, some had $50.
Some were going back more than once.

I bought a $2 ticket. It was dated "1989," and it looked like
a throwback technology, the sort of thing state lotteries offered
before scratch-offs became popular. These cards are called "pull
tabs." You lift off cardboard tabs that cover three slot-machine
payoff lines.

If you are an adult, and you are seeking entertainment on a
winter night in Savoonga, apparently this is where you go. Pull
tabs are one bad bet. The jackpot payoff for a $2 ticket is $200.
A large barrel was provided to collect the losing tickets; it was
nearly full.

Fresh on the icy wall beside the entrance, someone had
traced a message with a warm finger. It said, "Boring." Michael
and I had come to refer to this ubiquitous, plaintive graffito as
"the writing on the wall."

Outside, a gap-toothed man approached Michael, pointed
disparagingly at his hat, and offered to sell him a better one,
made from sealskin, for $150. The guy said he was in a jam and
needed the money for airfare to Nome, to serve a forty-five-day
jail sentence.

For what, Michael asked.

He'd been convicted, he said, of trying to smuggle liquor into
Savoonga. They agreed on $75 for the hat, and also that, under
the circumstances, he would not be named in this story.

He and Michael walked to his house. Michael forked over the money; the guy produced the hat and immediately got on the phone to plan his trip.

The linoleum floors at the man's house were eroded in places down to plywood. Seven children—some shirtless—sat around a TV set on grungy throw rugs, eating ice cream from a gallon container, watching a tape of *Gilligan's Island*. The oldest was a sixteen-year-old girl, sitting to the side, impassively playing Game Boy. The babysitter. It was not clear who would watch the kids for forty-five days.

"I love Gilligan," said a seven-year-old. "He always gets hit in the head with a coconut and goes to sleep."

Mostly, the kids' faces were frozen in the glow of the screen, silent against the sounds of the show.

> *The tale of the stranded castaways*
> *Who are here for a long, long time*
> *They'll have to make the best of things*
> *It's an uphill climb . . .*

Once he'd been paid, the man walked out with Michael, cash in hand. The last Michael saw of him, he was heading back toward Bingo Night.

———

AT THE GRANDSTANDS in the gym, I had met a friendly twenty-two-year-old named Collin Noongwook. In this place, you couldn't miss Collin. He had an orange crew cut. Personable, squarely built, wearing a Pure Playaz shirt, walking with a modified hitch and roll, Collin wouldn't look much out of place on the streets of D.C. Unlike most of the younger people we'd spoken to, Collin seemed not in the least personally dispirited. When I asked him what he wanted to do with his life, he outlined a plan.

He wants to get out of Savoonga and live somewhere warm—California or Hawaii maybe—and he hopes to do it through the National Guard. He's tried to interest his friends in joining him, he said, but he's failed. They haven't the will to leave.

If I really want to get a sense of what Savoonga is all about, Collin told me, I ought to talk to his dad.

That is how, the next day, I was sitting in Chester Noong-wook's home, at his kitchen table, perspiring in the heat. Chester is seventy-one, with a distinctively Eskimo face—flat, round, weathered, twinkly-eyed, resembling his father and grandfather, whose photos reverently adorn the walls, across from the big-screen TV, beside the socks hanging out to dry on a clothesline.

Chester immediately declared the impending end of the world. We were in the Christian end times, he thundered, and we'd better be ready for the Second Coming of Christ. The signs, he said, were everywhere: "Suicides, war, earthquakes, people asking too many questions . . ." His face remained impassive, and only after we burst out laughing, did he, too.

Like many of Savoonga's elders, Chester speaks in heavily accented English. He used to work for the U.S. Postal Service, delivering the mail from Savoonga to Gambell, back when mail came once a month, there were no snowmobiles, and it took two days "by dog." His last dogsled run was in 1963. He also was on the local team of fishermen that caught Savoonga's first whale in 1972. Chester still hunts, but less often, and it bothers him. He used to live on what he could trap and hunt, and that suited him fine.

"When I was going on foot," he said, "you might go out twenty miles to the Bering and back. A man used to walk sixty miles to get his family something to eat. Today we get something at a store, a New York steak for forty dollars."

He barked out a list of expenses he found abusive—heating oil! rent! propane!—then quickly offered to trade his camera, a cheapo Instamatic, for Michael's thousand-dollar Canon, as part of an important cultural exchange among new friends. There was a moment of stunned silence until Chester guffawed. He was having fun with the rubes from the South.

"When I was ten years old," he said, "I didn't even know what money was. We relied on ourselves and got our food from reindeer and fish and walrus."

Chester produced a slate-gray object made from fossilized ivory. It resembled a small rudder, like a seal's tail. "So much has changed," he said, "so much has been forgotten. This is proof of how we used to catch the walruses." He demonstrated how you would stick the object onto the wooden end of a harpoon, and then, with a quick, discuslike motion, whip the bone-pointed weapon across the surface of the ice. The rifled tail would act like a stabilizer, or the feathers of an arrow, to ensure the flight was true. It must have taken extraordinary skill, hunting walrus that way.

Nowadays, when Eskimos kill walrus, they use steel-tipped harpoons fired by shotgun. For whales, the tips are charged with explosives.

The whole Savoonga dilemma seemed to be playing out before us in that overheated kitchen, in an unscripted tirade responding to a question that hadn't been asked. Chester was delineating the Savoongans' reluctant, grudging, almost tragic acceptance of a sterile, technology-driven cash economy that in ways subtle and dramatic was turning a fierce and proud culture into a docile, dependent one.

Collin entered the room. I asked Chester what he thought of his son's hairstyle. He said he thought it was just fine. But across the room, Collin's mother was smiling and vigorously shaking her head no. Sally Noongwook was wearing a True Value T-shirt and a look of exasperated devotion.

Collin plopped down next to her on the couch. She's just

jealous, he said, because she's tried to dye her hair and failed. They started playfully shoving and tickling each other.

Here, in front of his dad, Collin lost a little of the swagger from the day before. When I asked Chester about Collin's plans to leave, he said that whatever his son chose to do was fine with him. But Collin blurted how he would never lose respect for his family, how his intent is to follow his father's footsteps in earning respect as a man. How, wherever he was, he would stay in touch with his family and honor them, and might one day build a walrus-skin boat to sail around the world.

Whatever despair was haunting the young people of this village, and dividing generations, it was not apparent in this home.

"I liked Savoonga better before," Chester said—back before government handouts, the modern advantages, state-financed housing and whatnot. "People would do things together. They would build a frame house, together, one hand, one heart, one thought, one mind, one man, working together."

I was just staring at the guy.

"I'm sorry," he said, "I wish I could say things better, but my English is not that good."

THAT NIGHT, MICHAEL and I took a detour, swinging back around the edge of the island, to find those two dogs. Or, with luck, one dog. My hope was that the sick one's suffering had ended quickly.

Both were there. As we approached, they bounded toward us exuberantly. The dog that I had declared half dead leaped up on me, tail whipping in the chill air, demanding a pat on the head.

From a house nearby, a man and a boy walked up. I told them that I had seen the dog the day before, and that he had seemed really sick. They laughed. The dog—his name was Headache—was fine. He'd been a little under the weather, they explained, because the island's walrus-meat inventory was low, and he'd been eating less protein-filled food.

The owners were really friendly people. And I, clueless in an alien culture, hadn't known what the hell I was talking about.

Also, lemmings do not commit mass suicide. It's a myth. I looked it up.

MICHAEL AND I appeared before a tribunal of Savoonga's leaders, to obtain permission to go ice fishing. Afterward, we got to talking with them. I asked how, given their isolation, Savoongans avoided the dangers of inbreeding. Did they have strict rules, such as prohibiting marriage between cousins? They looked at me like I was crazy.

"I am married to my cousin," said Linda Akeya, laughing. She is secretary of the village corporation, an attractive woman who is missing a front tooth. Then, she said, "When it's seventy or eighty below, our kids are at school."

Meaning?

"You have to be tough to live here."

The Eskimos of Savoonga are a particularly tough distillate of some of the toughest people on Earth. They are descendants of Gambell residents who left the comparatively easy village life to live in camps as reindeer herders; several reindeer camps coalesced into the village of Savoonga in 1920. What Linda Akeya was saying is that they will do what it takes to make the best of their circumstances, and they will survive, and they will propagate, and that doesn't mean living by the niceties, or rules, of mainlanders.

Morris Toolie, the president of the village corporation, said the community is facing many challenges—among them, the loss of language: The young adults today tend to understand Siberian Yupik but cannot speak it. The next step is as apparent as the passage of another generation.

Gingerly, I asked about the suicides. In the past few days, we had heard more details, more heartbreaking stories: The high school girl who had let it be known that there was a bullet with her name on it—literally—that she was keeping at the ready. The boy who shot himself after a hanging attempt failed. The girl who'd be dead today, except the rope broke. The fourteen-year-old girl whose rope did not break.

Understandably, this is a subject the adults of Savoonga are hesitant to talk about with strangers. Toolie spoke only obliquely of the youths' disaffection. He blames TV for much of it. Linda Akeya agreed: "There's violence, even in cartoons." But she added: "We have a lack of jobs, a lack of things to do. It's just boring for them."

What Savoongans need, she said, is more money for more jobs and more recreation, and this is how she said they need to get it: The kids need to leave Savoonga, get a college education, become expert in the ways of bureaucracy, then come back to help the village as community leaders, writing grant applications in a way that will ensure their approval.

I didn't ask the question that was in my mind, because it would have seemed impertinent, and culturally unthinkable: Isn't that assuming a lot, that they would come back?

———

THE NIGHT BEFORE it was time to leave, Michael and I decided to go back to the school. We realized this was becoming a story about the kids.

The basketball court was being spiffed up for the tournament. Mike Kimber was there—Mike is always there—but almost no young people.

Where were they?

Probably at Yugni's, Mike said.

Yugni's?

The place all the kids go, he said.

In four days of asking everyone about everything, this was the first we'd heard of Yugni's. No one had volunteered that such a place existed.

It wasn't easy to find, because from the outside, it looked just like a boarded-up house. Our clue was the cluster of little kids— six, seven, eight years old, hanging around the entrance, cracking open the door, peeking inside.

"They're smoking marijuana in there!" one of them giggled, pantomiming sucking on a joint.

Yugni's place had once been a single-family home, but that must have been a long time ago. The insides were stripped bare, the windows boarded up, the floors pitted plywood, the walls painted the color of industrial rust. All the furniture was gone, replaced by a foosball game and a battered pool table with duct-taped felt.

There was no pot that we could detect. The room smelled only of desperation and languor.

The lighting was dim, like a skid-row saloon. The place was wall to wall with Savoonga's youth, from eight to their mid-twenties. Some played pool, as little kids wove and tumbled through their legs. Most just stood around, talking, or not talking, just standing.

"Fuck you," an eight-year-old screamed to his buddy, as he wrestled him to the ground. It was, oddly, the first profanity we had heard in the village.

In the kitchen, coffee and watery Kool-Aid were for sale, 50 cents a cup, beside a photocopied drawing of Jesus and the words "Happy Holiday, the love of Christ controls us."

Pool was 50 cents a game. Collecting the cash was Yugni,

whose English name is Maynard Kava. He's the proprietor, and the mayor's brother-in-law. Yugni is fiftyish, toothless, with a sunken face and long stringy hair. He speaks in an unintelligible mumble. After he failed to sell us a carving of a walrus, he took his seat beside the cash box and paid us no mind. He ignored the kids; the kids ignored him.

Some older kids were playing pool, stone-faced, almost robotic. One hauntingly beautiful girl with long chestnut hair and charcoal eyes would lean over the table, barely aim, take a bad shot, return to her spot against an old bar rail, silent, impassive, her face a mask. She moved like a zombie.

Little kids swarmed us. They groped Michael's camera, queued up for the entertainment of serially peering through the fogged-up lens of my eyeglasses.

Throughout Savoonga, the Writing on the Wall had been an occasional sighting—a few furtive scribblings here and there. In this place, it was an entire infrastructure of despair. Every inch of wall space was covered in writing that had been scrawled in, or scratched in, or seared in by cigarette. Even the ceiling. It was overwhelming—almost unendurable:

"JDS—One Day Without Toking 1/20/05"

"We Were Here 1-26-2004, Bored Out."

"Boring Boring Big Time"

Next to a drawing of a daisy with a frowning face: "Really, Really Bored."

"I Wish I Die Now."

"Wanna Die Right Now."

"I Can't Wait Til It's My Turn."

I plopped into a seat at the only table, and younger kids descended on me. I didn't want to interrogate little kids, but they wanted to interrogate me. They told me their names, insisted I write 'em down. A ten-year-old boy pointed to a drawing on the wall behind me. "That guy is thinking about marijuana!" It was a cartoon of a man, with a thought balloon containing a marijuana leaf. Another showed me a wall inscription "P.I.M.P."

"That means pot in my pipe!"

Then he leaned forward, conspiratorially. "My mom is in jail. I can't say for what."

I recognized an older kid: Lanky and fresh-faced, Freeman Kingeekuk had been effortlessly hitting twenty-foot jump shots at the gym a couple of days before. Freeman, fifteen, likes Savoonga, is an avid hunter and fisherman. No complaints?

Booze and bingo, he said.

Bingo? "The [adults] go three nights a week, and if one night has to be canceled, they'll set it up for another night that week."

The beautiful, stone-faced girl is named Carolina Burgos. I learned that when I went up and spoke to her. She turned at the sound of my voice, her face unfroze, and she smiled, as though awakened from something. Carolina is a high school senior.

Yes, she dislikes Savoonga: "It's like we live in a freezer." She wants to go to college in Anchorage, to study finance.

I thought: This is Linda Akeya's dream. Maybe.

Does Carolina plan to return?

She rolled her eyes. No.

"When I was young," she said, "I thought Savoonga was the best place. There was so much to do. Now . . ." She just looked around the room, then down at her pool cue. "One of my cousins locked herself into a room and shot herself. I guess it was 2001. She was drinking that night."

Why did she do it?

"I don't know." That is what everyone in Savoonga says, when you ask why.

Watching the pool game, at the old bar, is Jason Noongwook, twenty-five. His sad eyes peek from under a Nike cap, on top of which is a cloth woodworker's mask. Jason is an ivory carver. He showed us a half-finished walrus. Nice.

Jason said he plans to stay in Savoonga, because he's figured out how to make a life here. It hasn't been easy. Then he started talking and didn't stop for a while.

"I lost my brother six years ago to suicide. He used to work for the water and sewer authority. He was a member of the [tribal] council. There was alcohol involvement. He didn't look like he was going to do it, before. I guess he was hiding it, holding it inside. He didn't come home for two days. He worked at the water plant, and he hung himself down there.

"Two months ago, my uncle attempted suicide. Actually, he attempted and succeeded. He shot himself. It was alcohol-related.

"Kids nowadays take a lot of pills and talk about suicide. I don't see why people do that. Well, I guess I do. I have been there. I got depressed a few months after my brother died. I loved my brother. He taught me how to shoot a rifle, you know? So I tried it two times."

Tried it?

"I planned it real hard. I didn't even know who to talk to. I love my father, but I didn't want to worry him. I was going to do it the same way my brother did. I used to work at the local washeteria. It was night work. I had a rope, tied it up, and I kicked the chair away, and the rope slipped off. I hit the ground.

"The second time, my girlfriend caught me trying it, and talked me out of it."

After that, Jason said, he decided life in Savoonga was livable, if you kept yourself occupied. "I carve and do hunting. I avoid stress and depression."

Digging outside of town, he recently found three fossilized ancient ivory dolls, one of which sold to a collector for $3,000. He's doing okay. And he and his girlfriend have a baby, a two-year-old girl.

"I think about my daughter. She keeps me around. I'm staying alive because of her."

Jason said he has a trick to keep his depression at bay: weightlifting.

"I lift rocks. That's what I do. That is how I take it out."

Take what out?

"My anger."

––––––––––

THE TEMPERATURE WAS practically balmy. It was zero. So was the visibility. We could see one another, but, a few feet beyond, everything dissolved into white. It was as though the rest of the world had disappeared.

Deno Akeya, 29, was looking around nervously. What was wrong? Nothing, he said. It's just that he had forgotten to bring his rifle.

Why did he need a rifle? I asked.

"Polar bear," he said. Oh.

His uncle, Arthur Akeya, unloaded a gas-powered auger from his snowmobile, set the drill bit on the ice, fired it up, and began drilling a Frisbee-size hole. The drill sank one foot, two, three. Finally, it punched through. Arthur pulled it back up, and with it came a furious rush of seawater. We were 200 yards offshore, out in the Bering Sea. It was lightly snowing.

I dropped a hook in, and before the line touched bottom, I felt a hit. What I brought up through the hole was as hideous a thing as you will ever see. It's a mottled beast the Eskimos call the uglyfish, the size of a shoe, full of warts and polyps and blebs. It looks to be a cross between a catfish and a bullfrog. It's great eating, Arthur assured us.

More holes were being drilled, more lines dropped, and the fish were chewing the lures like popcorn.

Next, the kill. A quick whack behind the eyes with the wooden spool, to break the spine. Then, you gut it the way Eskimos have done for 2,000 years: You tromp on it with your boot, and the insides shoot out of the mouth. I'm a city boy and an animal lover, and none of this felt wrong.

Nor was I surprised to learn, two hours later, that those ghastly-looking creatures, boiled for twenty minutes and then drenched in melted butter, were as succulent as lobster.

Out there in the enveloping whiteness, it had been possible to lose yourself, fishing with Eskimos in the Bering Sea the way it has been done since the age of the igloo. There was no village, there were no dead kids, no fog of denial, no generation in agony, literally bored out of its mind. There were no soul-wrenching choices between survival of self and survival of a culture. There was just an exhilarating ritual, as old as a civilization, irreducible, unencumbered by a sense of guilt, not subject to misunderstanding or misinterpretation through cultural chauvinism. It was clear and it was clean. It was possible to comprehend the joy of surviving by your skills and savvy on the bounty of the Earth alone, in defiance of whatever hell nature and fate throw at you. And it was possible to understand why, lost in that moment, you could want to live that way forever.

A Wing and a Prayer

As I walked from the Metro to my office on this day, police were everywhere. People were nervously scanning the skies. The government had just issued a terrorism alert of the gravest nature but of dubious practical value: An attack of some sort, they said, from unknown agents, might be imminent. Somewhere.

This is about what happened on my walk from the Metro to my office in downtown Washington, D.C. It's the shortest story in this collection. It's about the meaning of life.

February 14, 2003

BUNDLED AGAINST THE chill of a very bad morning, people hurried down 15th Street in downtown Washington yesterday, past the row of newspaper boxes with front-page headlines weighing the likelihood of annihilation by radiation, by ballistic missile, by airborne cyanide, or by the pedestrian body-mounted suicide bomb. They hustled past the Radio Shack that had already sold nearly every battery-operated radio in the store, even the crystal sets that require earphones. Then, at L Street, they stopped to look in the window of the Rite

Aid drugstore, which earlier in the week sold out of duct tape.

Many people went in, even those with nothing to buy.

"Do you know that . . ."

"Yes, we do," said the store manager. "We're working on it."

Around 6 A.M., when the store was still closed but its doors were propped open for deliveries, a starling flew in. No one saw this, but you can figure out what must have happened next. The little bird flapped above the aisles, observed, perhaps, the absence of anything resembling habitat, banked over the cough and cold remedies, reversed direction, and headed for daylight.

It did not see the glass. It thudded headfirst into the front display window, dropping like a stone past the Valentine's Day stuffed bears into a 5-inch-wide channel between the window and a dividing wall.

The starling was alive but trapped. It couldn't spread its wings enough to fly. So it paced its small enclosure, helpless. On the other side of the divider, near the cash registers, the humans were helpless, too. They could climb a ladder and look over the top, but the bird was three arm lengths away. The humans looked down, and felt pity. The bird looked up; what it felt can only be surmised.

The store opened at seven, and immediately the parade of concerned citizens began. Men, women on their way to work. Police officers. Utility workers. Vagrants. By 9:45, store manager Rick Bromley had made a phone call, then used the store's sale-tag printer to create two signs, which he taped to the front window. They were done in haste but with good intention. The first read: ANIMAL CNTRL. IS COMMING TO RESCUE BIRD.

That was for the Rite Aid's beleaguered employees, to help stanch the inquiries. The second sign had a different purpose.

"People were coming right up next to the window," Bromley explains, "and the bird was, you know . . ."

The bird was petrified. This tore at the humans' hearts. Animals may not understand that they are mortal, but in return for this comforting ignorance, they are denied a sense of proportion. They lack our capacity to rationalize fears, and prioritize them. They cannot be reassured by words. You just needed to look at this bird to know it was in an inconsolable panic. The humans were afraid it would die of fright.

Thus, the second sign: PLEASE DON'T SCARE THE BIRD THANKS.

So passersby mostly kept their distance, watching with concern as the starling paced and fidgeted, every once in a while sharply cocking its shiny, speckled head in that way birds do, as though they are alert to something you aren't. This makes birds look smart and shrewd and prepared for anything, but it's probably just an illusion.

At ten thirty-one, D.C. animal control officer Ted Deppner arrived, and, with a ladder and a net on a long handle, retrieved the starling and handed it to an assistant. She carried it outside and launched it free into the wind.

Everyone felt much better.

It's nice when you can do something.

By noon, Rick Bromley had reordered duct tape, but his store was almost out of first-aid kits.

Tears for Audrey

On the Sunday this story was published, I was work-ing in the office. My phone rang. The caller identi-fied herself as Linda Tripp—the mystery snitch in the Monica Lewinsky scandal, which was just begin-ning to unfold.

At the time, Linda was in self-imposed exile; she held the key to the whole affair, but she wasn't talk-ing. Journalists were slavering to interview her.

But Linda wasn't offering me that, at least not yet. She was calling about my story in the newspaper that day, about a grievously injured little girl beside whose bed religious figurines were said to be weep-ing oil. The story ends on an ambiguous note, Linda observed: It wasn't clear what I thought was really happening in that house.

Right, I said. The ambiguity was deliberate.

Well, Linda asked, what do I really think?

It was clear I was being tested, in some way. Pre-interviewed. I think I might have been willing to mislead Linda Tripp, just to gain her confidence. But I didn't know what she wanted to hear about little Audrey Santo, and the possibility of God. So I gambled and told her what I really thought.

It was the last I heard from her.

July 19, 1998

I N THE BED at the center of the room, beside a pink heart-shaped pillow, beneath a crystal chandelier and a cheerful bouquet of red, white, and blue balloons, lies the child. Her dark hair is shiny and fragrant, gathered at the crown by a red satin bow, cascading onto the pillow and 3 feet beyond. Her complexion is alabaster, without bruise or blemish. She is toasty to the touch. Her gray eyes have the luster of wet pearls. They are open. They march back and forth, slowly, as though she is reading Scripture.

She reads nothing. She says nothing. She does nothing. Her jaw lolls open in flat, dreadful stupor. From time to time spittle must be mopped from her lips and tongue. A breathing tube enters her neck, attached to a ventilator.

Eleven years ago, when she was not yet four, this little girl fell into the backyard swimming pool. She nearly drowned. Much of her brain died.

Upon the foot of the bed are letters. They have been mailed by people around the world, people sick in body or in spirit, pleading for a cure. Later, these will be opened and read aloud to the child, one by one. She will not respond. Against the far wall is a dresser cluttered with religious statuary: crucifixes, Sacred Hearts, Virgin Marys, bleeding Jesuses with crowns of thorns. Scotch-taped beneath the chins of many of these effigies are little Dixie cups, to catch the weeping oil.

Yes, weeping oil. You can see it, hanging from plastic chins, beading up on wooden cheekbones, painting ceramic tunics with a bright, damp sheen.

Mysterious events have been occurring in this home. Communion wafers have been said to ooze blood. Statues have been said to move on their own when no one is looking, pivoting to face sanctified objects. Chalices have been said to suddenly fill with sweet-scented oil. Sick people who have come here say they have been healed.

The girl's family claims to be mystified. For years, word of these events has been slowly leaking out, like the oil that puddles on the eyes of the painting of Our Lady of Medjugorje out in the garage. The garage has been converted into a chapel. Now tens of thousands know of this place. It has its own Web site, and a committed cadre of Roman Catholic volunteers who answer correspondence, organize masses, and call themselves the Apostolate of the Silent Soul. No money changes hands. No one's getting rich.

The events here have not been officially embraced by the Worcester diocese, but several area priests have become something of a kitchen cabinet to the girl's family, celebrating masses before groups larger, and more needy, and more enthusiastic, than they have otherwise known.

Today is Wednesday, so it is Pilgrim Day. Eighty people who made reservations as much as a year and a half in advance arrive at the simple one-story frame house. In groups of ten, they are escorted into a small room beside the girl's bedroom. In the dividing wall, a picture window has been installed. Venetian blinds are drawn. The pilgrims wait with hushed expectation. The blinds are opened, and she appears.

Children crowd wide-eyed to the front. Someone points a disposable drugstore camera and clicks.

Inside the bedroom, the girl's grandma fusses with the sheets.

"They have come to see you, Audrey," she coos. "Don't you look beautiful?"

Audrey does not respond.

Grandma takes a vacuum hose and suctions mucus from Audrey's nose. In the room next door, people fish for their rosaries and hold them out. The beads drizzle against the windowpane. A woman with haunted eyes and a twist and swing in her step approaches a padded kneeler placed beneath the window and painfully sinks to her knees.

After five minutes, the blinds are drawn again. This group shuffles out, and another is ushered in. At the end of the tour, each pilgrim will get a souvenir, a ziplock bag containing a little cotton swab, daubed in the oil of this holy home.

Spend time in the house at 64 South Flagg Street and you are likely to be either appalled or inspired. One of two things is going on here: a monstrous fraud that exploits a grievously injured child, or a startling declaration by God Almighty that He exists—is here, right now, in this very place, working miracles.

One or the other. No in-between.

Right?

———

THERE IS A scene in the movie *Oh, God!* in which the deity—in the irresistible person of George Burns—arrives in court to testify as a witness in a trial of a good man accused of slander. The judge is, understandably, skeptical. Burns asks: What, you want a miracle? "I got a cute miracle," he offers, pulling out a deck of cards. With a pass of the hand, it disappears. Happy now?

The message is clear. God does not perform parlor tricks.

But consider this. If God chose to announce His presence one day by appearing in the sky, a face a hundred miles high—a bearded patriarch who waved His arms and turned cats into dogs and dogs into trees and angels descended in gossamer chariots— well, instantly, there would be no agnostics on the face of the Earth. All men and women would embrace the Lord with a fervor built on certitude, and awe, and terror for their mortal souls. Everyone would have God.

But no one would have faith.

Faith is the foundation of religion. After His death, Jesus appears to Thomas and chides him for demanding proof of His resurrection. You must simply believe, Jesus says. In your belief is salvation.

So might it not follow that a God given to tests of faith might choose to say hello to the world through what seems like a cheesy stunt—a stunt so trivial that sneering debunkers have gone on TV to duplicate it? Thus, the believer looks like a fool or a criminal, his piety tested through the derision of others. Isn't that possible?

This is the sort of dialogue one has with oneself after leaving the house on Flagg Street.

As the millennium approaches, there have been reports of an increase in mystical phenomena worldwide, weeping statues in particular. Believers offer this explanation: Mary is crying for humanity because we have become too selfish and secular, distancing ourselves from God.

Some of these observed mystical events are famously ludicrous: Mother Teresa's face in a sticky bun; Jesus in a bowl of spaghetti on a billboard. Some have been convincingly exposed as hoaxes: A man in Montreal who drew thousands of penitents was found to have coated religious figurines with a waxy mixture of pig fat and his own blood, so when people crowded around, and the room warmed, the liquid ran. Some alleged apparitions have never been convincingly dismissed. Hundreds of thousands still flock to the hamlet of Medjugorje, Bosnia, where the Madonna has supposedly made periodic appearances since 1981.

But mostly, in these cases, one is left with proof of nothing, only a feeling of unease: An obscure priest in a Lake Ridge, Virginia, parish briefly became a national celebrity in 1992 when figurines began crying in his presence. Was he a faker? Maybe, maybe not. Journalists discovered that, as a young man, he had once sought a sort of wacko fame by riding for days nonstop in a roller coaster. Soon after this was published, the figurines dried up. Eventually, the priest was moved to another parish. End of story.

Now comes Audrey Santo, a comatose girl in whose presence statues weep and in whose bedroom thousands congregate.

What in God's name is going on here?

IT IS, AS it happens, a predominantly Jewish neighborhood. The back yards on Flagg Street are mostly communal, with few fences, just a broad band of grass with kids' swings and wading pools and the occasional vegetable garden. Then at the Santo home, a huge Virgin Mary stands sentry in a wooden grotto. The rest of the yard is a checkerboard of plastic folding chairs under a canvas canopy. The deck behind the house has been converted to an altar. Plastic flowers are taped to it. There are portraits of Jesus, and Mary, and Audrey.

Apostolate volunteer Mary Cormier is welcoming the Wednesday visitors.

"Audrey has become global. She is booked through 1999. She is beautiful. She is precious. She is not in a coma. She is very alive and alert."

In the audience, Joe Jardin, a sturdy man from Providence, Rhode Island, is discussing the pilgrimage he made to Medjugorje in 1988. The woman in front of him turns around, delighted. "I went to Medjugorje in 1988, too," says Bici Turiano of Phoenix.

It seems there is something of a miracle circuit. People travel from one apparition site to another. Lourdes, France. Fatima, Portugal. Medjugorje. Audrey's house.

One wonders what Jesus might say to these folk, gathered here in drip-dry short-sleeve shirts and pastel trousers, chatting amiably, sucking Tic Tacs, patiently awaiting Proof.

Sitting on the grass is a woman named Laurie Wilkinson, from Wakefield, Rhode Island. Her limbs betray a tremor. She is maybe thirty-five, but she walks with a cane. Around her neck and dangling down as far as her hips is a handmade necklace of religious medallions, each commemorating some site where a saint is said to have appeared. Her expression seems forever caught between euphoria and despair. This is Wilkinson's second visit to Audrey's home. She carries a scrapbook of Polaroids taken from her first visit. In photos of the outside of the house, Wilkinson has detected the face of a kindly man—maybe the pope—in an angle made by the rain gutter and the roofing tiles.

Wilkinson is here to be healed.

"I have chronic fatigue syndrome and fibromyalgia," she says. "Also, I broke eight of my toes. I have autoimmune problems, and my sisters have dermatic myositis and endometriosis and chronic fatigue syndrome and my husband has a bad disk and a bad knee. And I get head-to-toe muscle spasms and I get broken blood vessels, see?" she says, presenting the back of her hand. "I feel very close to Audrey." Wilkinson arranges religious icons about her in the grass, facing the deck-turned-altar, where Mary Cormier is wrapping up.

"And now, this is our movie star!"

Linda Santo pads out from the house, to enthusiastic applause. She is a tiny, sprightly woman in her forties, 4 feet 11 in bare feet. In fact, her feet are, at the moment, bare. She wears stretch pants and a loose blouse and her chestnut hair has been hurriedly cinched in a banana clip. She walks low at the hip, the no-nonsense bustle of a harried mom. She warmly welcomes the visitors to her home.

In Audrey, she says, there is a central message: "God doesn't make junk—all life is valuable."

"Sometimes you will see Audrey crook her finger," she tells the visitors. "She is saying, 'Come, see my Jesus, come adore Him.' And He will bless you, maybe not as profoundly as He blessed Audrey, but He will bless you."

———

LINDA SANTO RUNS this house. She is everywhere. She was there
when the strange manifestations began occurring more than four
years ago. If there is deliberate deception, she is almost certainly
complicit. Yet, to many, she seems beyond duplicity.

She is aggressively likable. Twinkly. Funny. Self-deprecating.
Down-to-earth. Above all, she is joyfully aware of how absurd this
all must look. She tells how people have arrived at her home unannounced, having driven all night from places like Nova Scotia.
"Nova Scotia!" she brays. "Why not call first, are ya stupid? I'm
washing the toilet, gimme a break."

She sometimes watches, bemused, as pilgrims kneel and
pray and then furtively pocket a scrap of carpeting or a clod of
dirt from the back yard.

"Ya gotta roll with it," Linda Santo says. She speaks with the
unpretentious blue-collar New England accent that sounds like a
happy amalgam of Boston Brahmin and Brooklyn bleacher bum.
"We're an ordinary family," she says. "This is a home, not a shrine.
Nobody levitates here."

Linda says she has no idea why these things are happening.
She knows it looks suspicious. But, she says, the quarts of oil that
have been oozing into her home are from no source known to her.
And she would have to know, she says reasonably, if someone else
were doing it. Someone other than God.

In the shattering weeks after the accident, Linda's husband
left her. Steve Santo was not a bad guy; he was an ordinary guy,
a strapping loading-dock laborer whose little girl would never be
the same. He just could not handle it. He spiraled into alcoholism, he lost jobs, he drove drunk, he went to jail. Linda was alone
with her three other children, and Audrey.

"Where are you going to put her?" doctors asked, meaning,
what institution?

"I will put her in my arms," Linda said.

And she did. She took Audrey home and lovingly administered round-the-clock nursing care. For years. Eventually, she lobbied successfully for free twenty-four-hour nursing assistance from the Massachusetts Commission for the Blind. Audrey has lived longer and with fewer health problems than anyone expected. Her arms and legs are stunted, but she continues to grow—last year, she entered puberty. She is kept immaculately clean and beautifully groomed. At least once a day she is propped up in front of a TV.

Supplicants come to this house almost every day. Mondays are reserved for people with terminal disease. Many are children. Linda welcomes them herself.

August 9 is the eleventh anniversary of the near drowning. For the occasion, Linda is organizing a huge open-air mass in a stadium at nearby Holy Cross College. As many as 20,000 people from all over the world are expected to attend. Audrey will be brought out, in an ambulance.

"I want one and a half million people!" Linda says, laughing, leaping nimbly onto a dining room chair. "Let's shut down Worcester. It's a Sunday! It's the Lord's day!"

If you have ever dealt with loss and have seen how it can break the spirit, if you value spit-in-your-eye stubbornness, if you are awed by selfless sacrifice, if you admire those who can find humor in the face of pain, then it is impossible not to like Linda Santo.

But what if she were making all this happen? Would you still like her, then?

"If people only knew," she says, "what was in our Dumpsters! Audrey makes five or six bags of trash a day. If I wanted to make a million dollars on this, I could sell the garbage!" She throws her head back and laughs, loud and cackly and unrestrained, straight from the gut.

Well, if she were making this up, could you dislike her, then?

"Ya want a sandwich?" she says.

THE HAGIOGRAPHY OF Audrey Santo has spread largely through word of mouth, but it got some help from the religious media. For years, Linda Santo permitted no publicity. But in 1996 she opened her doors to a producer from the Mercy Foundation, a nonprofit Catholic organization that filmed a slick one-hour documentary called *Audrey's Life: Voice of a Silent Soul.*

The tape has sold 2,000 copies, and has been broadcast several times on the Eternal Word Television Network, a religious cable channel. The video is clearly partisan. Inevitably, it points out that Santo means "holy one." It argues that Audrey is almost certainly a "victim soul," a person chosen to suffer for others; victim souls are said to speak to God, interceding on behalf of supplicants who petition them with prayer.

The documentary quotes a Boston chemist who says he analyzed the oil and found it to be a mysterious substance, not any known commercial oil. It interviews Audrey's pediatrician, John Harding, who says that her relatively good physical health cannot be explained by conventional medicine. Harding says the biopsy of an angry skin condition that once appeared on her legs revealed a rash typically suffered by persons undergoing chemotherapy, even though Audrey never had chemotherapy. The implication is that Audrey assumed into her own body the pain from some visitor being treated for cancer. And, most dramatically, the Mercy Foundation cameras actually filmed a mass at which a priest held up the host—a communion wafer—to discover it had a wet red spot on it roughly the shape of a cross.

His astonishment is captured right there, on tape.

IN SOME WAYS, religion is like abstract art. There is beauty and spectacle, but in both cases, one must reach into oneself to find meaning. And so it is that when outsiders behold the events at 64 Flagg Street, they tend to see different things.

The Reverend Mike McNamara, a priest from the Boston area, says Audrey's survival speaks against the evils of abortion, birth control, and government-sanctioned gambling. Father Mike has no doubt that what is happening on Flagg Street is divine. He says he has seen a chalice in the home well up with oil, spontaneously; it was out of his sight for seconds only, and no one approached it.

Father Mike believes in miracles. He himself has traveled to Medjugorje. He stood on a hillside, he says, and watched as the sun spun in the sky like a pinwheel, giving off sparks. Then he felt some energy pierce his heart, so strong he doubled over and let out a yell. He felt it was "waves of God's love for me."

John Harding, the pediatrician, believes Audrey's message is meant for doctors. Her survival speaks against physician-assisted suicide, proclaiming that there is value in all life, and dignity in suffering.

Harding—former chief of pediatrics at Hahnemann Hospital in Worcester—notes that he first met Audrey not as a doctor but as a penitent, when he came to her house to pray and say a rosary. He once sat at her bedside and asked her to help a friend who had cancer.

Once, he says, a priest asked him to examine one of Audrey's communion wafers allegedly containing blood. He brought his microscope, he says, but at the last minute he decided not to use it. Catholics believe the consecrated communion host is literally the flesh of Christ, and Harding says he felt uncomfortable "putting our Lord under the microscope." Instead, he says, he used a small magnifying glass.

He knows this sounds strange, but he is a straightforward man, and he is not embarrassed by his faith. What he saw in the bleeding host, he says, was "a Madonna and Child."

The Reverend Emmanuel Charles McCarthy, a genial Eastern Rite Catholic priest, was the cleric initially summoned by Linda Santo when she first reported the leaking oil. He remains a close family friend.

Father Emmanuel Charles looks like Santa Claus. A former attorney, he speaks with the engaging gravitas of a theologian-philosopher. He doesn't buy the "victim soul" thing, the notion that God would cripple a child to serve His purposes.

That turns God into a monster, he says. "God is not a monster."

The message of Audrey has been somewhat misunderstood, he says. She is not about physician-assisted suicide, or abortion, or gambling, at least not primarily. He says she represents a thunderous condemnation of war and murder.

This message—that Christians should not kill—is Father Emmanuel Charles's life's work. He first became interested in Audrey when he learned that her accident occurred on August 9, 1987.

He explains: August 9, 1945, was the date that an American bomber crew incinerated Nagasaki. Ground zero was a Christian church. The bomber crew was all Christian. "No Jews, no atheists. Christians killing Christians, y'see?"

August 9 was also the date, during the Holocaust, that a nun named Edith Stein died. Sister Edith has since been canonized; in fact, one of the miracles ascribed to her was the recovery of McCarthy's own infant daughter, Benedicta, from a massive accidental overdose of Tylenol a few years ago. Edith Stein died at Auschwitz. "Auschwitz was totally run by Christians," McCarthy says. "The Nazis had *Gott mit Uns* on their belt buckles, y'see? 'God is with us.' Christians using the church to justify killing!"

It all fits in, says Father Emmanuel Charles: Nagasaki, Nazis, Audrey Santo. Plus, August 9 also happens to be the date of his own ordination.

It's his life's work, and it all fits in.

BOGUSLAW LIPINSKI IS a Boston biochemist who appears on the Mercy Foundation tape, testifying to the mysterious nature of the oils. He says he ordered a chemical analysis and discovered it to be without the characteristic chemical signature of any known commercial oil. As the legend of Audrey has grown, the description of this oil gets more and more supernatural. "Not of this world," is how pediatrician Harding now describes it.

This is not exactly right. According to Barbara Rybinski, the Kraft Foods chemist who supervised the analysis, Audrey's oil did not have the signature of any pure commercial oil. But it could have been a simple mixture of commercial oils, Rybinski says, and it could have been a partially hydrogenated oil, available under many labels.

Lipinski disagrees. His own analysis of the test results suggests that the oil would be hard to duplicate through ordinary means. It is strange, Lipinski says, but he has seen stranger things. His hobby is scientifically documenting paranormal religious phenomena. A few years ago, he says, he went to Medjugorje and tested the air with a type of Geiger counter. He was surprised to discover an unusually high concentration of ions.

He tested the air in Audrey's house, too. Elevated ions, again.

Lipinski is a scientist, so he won't engage in conjecture as to what this all means. But like anyone, he has a suspicion: It is the thumbprint of God.

FINALLY, THERE IS the Reverend George Joyce, retired Catholic priest from Springfield, Massachusetts. Father George is eighty-three, a kindly man with liquid eyes. Of the four communion wafers that are said to have bled in the Santo home, only one occurred directly in front of an independent witness. That was

Father George, who was in the middle of a mass in 1996, as the Mercy Foundation cameras were rolling.

In truth, when you rewind and replay the tape, you cannot actually see the wafer bleed. It is lying on a plate beneath another wafer. When the top wafer is lifted, the one with the wet red cross can be seen. Tests would later show it was human blood.

Father George says everyone denies having tampered with it, and he believes them.

What is happening in the Santo home, he says, is pure good.

He knows evil when he sees it. "I have dealt with the Devil," he says.

One day five or six years ago, the priest says, he trapped a man into revealing that he was demonically possessed. He did this by secretly blessing the salt in the man's home. That night, the man's wife used the salt on his food, and the man "ranted and raved" and ordered her to throw the food out. In a subsequent ritual, Father George says, he drove Satan away.

A priest can reliably tell when people are possessed, Father George says, because "when you throw holy water on them, they start screaming."

Audrey Santo, he says, is a victim soul. Of this, he is "100 percent certain."

———————

IN THE BACK yard, the Reverend Mike McNamara is celebrating mass. Linda Santo takes a consecrated wafer on a brass plate and disappears into the house with it. Every day she gives communion to Audrey. (Audrey has a feeding tube; the wafer is the only solid food she receives by mouth.)

A few minutes later, Linda returns. There is a peculiar look on her face. She is holding the empty communion plate gingerly, and replaces it on the altar.

Liquid sloshes out and onto the tablecloth.

"Sorreee," she whispers to the priest.

After the ceremony, four priests crowd around the communion plate. It is filled halfway with opalescent yellow oil, maybe three or four tablespoons of it, and on top of that is a large, floating bead of clear liquid. It smells of pure roses, eerily strong. It wafts up and out into the sweltering summer air.

Linda Santo meekly explains that the plate quickly welled up with this substance as she walked alone from Audrey's bed to the back porch, a trip of some 30 feet.

The priests nod. It is a miracle, everyone agrees.

———————

When paranormal phenomena are reported, lay people sometimes expect that Catholic church leaders will eagerly embrace them. After all, anything that brings people closer to God cannot be bad, right?

Actually, these things make the diocese uneasy. The Vatican is wary of lending its imprimatur to something that may, ultimately, be exposed as a chimera. The church wants to be the voice of reason, caution, restraint.

The Reverend F. Stephen Pedone is the judicial vicar from the Worcester diocese. He is overseeing an investigation, ordered by the bishop, into the events occurring at the Santo home. The investigation is headed by John Madonna, a local psychotherapist who has been asked not only to try to verify the occurrences, but also to see if there are any human pathologies afoot in the household that might explain what is going on. (Madonna says he and a team spent several days at the house, and even slept there overnight. So far, he says, he has found nothing to indicate deception or sociopathy. In fact, he says, he has observed physical events involving religious icons that cannot be readily explained.)

Father Stephen is a trim, square man with orange hair and piercing eyes. He says he does not want to prejudge, or prejudice, the investigation. He has, however, been to the Santo house, and has an observation.

"I was uncomfortable. The house was filled with people. A little girl was on display in a bed. One priest was bending over her, whispering intercessions in her ear." That means the priest was reciting the names of sick people, on whose behalf Audrey was to speak with God. "The grandmother kept saying, 'You remember Father Steve? Father Steve is here!'

"My impression," says Father Stephen, "was that it bordered on the bizarre. It seemed like an invasion of her privacy."

But isn't it good that the events in this house are giving people hope?

Father Stephen smiles painfully. Yes, he says, people are desperate for reassurance, and reassurance is good. "The downside is, if the faith lacks basis, it is going to quickly evaporate. The church is looking for more long-term faith. You don't draw a circle and say, 'Okay, God, dance for me.'"

Sometimes, he says, people are so desperate for tangible miracles that they get blinded to miracles happening every day: "We wake up in the morning. That is a miracle."

OUTSIDE AUDREY'S BEDROOM is a sign, made to resemble an old-fashioned needlepoint sampler. It says SHH—I'M TALKING TO GOD.

Inside, with Audrey, is Pat Nader, Audrey's grandma. She is small and slightly stooped and determinedly cheerful, a woman who lost her favorite grandchild one day in August 1987, and then discovered she didn't lose her at all. Pat Nader found that Audrey was still around. Just different.

Nader spends hours every day at Audrey's bedside, as she is right now. She talks to her constantly.

"She is what you call a typical teenager," says Grandma Nader. "She is spoiled. She doesn't have to do anything for herself!"

Friends and family contend that Audrey is completely aware of her surroundings, alert, perks up when priests or family members are around, gets agitated when someone says something of which she disapproves. They say medical experts support this.

"They told us she understands everything," says Grandma Nader. "She's perfectly healthy. She'll come out of it one day."

A newspaper photographer bends and focuses.

"I think they want to take a pretty picture," Grandma tells Audrey. "Remember that you are gorgeous, remember that."

Audrey does not respond.

Grandma kisses Audrey's face. The camera clicks.

"I'm the one she loves the best," says Grandma Nader. "I am the grandmother. She is the love of my life, aren't you, Audrey?"

Audrey does not respond.

———

EDWARD KAYE IS a pediatric neurologist at St. Christopher's Hospital in Philadelphia. For eight years, beginning a short time after the accident, Kaye was Audrey's doctor. He has done extensive examinations of the girl's brain.

How injured is she?

"The cell death is about as bad as you can get and still be alive," he says. "Her EEGs are profoundly abnormal. She has brain stem activity, but very, very little above the brain stem."

Is she conscious? Aware of her surroundings?

"There is little objective evidence that she can respond to external stimuli. There is no evidence to suggest that something gets through and gets processed."

Dr. Kaye says he understands how a loving family, ministering selflessly to a terribly injured child, might take comfort from what it interprets as subtle signs of cognition.

What is Audrey's prognosis?

In such cases, the doctor says, "the prognosis is abysmal."

Is he saying she is dead?

"She is not brain-dead because she has brain stem activity. From a cognitive standpoint, she is dead."

IT IS THURSDAY morning. The Santo family and some apostolic volunteers have assembled in the garage chapel for a mass offici- ated by Father Mike. Mass is a daily event at the Santo home.

First, a brief, homey sermon. Father Mike tells an amusing story, at his own expense. He says he was about to host a fam- ily birthday party one Sunday when he realized there was not enough ice-cream cake for all the children. So he stopped at a bakery. Several of his parishioners were there. He was caught red-handed, violating the Sabbath!

Linda Santo pipes up, offering the opinion that this is a for- givable transgression.

"It is like if you have kids in a burning house," Linda says. "You have to get them out, but they want to stay. So you tell them there are toys outside. So you lied to them, but it's okay."

There are two seconds of absolute silence.

"I'm not sure I like your example!" Father Mike says finally.

Everyone laughs.

"I KNOW I seem insane," says Linda Santo. "I'm in good company. Half the saints were insane."

In fact, Linda does not seem remotely insane. She seems delightfully solid. Her youngest son, who still lives with her, is a happy, boisterous teenager who appears well adjusted, close to his mom, joyfully teasing her at every turn. It is a bracingly normal relationship.

Linda is seated in her side yard. Beside her is her husband,

Steve. Steve came home to his family two years ago, after an eight-year absence.

Steve Santo is the sort of guy you would describe, affectionately, as a big lunk. He is cinematically handsome, thick through the chest, square-jawed. His accent makes Linda's seem like *Masterpiece Theatre*. He, too, is instantly likable. Asked if anything in the house other than religious artifacts has ever wept oil, he laughs and says, "Yeah. The top of a pizza box."

He says at first he strongly suspected that his wife was doctoring the statues, until he saw some things he could not explain. Once, he says, an effigy hemorrhaged oil. Linda, as he recalls, was nowhere around.

Steve Santo had years when he abandoned God. But he is back for good, he says. "I like to say the rosary now."

He has to leave for work. But first, he has a question: What sort of results can he expect from this newspaper article? "Will it be a made-for-TV movie?"

Well, maybe. Publicity is starting to pick up; *20/20* is planning to film the August 9 mass.

Linda says it is amazing, and a little sad, that God had to go to this extreme, to do this miracle thing, to attract attention. "If there weren't four bleeding hosts," she asks, "if there was just a child in a bed, would anyone pay attention to this?"

In retrospect, she says suddenly, all of it seems foreordained.

When Audrey was born, she says, she prayed not for a healthy child but for a saint. "I can give life, but only God can give eternal life," she explains.

Linda also says that doctors once X-rayed Audrey's ovaries, expecting to find a tumor. Instead of a tumor, she says, they were astonished to find, literally, right in the X-ray, the figure of "a little angel."

She has this X-ray somewhere, she says, but when asked to locate it, she cannot.

Linda also says she once saw two moons in the night sky. That was in 1988, when she took Audrey to Medjugorje. There was a clamor out in the street, she says. The townspeople were shouting that the little American girl's face had appeared in the moon. Linda looked up in the sky, she says, and there, unmistakably, in the face of the moon, was Audrey.

Then she looked again, she says, and there was a second moon, beside the first one. This one had the face of an old nun in it.

Linda does not apologize for, or explain, these things. God works in mysterious ways, she says.

And so Linda is asked this: Let's say that someone in her house, unknown to her, is making these mysterious events occur. Let's say that this person looked around at the sorry state of the world and saw good people far from God, facing eternal damnation, a billion children in burning houses without the sense to rush outside to safety. Could a little lie be so bad? Would such a person be a bad person?

"God might say that's not a lie," Linda says. "God might forgive it."

Silence.

But it would still be wrong, she says. "A lie is a lie," she says.

Silence.

If someone were doing it, she concludes, it would be a betrayal. She would probably forgive this person, but she would still have to dismiss him or her from her home ministry, she says.

Then she offers you lemonade.

————

LINDA SANTO PERMITS the *Washington Post* to remove a small sample of the mystery oil, to send to a lab for analysis. "I'd like to know what it is, too," she says.

According to Microbac Laboratories of Pittsburgh, the sample contained 80 percent corn or soybean oil, and 20 percent chicken fat. Microbac chemist Tom Zierenberg says it is a simple mixture, reproducible in any American kitchen.

Which is interesting, but hardly evidence of deceit.

God, after all, makes corn. And soybeans. And chickens, too.

THE TRIAL IS over. God has given his testimony.

"I'm not sure how this whole miracle business got started," George Burns tells the courtroom, "that idea that anything connected with me has to be a miracle. Personally, I am sorry that it did. It makes the distance between us even greater."

He walks to the door.

"I know how hard it is in these times to have faith. But however hopeless, helpless, mixed up, and scary it all gets, it can work. . . . If you find it hard to believe in me, maybe it would help if you know I believe in you."

And then the door swings shut, and God is gone.

IT IS AUGUST 9, 1987, at 11:03 in the morning. Linda Santo is at home. Her sixteen-year-old daughter Gigi is upstairs, on the phone. Matthew, twelve, is on the floor, sorting laundry. Outside, three-year-old Audrey and brother Stephen, four, are playing in the driveway with a new toy, a remote-control truck.

Audrey is a lively little girl. She is already reading Garfield comics. She is all mischief and moxie. "I'm gorgeous," she says all the time. And she is.

Like all young mothers, Linda is doing twelve things at once. Suddenly, she looks up with a vague sense of dread. What?

Gigi is coming down the stairs from her bedroom.

Matthew is still on the floor.

Stephen is coming in from outside.

The German shepherd, Sting, is usually patrolling the yard. Sting protects Audrey. When Audrey strays off the property, Sting grabs her butt and yanks her back. But Sting, for once, is inside the house.

Where is the baby?

"She's outside," says Stephen, out in the driveway.

But she is not in the driveway.

Matthew and his mother race out back, toward the pool.

No. No.

It is a 36-foot aboveground pool. There are retractable steps leading from the top to the ground. The steps are supposed to be up. But someone left them down.

No. No.

Two seconds. Three.

Matthew is in the air, spread-eagle, launched toward his baby sister, who is face down, at the far end, floating, arms spread, like a snow angel, motionless.

Linda hears a bloodcurdling scream.

It is, she realizes, coming from her.

———————

ELEVEN YEARS LATER, Linda is preparing for a gigantic mass of the faithful in honor of her daughter, who is not a dreadfully brain-injured child, but a living saint, selected from birth, anointed by God, nestled in His lap, whispering in His ear.

Week after week, Linda is visited by admiring priests.

Week after week she is applauded by a hundred penitents.

To some, she is a modern-day Mary.

Statues are weeping. Oil is flowing. Wafers are bleeding.

It's a miracle, says Father Mike.

It's a miracle, says Dr. Harding.

It's a miracle, says chemist Lipinski.

It's a miracle, says Father George.

Linda Santo has defied conventional wisdom and kept her child alive through heroic love. She has stayed strong and resolute in the face of unimaginable tragedy. Her joy and spirit have inspired thousands. She has given solace to the sick and dying. Her fortitude outlasted her husband's despair, triumphed over it, brought him back to the home, and to his faith.

Okay.

It's a miracle, says the *Washington Post*.

———

Postscript: The Roman Catholic Diocese of Worcester ended their investigation without an official verdict on whether the events occurring in the house on Flagg Street were miraculous. The report complimented the Santo family for the love and care they gave Audrey, but pointedly cautioned parishioners not to pray to the girl or worship the unconsecrated oil from the house.

Audrey lived almost nine years longer. She died on April 14, 2007, at the age of twenty-three.

If You Go
Chasing Rabbits . . .

I've never been a fan of stories linked to holidays—they seem opportunistic and contrived. But I proposed this one, in time for Valentine's Day. The idea was to find the girl I'd had a crush on in second grade and hadn't seen since. I would take her out on a date.

Thanks for asking, but, no, I didn't score. Yet I've never walked away from a story feeling quite so naked.

February 11, 2001

THIS LOVE STORY, which is about science and not emotion, begins on November 17, 1947, in an electronics lab in suburban New Jersey, when a man dunks a silicon wafer into a beaker of water and invents the modern semiconductor. Thus would become possible not only the storage of vast quantities of data, but its nearly instantaneous retrieval from remote-access sites such as the personal computer at which I sat one day in January 2001 and idly fed the name Shari Basner into an Internet search engine. (Nonspecific curiosity is a Darwinian adaptation of the human species.) Approximately 1.4 seconds later, the computer informed me that Shari lived a mere twenty-five miles away, precipitating an involuntary secretion of norepinephrine from my adrenal glands, which are located above the kidneys. Norepinephrine stimulates the heart.

I knew Shari Basner in 1958 and 1959, in Miss Endler's second-grade classroom in P.S. 26 in the Bronx. I was a very small and very bashful little boy, and Shari was the loveliest girl on Earth. She had silken chestnut hair and eyes like a fawn and a guileless smile of Crayola Red. Her physical presence awakened in me urges and longings as overpowering as they were indecipherable. I knew certain things, however: that I wished to spend eternity with this person, that we would have children through some mysterious and frightening process, and—I remember this specifically—that she would call me "darling."

I was only seven, but not without savvy. And so I promptly developed a two-tiered strategy to deal with these feelings: flight, and paralysis. I never spoke to Shari unless it was unavoidable, and on those occasions I exhibited the conversational skills of a Pleistocene hominid.

I was relieved of this hideous burden after second grade, as I recalled, when Shari and her family moved away. I never saw her again.

And here she was, on my computer screen. A single hit, but a solid one—nailed by an account of a conference she'd chaired in 1998. Shari appeared to be an expert in business communications: diversity awareness, team building, consensus forming, that sort of crap. She is married with kids—as I am. She lives in Columbia, Maryland. And this gave me an idea. I would call her up and invite her to dinner. A date.

Once we were together, I would 'fess up to my crush, forty-two years late. We'd laugh and laugh. And I'd write about it, for Valentine's Day. It would be a dispassionate examination of the origins of romance and the phenomenon of juvenile infatuation. You know, for science.

I dialed Shari's phone number, but before the first ring, I hung up.

No, that's not why. I am a grown-up now, for cripes' sake, not a bashful schoolkid. I simply decided I had not done enough research. I wasn't . . . ready.

———

THE EMOTIONAL RELATIONSHIPS between human males and females can be a complex and imperfect thing, a fact I discovered when I telephoned Professor Robert Billingham at his home. His wife answered. When I told her that I wished to interview her husband as an expert on the subject of romantic love, she burst out laughing.

At Indiana University, Billingham teaches adolescent and preadolescent human behavior. My crush on Shari, he said, was completely normal and ordinary, even at age seven. This sort of behavior is a matter of evolution and adaptation.

As recently as the 1400s, Billingham said, the median life expectancy was twenty-four years. "As soon as sexual maturity was in place, it was time to reproduce, or humans would cease to exist. The problem is that human biology hasn't changed one iota since then." We are still genetically programmed to have intense sexual curiosity at twelve or thirteen. Ages seven through eleven, he said, are a "practice period. The biology is being primed."

But why is it so awkward?

"Have you ever primed a pump? The water doesn't come out in a rush. There are false starts—gurgles and burps and hiccups."

Yep, that's me, at seven. Some kids will take my shy route. Others dip pigtails in the inkwell. Either way, it's inept.

"That's also explainable in Darwinian terms," Billingham said. Nature, he said, wants us to practice, but fail. You don't want seven-year-olds communicating their desires competently, because then they might act them out. Not good.

So bumbling, inarticulate, doofuslike childhood crushes are a dirty trick by God?

"Precisely."

Rummaging through old photographs, I found the one that appears with this story. It is from a P.S. 26 Easter play. I am the petrified-looking rabbit standing immediately at left of the seated rabbit. That's Shari beside me. The exquisite one.

I recall this theatrical production not at all. My only thought, upon seeing the photo, was astonishment that I had actually once been that physically proximate to Shari Basner and not fainted dead away.

I did remember the name of one other person in the picture. The constipated rabbit at the table, spectacles askew, is Clayton

Landey. He and I were friends. Again, the Internet came through. I found Clayton at his home in L.A.

It's funny about memory. Clayton remembered me only vaguely. He remembered Shari not at all. But when I described the photograph, he was there.

"I played Papa Bunny! It was my first stage appearance!"

Clayton Landey, it turns out, is a successful Hollywood actor. He had small roles in the movies *Norma Rae* and *A Civil Action*. He's had big roles off-Broadway. He appeared on *Knots Landing* for three seasons, as Donna Mills's attorney. He was on an episode of *The Practice*, playing a rich guy charged with the hit-and-run of a homeless person. His is one of those faces you recognize, kinda.

("Let me get this straight," he said. "I'm finally going to get my picture in the *Washington Post,* and it's in the [expletive] bunny suit?")

I asked: How could you possibly not remember Shari?

"Back then," Clayton said, "I was aware females were attractive, but I was focused on older women. The kindergarten teacher was a battle-ax, but her assistant was beautiful. I had hot dreams about her."

At seven?

"At six. In the dreams, she would have to walk through my neighborhood to get home, and I would save her from the bad guys."

Pump priming.

———

WHEN I TOLD colleagues what I planned, most had the same question. It's the same question you would have if you are married, or have ever been married, or are seven years old hoping that someone, someday, will call you darling. The answer is, no, the wife didn't mind.

Apart from the unnerving idiosyncrasy of getting dressed sock-shoe-sock-shoe instead of sock-sock-shoe-shoe, my wife of twenty-one years is the most self-confident and levelheaded person I know. She is a lawyer, a prosecutor by training, and she doesn't believe in building cases out of nothing. There is no room in her psyche for an emotion as foolish and self-destructive as jealousy. Plus, she is a looker who is married to an eyesore, and this combination tends to militate against jealousy.

So, yes, my wife said fine when I asked her about Shari. (Or, as she referred to her, without a hint of resentment, "your bunny girl.")

Armchair ethicists might well pose the question: Shouldn't Shari's husband also be given the opportunity to weigh in on this subject prior to our date?

The hell with armchair ethicists: The answer is no. Shari has no moral obligation to inform her husband of our date because I have her on the phone right now, and I am not telling her it is to be a date. I am telling her I want to interview her for a story, over, um, dinner at a fancy restaurant.

"What is the story about?" she asks.

"I can't tell you," I say.

I was counting on her curiosity. But I was not counting on this:

"Do I know you? I grew up with a Gene Weingarten."

It had not actually occurred to me that Shari would remember my name. Yes, I tell her, same guy.

Why would she remember some weenie whom she knew for a year and who could not look her in the eye? And what did she mean by "grew up with"? And why, when she somewhat dubiously agreed to do this, did I put down the phone and go for a long walk in the cold?

———————

I DECIDED TO wear a suit without a tie because, since Shari didn't know it was going to be a date, she might be comparatively underdressed and that might make her feel bad. I decided that I would quickly work in a reference to my wife, kind of casual-like, so that later, when I explained what I was doing, she would understand the totally innocent and hilarious nature of this event and not think that I was some sort of creep with a shrine to her in a dank basement lit by candelabra. I decided that maybe it was better to wear the tie, after all, because I could always take it off if we were incompatibly attired. I decided to use my daughter's car, because it is clean, as opposed to my car, which is filled with old newspapers and soda cans and stray bits of food products decaying in aluminum foil. I decided I had not prepared this rigorously for my interview with George W. Bush.

In second grade, I never confessed to anyone my longing for Shari. The closest I came was the day our class picture came out. My mother was commenting how attractive a certain girl was. I forget which one. One of the Others.

And I said, "I think Shari is sorta pretty."

And my mother said something that I never forgot. It was a pronouncement I simply accepted because grown-ups knew all kinds of stuff. My mother said, "Shari is pretty now, but she won't be pretty as an adult."

———————————

Dear Ma:

How are things in Heaven? I miss you.

Listen, remember when you predicted that I would wind up regretting my choice of roommate in college? Well, you were right.

But you were really, really, really wrong about Shari. Just FYI.

So, we sat down to dinner, Shari and I, me feeling like an eyesore with warts. At least I am taller than she is. Finally.

The first thing I did, right after sliding in the obligatory and entirely casual mention of my wife, was to ask her to volunteer everything she remembered about me. I was going to tell her how I remembered her—the dancing cherubs and symphonies—but only after establishing, for the record, for humorous effect, that I was barely a mote in her memory.

But Shari began talking and did not stop for some time. She wasn't Clayton. She remembered I was shy. She remembered that she sat next to me, which was news to me. She remembered once visiting the home of my cousin Margaret, who was also in our class, and that I had lived in the apartment below.

(Actually, I remembered that day, too. I hid in my room, terrified that the girls might come downstairs and that I, forced into casual physical congress with Shari, might toss my cookies.)

"There's something else," Shari said, "but I'm not sure you want to hear it."

Sure, I said.

"One day we had an assignment to cut out paper flowers, and . . ."

Well, I knew where she was going. I was back in my second-grade classroom, where I was the youngest kid. I entered second grade at age six—too young, but my mother had pulled strings. She believed, strongly, in a popular educational theory that smart kids foundered if they were not adequately challenged, and so they should be taught at their level of academic competence even at the cost of some awkward social adjustments.

". . . and you were having trouble, and getting frustrated . . ."

As I look at the picture of my second-grade class, I am astounded by its size. Miss Endler had to deal with nearly forty children every day; I remember her as a witch, but that doesn't seem fair, in retrospect. She was an overburdened teacher with an impossible job. She could not permit any sort of discipline problems to get out of hand, particularly an immature kid who was always . . . crying.

". . . and you couldn't cut out those flowers the right way, and you started to cry . . ."

The school year 1958–59 was a time when I was forever losing control of myself in class, and Miss Endler was forever dealing with this in a manner less understanding than one would expect of, say, one's kindly old aunt. The humiliation brought more tears. I recalled the flower-cutting moment as one of the bad episodes in a series of bad episodes in a year that to my memory consisted entirely of loving Shari and crying in class.

". . . and I was so upset that you were so upset that I leaned over and cut out your flowers for you."

A waiter came for our order. I waved him away.

"You did?" I stared at her. I had no memory of this.

"Yes."

Shari has beautiful eyes.

Journalists are fascinated by, and skeptical of, theories of personality that place great weight on the impact of past events. We love this stuff because it permits us to believe that if we root around deeply enough in someone's history we can figure out the single reason he is the person he is. (And because, so often, when we do discover such things, the fit seems right.) On the other hand, we are wary: We know that there is seldom a single reason that explains anything. These historical theories can be incomplete at best, and total hooey at worst. So sometimes, in writing stories, we report what we find, and leave it to the reader to weigh its significance.

At the end of the school year 1958–59, my mother came to me with wonderful news. I and five of my classmates had done so well on a test that we were going to skip third grade. Soar right over all those ordinary ninnies, right into the fourth grade! The school system had objected in my case on account of my age, but she had written letters, and they relented.

So, now, at seven, I was to be *two* years younger than most of the kids in my class.

Dear Ma—

One other thing . . .

———————

"I SKIPPED THIRD grade with you," Shari said. "We went into fourth grade together."

Again, the waiter came. Again, I waved him away.

Shari was showing me other photographs now, pictures she had brought with her, ones I didn't have. Here was my fourth-grade class picture, and fifth, and sixth. I was in every picture. So was she.

How was this possible?

We realized that some of the other kids in the bunny picture were not from our second grade at all—they were from our fourth-grade class. Clayton was there because he had skipped with us, too. This picture was a fourth-grade Easter production, not second.

Shari said she didn't move away to Queens until after sixth grade.

So she was right: I had "grown up" with her. Somehow, I didn't remember her in those last three years. And now, sitting across from her forty-two years later, I was beginning to remember why not.

During the summer between second and fourth grade, I spent a lot of time alone in a hammock behind our family's cheerfully decrepit summer house in Hopewell Junction, New York. I remember squinting into the afternoon sky, swatting mosquitoes and hashing things out in my head.

I was, I told myself, at a crossroads. If I remained a crybaby,

I was doomed. In this new class of really old kids, my immaturity would stand out like a sucked thumb. And yet I had been handed a gift, in a way. Almost no one would know the second-grade me. If I tried, I could become a different person altogether—any person I wanted to be. And so I did, with the sort of melodramatic intensity only a seven-year-old can muster. What I decided was that I was simply going to erect a barrier between the part of me that felt things and the part of me that interacted with other people.

And so that summer, I built it, brick by brick. I remember thinking sad thoughts—that my dog had died, for example—and then practicing holding back tears. I worked at it until it was a different kid who walked through the doors of Mrs. Nolan's fourth-grade class.

It proved easier than I'd thought. I carved out new friends, new relationships, all constructed around the premise that I was a worldly, even cynical, individual. And the love of my life? A guess: She was part of the past from which I had to disassociate myself. She, more than anyone else, knew my weakness. She was not part of the new program.

I never cried in school again.

I felt things. Tears would come. But never in front of another person.

Never. Didn't cry at my own mother's funeral, thirty years later.

OF COURSE, THIS is about Shari, and she has been waiting patiently for nearly an hour to find out why the hell I have asked her to dinner. So we order our food, and I tell her. I tell her about the silicon wafer, and how I am going to explore the biochemical nature of juvenile crushes, and how I was in love with her at the age of seven, and how I never told her about it, and how I was now, as an adult who is able to confront such things with humor and maturity, taking her out on a date. For Valentine's Day.

She was appalled.

Not at the story. She liked that. But she hadn't known about my crush, or even suspected it, and was dismayed that she could have possibly created an atmosphere, back there in Miss Endler's class, in which she had seemed aloof or unapproachable.

I tried to explain why she was blameless. You know: Darwin, human biology, pumps, water, etc.

Shari would have none of it. She was really beating herself up. "It's hard to believe anyone would find me intimidating. I consider myself approachable. I wonder if it was something I was projecting . . ."

The woman's professional career has involved teaching people how to relate to other people in a straightforward manner; how to share feelings; she has advised organizations how to repair breakdowns in communication.

Burps and gurgles: the ultimate nightmare.

When we'd spoken on the phone, Clayton Landey and I had reminisced about growing up in the South Bronx in the late 1950s, a place in restive ethnic transition. We Jewish kids had been picked on by what seemed to us to be larger and angrier Irish kids. "To get to school," Clayton said, chortling, "you had to fight your way through the freckles."

Shari remembered it, too.

"In winter, we had to walk to school in a convoy. They would nail us with ice balls."

I nodded and laughed.

She looked at me quizzically.

"It hurt."

Well, yes. It did hurt. I had forgotten that.

I had forgotten a lot of things. She'd forgotten nothing. She remembered the smell of P.S. 26, how the old building had been an architectural delight, with gargoyles, columns shaped like minarets, ornate Gothic and Moorish details.

Clayton's memory had been even shabbier than mine. He had recalled being a bit of a hellion in P.S. 26. What he had not recalled was that, after fourth grade, he and I had hung out together some. We were real smartasses. I was carefully crafting my new iconoclasm: All of human behavior was fodder for deconstruction and ridicule, in a sort of primitive, snotty, nine-year-old, polite-to-adults, slicked-down-hair-with-cowlick fashion. Part Bart Simpson, part Eddie Haskell.

Clayton told me that in his teens, he finally changed who he was: "I realized there was only so much the world was gonna put up with and let me keep breathing."

And that's when he started taking life seriously, learning to emote, beginning an acting career in earnest.

"And you?" he asked.

"I'm still a smartass," I said. "I do it for a living now."

For most of my adult life, I have been involved in the writing or editing of humor. Humor is designed to deliver joy to others, but there is something about it that permits—even demands—an emotional distance from your subject. Part of it is that humor often requires a bloodless hostility; laughs usually come at the expense of something or someone. And part of it involves the nature of humor itself—it exists, on the deepest level, as a perverse denial of pain and fear. No one has ever explained this more succinctly or ingeniously than Dave Barry did in a tiny essay he wrote for a newspaper magazine I edited in the 1980s. I had asked him to create a definition of "sense of humor." He took three days. This is what he wrote: "A sense of humor is a measurement of the extent to which you realize that you are trapped in a world almost entirely devoid of reason. Laughter is how you release the anxiety you feel at this knowledge."

Sometime afterward, Dave's mother died suddenly. I was

making plans to replace his column that week with something we had on file, for emergencies. But before I could, he delivered a column. It was about his son's pet gerbil. It was really funny. I asked him how he could possibly have written that under the circumstances, and he said, "Writing humor is the greatest possible escape from emotional pain."

Shari hustled her way through school, as I did. She even skipped eighth grade (the school system had, finally, flatly refused to let me do that) and so, like me, she wound up entering college at sixteen. Like me, she wound up doubting the wisdom of it: "Intellectually, it was liberating. But socially, it was a disaster. I often thought, why was I running so fast? What was the point?"

Shari tried the sorority route for a short time, and found it empty. As the Vietnam War escalated, she was drawn into the antiwar movement at Queens College. Meanwhile, I was at NYU, drawn into the drug, uh, movement. It was a time of robust experimentation, and I was right in the middle of it. You may remember the time: People were getting in touch with their inner selves. They were tripping on LSD and smoking weed and learning to commune with nature and each other in a slap-happy commingling of souls and tongues and flowers and incense. Happy, daffy, people-grooving-on-people stuff.

Me, I liked heroin.

On May 4, 1970, when federal troops opened fire on a crowd of demonstrators at Kent State University, killing four, Shari's sense of security about the world was shattered. There was no sane way to react, so she did the insane.

"What do you do, how do you make your voice heard when you are at a suburban college where everyone goes home at the end of the day to Mom and Dad?"

Here's what: With a handful of other students, she walked out onto the busy Long Island Expressway and put her body in front of the cars. When they screeched to a stop, she told the drivers, "You have to do something about the war."

"I was so filled with despair," she says, "that it didn't matter what happened to me. I was well past the point of thinking about my own safety." She was nineteen.

At nineteen I was writing about Vietnam protests for the newspaper at NYU. It was a way of being involved intensely, but at a distance, as an objective observer.

I remember distinctly the day I first saw the wrenching photograph of that nine-year-old Vietnamese girl, racing naked in terror down Trang Bang highway, her clothes incinerated by a napalm attack. Trapped in a world almost entirely devoid of reason. It was an image of transcendent horror. I found a way not to feel it. The caption reported that the little girl's name was Kim Phuc. I looked at this picture and . . . laughed.

Shari's husband is a philosophy professor who now works in computer technology. Most of Shari's professional life—in communication, human resources, and adult education—has been tailored to follow his two- and three-year posts at various universities; she's taught in some of the same schools, including Cornell and the University of Wisconsin. Now she works as an education and training coordinator at a health-care facility.

Two health crises have shaped her identity: The first was when her mother died after a long and difficult illness that required Shari to abandon plans for a doctorate. The second occurred with the birth of her second daughter, Jenny. Jenny was dauntingly premature—arriving at the twenty-sixth week of pregnancy, at 1 pound 10 ounces. Nothing looks as vulnerable as a baby that small. Nothing alive looks as close to death.

"It was shattering, the most painful thing I ever experienced. I found myself praying for the first time in my life."

She took a swallow of wine.

"It's an example of moving from macrocosm to microcosm.

It's one thing to protest mass loss of life. It's another to face the loss of a single life. A sense of randomness overwhelms you. I have always prided myself on being someone who could do things, who could find a way, if I tried hard enough. But here was a total lack of control. There was nothing I could do."

Jenny survived. She is seventeen, and healthy. Shari wiped a tear.

"I can't imagine life without her."

Two health matters helped shape my identity, too. For years I was a silent hypochondriac—comically enslaved by fear of illness, inclined to diagnose any minor symptom as the onset of a fatal disease. I wrote a book about it, a funny book in which I gleefully provided the amateur hypochondriac all the medical information necessary to turn pro. (Yes, hiccups can mean cancer.)

One of the few serious moments in the book comes when I try to explain why someone who is relatively fearless in the conduct of his life—a natural risk-taker—can wind up being such a baby about his health. Hypochondria, I said, suggests a morbid fear of losing control of one's emotions in front of the world: If you're prepared for death—if you're braced for the Bad News because you have seen it coming—you won't get caught crying.

In this book I also revealed the surefire cure for hypochondria: Get really sick. This was the second health matter that shaped my life: In 1991, I was diagnosed with a potentially fatal liver disease.

I recovered. But when I wrote the book, it looked as though I had about five years to live. The final chapter was titled: "Is Death a Laughing Matter? Of Corpse Not."

One of Shari's great regrets is that the South Bronx she knew—a comfortable place with a strong sense of community—seems forever gone; it disappeared in an ugly ethnic upheaval in the early 1960s that transformed it into a sullen moonscape of gutted buildings, drug supermarkets, and cringing, three-legged dogs.

"I feel like a displaced person," she said, "like someone who grew up in Sarajevo. Someone who can never go home. It was like an epidemic had hit. I can't help but think that if it hadn't happened so swiftly, maybe the chasm would not have been there. Maybe people of goodwill could have stepped into the void—shopkeepers, educators, they could have drawn people together to work for a common good."

Maybe. Shari's a problem-solver. To me, the ruined Bronx had been a gold mine: My first big break as a journalist came when I infiltrated the teenage street gangs there and wrote about it for a national magazine.

It was time for coffee. Shari had to put on glasses to read the fine print on the menu. I had to take mine off. I am forty-nine. Shari turned fifty the day before our date.

Man, that one year seemed huge in second grade.

When it was time to go, Shari asked me what the theme of my story would be, and I told her that I did not know for sure. Definitely about the search powers of the Internet, and juvenile romance.

"Also, maybe the pull of history," she said.

Yes, I said. That, too.

"You know, I am not sure I would have agreed to do this with anyone else," she said. "When you called, it brought back a flood of memories. There was something there. For what it is worth."

It occurred to me, for what it is worth, that Shari is probably really good at what she does: team building, consensus forming. Feelings. You know, that sort of crap.

We hugged and said goodbye.

As I drove away, I noticed there was a cassette in the tape player and punched it up. Turned out to be a collection of tunes Buddy Holly recorded in 1958 and 1959. His songs are musically brilliant and, like much early rock, lyrically infantile. No depth at all. Just naive, explosive expressions of excitement and wonder at the visceral power of young love.

> *Heartbeat,*
> *why do you skip*
> *when my baby's lips*
> *meet mine?*

Buddy never had to learn that things get more complicated. He was twenty-two when he stepped onto that plane, in the middle of my second-grade year.

I drove home to his music. And I can report that, still, no one ever sees me cry.

Fear Itself

This is the only assignment I ever had that I thought might get me killed. Before I flew to Jerusalem, where I would ride a public bus during the intifada to see what pure terror felt like, I left a love note for my wife and children buried deep in my sock drawer.

I discovered it four months after my return and threw it away, unread. Why? Because the idea of opening all that up again, of revisiting my worried state of mind, unnerved me. Better not to think about it.

And that, in a way, is the point of this story.

The meaning of life is that it ends.
—Franz Kafka

August 22, 2004

YOU ARE NOT afraid of terrorism, really. You have weighed the facts and have concluded, rationally, that even if terrorists strike again in this country, the chances are negligible that you or anyone you know will be killed or injured. You feel no special tension when you place your seat tray in the upright position. You are old enough to have lived through other supposedly apocalyptic times, or you've surely heard about them—most famously, the silly spectacle of 1950s-era schoolkids giggling under their desks in anticipation of the Big One.

The recent warnings about terrorism during the election campaign have ratcheted up your concerns a little, but so what? You are going on with your life not as an act of defiance so much as a celebration of rationality. You will be fine.

So here's a question: Would you ride a bus in Jerusalem? Right now? Here's your 5½ shekels, go take a bus to market, buy some figs. Pick a bad day, after the Israelis have assassinated some terrorist leaders and everyone is waiting for the second sandal to drop. There are *lots* of buses in Jerusalem—the odds are still long in your favor. Do you take that dare?

A few weeks ago, I did just that: boarded a bus on just such a day and rode for nearly an hour. I did it because I wanted to better understand the psychology of terror. Not the psychology of the terrorist—the psychology of the terrorized.

After 9/11, Americans are concerned enough by terror to be waging a costly war against it. But, by and large, the fear of terrorism has not seeped into our bones. We are new to this thing. The Israelis are not. Terrorism creates a hierarchy of fear; theirs is greater than ours.

Hence, this trip. Call it a scouting report.

The bus I chose was the No. 18. Its route is a vital artery, traveling down Jaffa Road through the heart of Jerusalem. Twice in the last decade, someone boarded a bus on this route, reached into his pocket, thumbed a button and detonated. As is dictated by the grisly kinetics of suicide bombing, the bombers' heads remained intact, shooting skyward with the roof of the bus. But their bodies were frothed into pulp. Forty-six other people died. Some of those were torn apart; some looked almost unscathed, but their organs had been jellied by the shock wave, a medical syndrome common to bus bombings and almost nothing else. Dozens of other people survived, but were crippled or disfigured by shrapnel: Customarily, suicide bombs are jacketed by nails, nuts, screws, and ball bearings, for maximum damage.

Like everyone else, I waited in line, deposited my fare, and stepped aboard the bus. Early afternoon. Sixty-odd people seated and standing, some with shopping bags, some without. Eyes forward, no one saying much to anyone else. It was hot.

TEN TIMES IN the last three years our leaders have told us that something was up. They didn't say what exactly: ominous "chatter" of an undisclosed nature in unspecified channels of communication among unidentified individuals planning an unnamed atrocity of uncertain dimensions in an unknown location at an indeterminate time. So what should we do about it? Unclear.

When there was finally an intelligence breakthrough early this month—a named source, a likely weapon (truck bomb) and five specific targets in three specific cities (New York, Washington, and Newark)—it was followed by the sheepish disclosure that the information was mostly four years old, which was followed by charges of political fearmongering, which was followed by indignant denials, and at the end of it all none of us had any idea whether anything important had just happened.

The day after the initial alert, I walked into one of the target buildings, the World Bank on Washington's Pennsylvania Avenue. At the front desk, I asked a question about security. An important-looking man came striding up. He was the building's security manager. "How did you get in here?" he asked. "I walked in the door," I said. He escorted me out and began berating a subordinate.

Our preparedness, at least those measures we can see, sometimes seems almost comical—from our primary-color danger alert codes to those video displays on the Beltway urging us to report anything suspicious. (What is one likely to see on the Beltway to arouse suspicion? I ♥ BIN LADEN?) At the Gateway Arch in St. Louis, visitors are wanded, their backpacks fed through metal detectors. A sign stipulates what size and shape of pocketknife is permitted inside. A visitor from Washington takes this in, thinking: Someone is going to hijack the Arch?

Hierarchies of fear. Ours is worse than yours.

Interesting fact: In the year after 9/11, many people stopped flying. Road deaths spiked.

There has been terrorism in the world, more or less nonstop, since twelfth-century Syria, when a persecuted Persian religious sect called the Assassins knifed people to death in crowds. Terrorism has persisted because terrorism works. It makes people crazy. It is a cost-effective method of waging psychological war by those who see themselves outnumbered or disenfranchised.

A disenfranchised minority cannot sack Rome, rape Nanking, burn Atlanta, or firebomb Dresden. Those things are terror attacks by nation-states, military sieges with the primary goal of sowing despair among the enemy and weakening their will to resist. A disenfranchised people—whether Palestinians in the Middle East, or Tamils in Sri Lanka, or Islamic zealots who see the spread of Western culture as an assault on their religion—will use the means at their disposal. Amoral though it may be, terrorism succeeds in focusing attention on whatever cause its practitioners espouse. It does this in a particularly insidious way.

A quarter-century ago, a cultural anthropologist named Ernest Becker wrote a Pulitzer Prize–winning book called *The Denial of Death*. For a time, during the primacy of Freud, it was huge. It's not about terrorism, it's about the psyche, and its central thesis is one of the most disturbing analyses of human behavior ever set in print.

Everything we are, Becker argued—our personalities, our attitudes, our very being—is an elaborate lie, a carefully crafted self-delusion constructed to avoid having to face a fact so terrifying it would drive us mad: Not only are we certain to die, but death could come at any moment, followed by an eternity of nothingness. Lower animals, blessedly unaware of their mortality, plod thoughtlessly through their lives on instinct alone.

Lacking their ignorance, Becker says, we compensate by making ourselves stupid. We tranquilize ourselves with the trivial; we make friends, raise families, drink beer, follow the Redskins, find comfort in religions promising eternal life, all of which takes our minds off the potentially paralyzing truth. We deceive ourselves into believing—not literally, but emotionally—that we are immortal. Paranoiacs and depressives are in some ways the sanest among us, according to Becker, because their layer of denial is so fragile it fractures. Most of us, though, are able to retain our sanity so long as our anxiety is held at bay, and our anxiety is held at bay so long as our bold illusion remains manageable.

This is not exactly the anthem of romantic poets or motivational speakers, but no one has ever successfully challenged Becker's central thesis. On some level, we attempt to smother our elemental fear of death with a grand lie.

That's where terrorism comes in. Terrorism penetrates that self-deception in a way that few things can.

During the Cold War, Americans knew that the Soviets had missiles pointed at us, and we at them. And yet, paradoxically—applying Becker's paradigm—this gave comfort. Mutually assured destruction seemed to offer an anodyne, a plausible measure of deterrence and thus a toehold for our state of denial.

It would take something truly diabolical to dislodge that toe, something that existed only in fiction. Remember SPECTRE, the shadowy international organization that was James Bond's nemesis? The acronym stood for "Special Executive for Counterintelligence, Terrorism, Revenge, and Extortion." It was an absurd concept, really—an entity of no fixed address, affiliated with no state, answerable to no constituency, diffuse, elusive, nihilistic, unavailable for negotiation, promiscuously cruel, fueled by hatred, with no comprehensible agenda other than mayhem, destruction, and death.

You know, al Qaeda.

With al Qaeda, however, there is an additional fillip, a small, elegant frisson. It was probably best expressed in a quote attributed to Osama bin Laden himself, a few weeks after 9/11: "We love death. The U.S. loves life. That is the big difference between us."

SPECTRE, with a suicide wish.

My terrorism field trip had destinations other than Jerusalem. The itinerary would take me to Madrid, to ride the same train route that al Qaeda blew up on March 11, killing 191 and injuring nearly 2,000. Then, Jerusalem. And then I would fly home on British Airways Flight 223, the one that kept getting canceled because of reports that terrorists were going to bring it down. There was really nothing to worry about, from a rational standpoint. Just a few days on vehicles of public transportation.

I brought *The Denial of Death* with me. Also, Kafka.

AWAITING TAKEOFF FOR the first leg of my trip, Dulles to Heathrow, I found myself seated on the aisle watching the last of my fellow passengers boarding the plane. It looked as if I might luck out, with the middle seat beside me unoccupied. But at the last moment a man arrived, struggled to stuff a large duffel bag in the overhead compartment, then plopped down next to me. I nodded, smiled, and looked away to compose myself.

A few months after 9/11, I told a coworker that I thought the Pulitzer Prize for news photography for the year 2001 should go to a machine. I couldn't decide which machine—the overhead camera in an airport in Maine that caught a shirtsleeved Mohamed Atta passing briskly through security on the morning of

September 11, or the ATM camera in Maryland that snapped hijackers Hani Hanjour and Majed Moqed withdrawing cash.

Both photos were riveting for their grainy banality, and for what they say about the duality in all of us. Here were ordinary-looking people engaged in ordinary-looking activities, indistinguishable from any of us, with dreadful secrets in their head. I hadn't thought about those photos in a long time, until now. I gathered my thoughts, prepared my face, and looked back at my seatmate, Hani Hanjour.

In the ATM snapshot, Hanjour—the Saudi national believed to have piloted the plane that hit the Pentagon—is standing behind and to Moqed's right, both looking placidly down as their money plops into place. I had pretty much the same view of him, here in the plane, to my left. Small guy, lithe build, olive complexion, angular face, sparse goatee, hard eyes.

If you Google "Hani Hanjour" you will find a spiderwork of conspiracy theories speculating that he is still alive—a demonic Elvis who has recently been seen walking the streets of Riyadh. He wasn't on that plane at all; his piloting skills were too feeble to have maneuvered a 757 through a hairpin turn at breakneck speed and bring it down onto a target that was, comparatively, the height of a Necco wafer.

"So," I said as cheerfully as possible to my new seatmate as the plane taxied for takeoff, "where are you from?"

"Saudi Arabia," he said.

Yes, yes, security for this flight had been formidable. This was the sister flight to the infamous Flight 223—the return leg on the Corridor of Terror. There were two separate inspections of our persons and our belongings. The second machine was so sensitive it busted a woman with a gold chain no thicker than a yo-yo string. Security officers took aside a little girl, five or six years old, with a gappy smile, and wanded her thighs up under her skirt.

This sort of thing went on for twenty-five minutes, until it

came time to board, at which point the final twenty or thirty
people in line, and their carry-ons, were waved aboard with no
inspection whatsoever. I was one of those people. Hani, here,
came in after me—he must have been one of them, too. His duffel bag was enormous.

So, what does a terrorist seem like, anyway? How do you
know one if you see one?

Social scientists and law enforcement agencies have been
focusing on this question for more than a quarter-century, with
no coherent results. In the late 1970s, a psychologist interviewed
eighty imprisoned terrorists in eleven countries and concluded
that most of them had defective vestibular functions of the inner
ear. This was an exciting finding, until it fell apart under further
scrutiny. More rigorous studies have found, disturbingly, that terrorists tend to be fairly ordinary people—relatively sane if politically extreme individuals of ordinary appearance and demeanor.
Like Hani, my seatmate.

What should I do? Summon a flight attendant? Stop the
plane on a wild suspicion? Too late anyway, we were in the air.

I think you know where this is going. My seatmate's name
turned out to be Tareq Ali Alghamdi. He's twenty-two, an en-
gineering student at the University of New Haven—a nice guy,
no more of a terrorist than I. I know all about him because he
burbled it all out within minutes of takeoff, even showing me his
visa papers, unbidden. I'm guessing he does this all the time—he
knows what he looks like, and is aggressively and engagingly open
about himself in a preemptive defense. I know, for example, that
he's a Muslim but no fanatic. He will have a beer every once in a
while and is, he emphasizes, a regular guy: "Hey, if I see a pretty
girl, I'll look at her ass, too."

Tareq says customs officials often detain him for unreason-
able lengths of time, simply by virtue of his passport and his general appearance. He says that his brother, who is diabetic, has

been held for questioning for hours without access to his insulin.

As we began our trip across the Atlantic, Tareq and I solemnly agreed that terrorism is making people too tense, that ethnic profiling is a dreadful indignity, and that dumb Americans are too darn willing to leap to unjustified conclusions about people on slim evidence.

Life is possible only with illusions. And so, the question for the science of mental health must become an absolutely new and revolutionary one, yet one that reflects the essence of the human condition: On what level of illusion does one live?

—Ernest Becker, *The Denial of Death*

IF THERE WAS anxiety, it was not apparent on the faces of the people on this double-decker commuter train that brings workers into Madrid from the blue-collar northeastern suburbs. People dressed for work sat quietly, in that state of swaying, hypnotic detachment familiar to subway riders everywhere. Some glanced at the time and temperature, which flashes continually in these trains on a dot-video display. But no one seemed to be noticing a large hiker's knapsack, left unattended. It was getting stares only from me, and only I bothered to nudge awake a dozing man across the aisle, to ask if it was his. It was.

Of course, most of these people had ridden here fifty times since the day that this very train—same destination, same time of day—exploded. That was ten weeks before, March 11, one of four bombings that occurred almost simultaneously, in different rush-hour trains, along the forty-minute commuter line. The instruments of destruction were backpacks detonated by cell phone. Al Qaeda masterminded it; Spain was said to be a target because of its cooperation in the war in Iraq.

This train took the worst hit, multiple bombs detonating a minute before it was to roll into the giant Atocha station—Madrid's version of Grand Central. Dozens of people died in unspeakable ways. When some survivors tried to describe for TV crews what they had witnessed, they began, but fell grimly silent.

On this day, on this train ten weeks later, there was nothing. Soldiers with assault rifles had been very much in evidence at the park-and-ride suburban station of Alcalá de Henares, where I had boarded. Alcalá was where most of the terrorists were thought to have entered the system with their deadly cargo.

But the train itself held only commuters, staring blankly ahead as they passed through gray industrial parks, clotheslined shantytowns with rusted corrugated-metal roofs, and the familiar New York–style graffiti that turned rocks into gaily spray-painted monogrammed pastel pillows. For many people on 3/11, this was the last sight they ever saw.

The train I was on was now standing room only. As we neared Atocha and the display time hit 7:39—the moment of the bombing—I approached a small, trim woman in her forties and asked her if she was nervous. Celia Alves, a secretary, was headed for work. Nervous? She shrugged no, and nodded disgustedly toward the newspaper I was carrying. It was that day's *El Pais*; I had picked it up at the station but hadn't yet looked at it.

"Obtuvieron lo que desearon," she said. They got what they wanted.

This was May 25. The headline read "Los Últimos de Irak." It reported that the final group of Spanish advisers had returned from Iraq. The troops had been ordered home by Spain's new antiwar government, elected in a backlash after the bombings.

They got what they wanted. Nothing to worry about anymore.

Can it be that easy to banish fear? Just find a reason for optimism, and optimism returns. But is the threat really gone? Isn't Spain still a modern, Western, capitalist, secular democracy, flagrant corrupter of a large Muslim population—as despised by radical Islam as any country other than ours?

The fact is, the Spanish economy has rebounded nicely from 3/11. When I was there, the country was giddy over the marriage of the dashing Crown Prince Felipe to a pretty TV anchorwoman. And at Atocha station, when I got off the train into a crowd five deep waiting to board (this disaster would have been much worse had the train detonated in the station), things were at a brisk and seemingly normal morning pace—though everywhere, a police presence was evident.

The public consciousness of the dead and wounded of Madrid's 3/11 wasn't gone; it was tucked away at one corner of Atocha, behind barriers, next to vending machines that sell Doritos and Toblerone and ham sandwiches. The improvised shrine was similar to those spontaneous memorials in downtown New York that sprang up after 9/11—personal messages, religious icons, photos, flowers, teddy bears. But there was an additional element that made this particularly powerful.

I felt it before I actually understood what it was. Many people who left a letter or a message also left a votive candle, contained in a broad, foot-deep glass cylinder. These candles have stout flames that burn for a week or more. Hundreds of them were on the floor, maybe a thousand in all, and, as I approached this shrine, I literally felt its warmth. I knew none of the dead, and yet, standing there at the barrier, at this small furnace of grief, I was startled to feel a tear on my cheek.

Weeks later, a wire story would report that the candles at Atocha had been removed and replaced with video screens and computers on which passersby can leave messages. People had complained that the candles were too emotionally powerful, preventing them from putting the attacks behind them.

> *But of the tree of the knowledge of good and evil, thou*
> *shalt not eat of it: for in the day that thou eatest there-*
> *of, thou shalt surely die.*
>
> —Genesis 2:17

ADAM AND EVE'S punishment for getting too curious was banishment from the Garden of Eden. But that was the least of it. The Bible is unclear about whether the first couple were immortal before their expulsion, but in a way, it is immaterial. What matters is that, as their punishment, they *learned* that they would someday die. That's when their Hell on Earth began.

To enter the modern, stone-porticoed building on King David Street in Jerusalem, I needed to give my name and show ID to an armed man who stood outside with a walkie-talkie. He radioed the information to a woman inside, who checked the name against her manifest and radioed back a clearance. Only then was I admitted.

"Welcome to Jerusalem," the guard said, deadpan. I was not sure if this was meant ironically or not. Probably not. This was my hotel.

Things are different in Jerusalem, different from anywhere you have ever been. Before entering a grocery store, or a bus station, or a movie theater, you are stopped and wanded, often questioned, and sometimes frisked. Many restaurants keep their doors locked and buzz their customers in. At Ben-Gurion International Airport, the X-ray machine is the size of a panel truck, and the inspection of a single laptop computer can take fifteen minutes. Ordinary citizens walk the streets of Jerusalem carrying concealed pistols—this is not only legal but encouraged, to maintain an omnipresent citizen militia. Soldiers on weekend leave stroll the street in civvies, but with assault rifles slung over their shoulders, like ugly, 15-pound handbags. This, too, is encouraged. Soldiers are also under orders to carry tourniquets, just in case. All of this is to make ordinary people feel safer, against the onslaught.

There is a Hebrew word, *hamatzav*, that is used to describe the state of dread that has swaddled Jerusalem like damp, clammy gauze since the Palestinian intifadas made merely living a daredevil act. *Hamatzav* literally means "the situation," and it seems to cover everything: the high security, the high anxiety, the high-stakes game of chicken. Palestinian militants believe they can make the Israelis so fearful, so desperate for peace of mind, that they will end their occupation and surrender more land than they ever bargained for. Israeli leaders believe their fierce reprisals will, in time, crush their attackers' will to kill. Both sides, of course, know fear: Plenty of innocent Palestinians have been killed in Israeli military actions—for Palestinians, the act of living must also, at times, seem like a mortal risk. Each side accuses the other of terrorism. Each side describes its own actions as self-defense. And so it goes.

On my first night in the city, I walked from my hotel to the Western Wall, Jewish Jerusalem's holiest site, and there I met Ozer Bergman. It is hard to miss Bergman. He stands 7 feet tall—6-feet-5 of it is Ozer, and the rest is hat, a dramatic, thick cylinder of fur. It was sundown on the holy day of Shavuot, and Bergman, a Hasidic Jew, had come here to pray. He works for a research institute that translates the writings of Nachman of Breslov, a revered nineteenth-century rabbi.

"That's a full-time business?" I asked.

"In Jerusalem it is," he said with a laugh.

I almost didn't approach him, anticipating a language problem. It turns out that Bergman is originally from Long Island. Devout Jets fan.

We were speaking outside the Western Wall's security gate, where Bergman was waiting in a crowd of hundreds to board the No. 2 bus, which carries the faithful to the ultra-Orthodox neighborhood where he lives. It's a mob scene, with an empty bus arriving every minute or two and leaving moments later, packed cheek by jowl. Eight months before, one of these buses—crowded just like these, on a similar day—blew up, killing 23 people, many of them children. Many more were grievously injured. The suicide bomber, a father of young children, was black-bearded like Ozer and dressed to resemble a Hasid. He had boarded the bus, wedged himself in the middle of a crowd of riders, patiently waited until his bus passed another bus to assure maximum loss of life, and exploded.

Bergman is not afraid to take buses?

"Never!" he thundered. "I take buses all the time. My wife, too. It's my country, I will not let them push me around." Bergman, forty-eight, said that if a Jew dies in a terrorist attack, he is in a state of martyrdom and is guaranteed the highest reaches of Heaven.

Isn't this more or less what the suicide bombers believe, about themselves?

There are ironies in this situation, Bergman conceded, that "sound obscene." But it doesn't matter, he said. Bergman believes what Rabbi Nachman taught: that God intends all things, good and bad, to happen for a reason—that there is pain in the world but no evil, because whatever occurs is part of an eternal plan leading to a state of utopia for all mankind. It's all predetermined: "If your number's up, your number's up," he said. But since it's all for good, in the end, there is no need for fear, and no reason to meet apparent misfortune with sadness or regret.

It was time to go. Bergman gently took the hand of his adult son, Nachman. Nachman Bergman wore a black suit, side locks that curled down from his temples, and the sweet, trusting eyes of the mentally retarded.

Hand in hand, father and son headed for the No. 2 bus.

What's the point of truth or beauty or knowledge when the anthrax bombs are popping all around you? . . . People were ready to have their appetites controlled then. Anything for a quiet life.

—World Controller Mustapha Mond, explaining
the origins of the dehumanized but anxiety-free
dystopia in Aldous Huxley's *Brave New World*

WHAT IS THE toll of terrorism, once terrorism has become not an occasional horror but a fact of everyday life? How do people adapt, and at what cost? Looking to the future, these are questions Americans might ask.

Everyone in Jerusalem deals with *hamatzav* in his or her own way, depending on one's personal threshold for danger, or one's personal calculus for safety. These are highly subjective matters.

Ilan Mizrahi is a freelance photographer who has covered the latest intifada since its inception. He negotiates the city on a minibike, fearlessly threading through traffic, and is often among the first on the scene when carnage occurs. In his travels, Mizrahi will pass a bus, if he must, but will not squeeze between two of them. With two buses, he feels, the odds of an explosion are doubled, elevated to the point that he is uncomfortable. That's his threshold.

In the late 1990s, Mizrahi said, his mother would frantically phone him as soon as word got out that there had been a suicide bombing. She wanted reassurance that he was safe. But within a few years, after bombings had become commonplace, she no longer called. One day, he arrived at the scene of a blast at a coffee shop and realized that it was right below the bridal shop in which his mother worked. He went up there to get an overhead shot from her window. Oh, hi, she said. She said she'd gone downstairs, checked out the three bodies, made sure it was no one she knew, and then gone back to work.

Israel has assimilated terror and institutionalized it. A bombing scene is cleaned up in hours, and one day later, there is often no sign it ever happened. Aleph Aleph Glass, once a small glazier company, is now a huge glazier company. It got the government contract for repairing windshields and is good at working quickly. For the first few days after a terror attack, when people are afraid of public places, many restaurants will start offering takeout menus. Then things return to normal.

I found myself remembering Terry Gilliam's macabre 1985 movie, *Brazil*, about a dysfunctional society that has given itself over to fear. Government officials are forever assuring that the war on terrorism is going well. At one point, the characters are seated in a fancy restaurant and a terrorist bomb explodes. Obsequious waiters instantly swarm the scene, putting up room dividers, dragging away corpses and apologizing profusely to diners for the disturbance.

Mizrahi and I were seated in Moment, a café just a few blocks from the residence of Prime Minister Ariel Sharon. Two years before, on a Saturday night in March, this popular dining spot became a charnel house when a suicide bomber walked in— right over there—and blew himself up in the middle of a packed young crowd. Eleven people died. Their names are inscribed on a stone tablet outside. Memorial tablets like that are all over Jerusalem, sometimes more than one on the same street corner.

"Our bill here will be one shekel higher," Mizrahi said, taking a forkful of salad, "because you're paying for that guy outside, sitting in the sun, waiting to explode to save your behind." He's talking about the security guard outside the door, a taciturn African Jew who has been a fixture at Moment since it was rebuilt. He'd frisked us as we entered. Not infrequently, when an attack is averted, it is done so by these security guards—ubiquitous in Jerusalem—who spot an attacker and bearhug him to the ground. Sometimes, if the guard can't immobilize the attacker's trigger hand in time, or if the bomb is rigged with a preset timing device, the two of them blow up together. Security guards are paid well.

Mizrahi carries with him, in a little leather pouch, a thick metal machine nut he picked up from the street outside, part of the body-piercing shrapnel the bomber wore. The nut was deformed, the hole in the center now a squashed crescent. "Can you imagine," he asked, "the strength of the explosion that could cause that?"

Mizrahi is a regular patron at Moment; he was planning to be there at exactly the time of the bombing, but he had stayed at home for a while to watch a TV news report of another suicide attack. In Jerusalem, such almost-but stories are legion. There is a famous picture of the bartender at Moment a few seconds after the blast. He had ducked down behind the bar to get a glass, and in that instant the bomber detonated not 15 feet away. The bar shielded the bartender. In the photo, he has just stood up, and is staring in disbelief at the bloodbath around him.

We climbed on the minibike, and Mizrahi wove through the streets of Jerusalem, shouting over the engine: "See that, that's bus number thirteen, the lucky one. It's never been hit. There's Netanyahu's house. Hey, we have a joke—When a suicide bomber gets to Heaven, he finds out it's not seventy-two virgins, it's a seventy-two-year-old virgin."

Mizrahi is Jewish but of Kurdish and Spanish descent; with his copper skin he has the look of an Arab, and with his camera case he has the look of an Arab Carrying Something. He is stopped by security guards all the time and submits good-naturedly. Actually, few people in Jerusalem resent these searches.

We parked and walked toward Zion Square on Jaffa Road, a commercial strip similar to one you'd find in any large city. Mizrahi was talking, and I was taking notes. His memory is encyclopedic.

"See the stone lion on that building, four stories up? Body parts hung there from the second bombing of the eighteen bus in '96. Down the street, see the Sbarro sign? Fifteen dead, August 2001. It's closed now. They moved it, but no one goes there anymore. That falafel place to the left? It exploded the same day as that pub over there. See the flower shop?"

"Where?"

"There. One person died, 2002. Right here, there was a suicide gunman, firing on people. A friend of mine, a civilian with a long ponytail, pulled out a gun and wounded the guy. January 2002. The guy ran, but the police finished him off. See that man, with the yarmulke? He's got a gun in his pants pocket, see the lump there?

"A refrigerator was abandoned over there, across the street, and it exploded. Thirteen people died. That was a famous one, a long time ago, I was a kid. Right over here, three years ago, a guy parked his car, walked right over there into a crowd, and exploded. He left another bomb in the car, with a timer, so when people came to help the people injured from the first bomb, they were killed. Eleven died."

"A woman walked into that clothing store and blew up. See there . . ."

I asked him to slow down. I was having trouble getting it all down.

"Way down over there, at the vegetable market, sixteen dead in 1997. Two bombers. That guy selling earrings from the stand in the street? His son died in a shooting attack."

Up to this point, we hadn't moved an inch. Mizrahi was just pivoting and pointing. Now we started walking. We passed a bearded man wearing jeans, a tie-dyed T-shirt and a submachine gun. "See that bank machine?" Mizrahi continued. "Five girls were shot there, waiting in line. One was the daughter of my family doctor. She was just trying to get twenty shekels. People don't wait in lines much anymore. You'll see them scattered around, keeping a distance from each other, less of a target."

Mizrahi stopped, smiled wryly, and nodded toward a street kiosk with a tattered advertising poster. It was for the national lottery. It said HAPA'AM YEHIYEH LECHAH MAZAL. What does that mean? I asked.

"This time, you'll be lucky."

Mizrahi is an adrenaline junkie. He loves Jerusalem, wouldn't live anywhere else, least of all Washington, which he considers too boring for words. He moves effortlessly through his city with his camera, chronicling the madness, absorbing it all with an attitude between stoicism and bemusement. He is an Israeli patriot, but no moralist. He says if he were a Palestinian, living out there in the occupied territories, in a life without hope, he might well become a suicide bomber, too.

Mizrahi has photographed more than twenty bus bombings in the past eight years. His portfolio is, in a word, heartbreaking. He knows that the vast majority of buses don't blow up, but he won't ride one, and he recently got angry with his wife when she did. "I can't help it," he said. "I see a bus, I see death."

"We have to ride a bus now," I said.

"Okay," he said. Work is work.

IT HAD BEEN two months since the last suicide bombing, an eternity in Jerusalem time. In the meantime, Israel had carried out brazen assassinations of Hamas leaders Abdel Aziz Rantisi and Sheik Ahmed Yassin, the latter an elderly paraplegic in a wheelchair who was considered the father of the strategy of suicide bombing. No Palestinian reprisals yet. So this was not the best moment, perhaps, to be riding a bus.

Mizrahi photographed both bombings of the No. 18, which came a week apart, in 1996. While standing on the roof of a building shooting down on the carnage of the second explosion, he had to step over body parts. On the balcony below him, he saw the bomber's head.

Before you get on a bus on Jaffa Road in Jerusalem, you get the once-over from security guards who are posted at every bus shelter. These are tense young men in tan vests, with sunglasses and wires snaking down from ear microphones.

They fidgeted over Mizrahi, eyed me cursorily, and let us aboard. The bus was packed. Jerusalem is a big city with no subway, expensive taxis, $3-a-gallon gas, and bad traffic. Most everyone rides buses.

"I don't ride buses," said Assaf Gershoni.

Assaf Gershoni was our bus driver. He meant when he is off duty. Work is work. A few minutes into the route, we passed a curious sculpture on the side of the road. It was a memorial, an enormous Star of David that appears to be made from scrap metal. It is. It is made from the twisted remains of the first No. 18 bus.

The people on the bus tend to be philosophical about their plight: What are you going to do? They will tell you their anxiety is reduced because of the guys in the tan vests outside, and because of the driver, whose judgment is, as far as they see it, the last line of defense.

This was interesting because at the bus stop, a tan vest had told us he'd never let his own relatives ride the buses. I asked Gershoni, the driver, if there's anything special he is trained to do if he thinks a bomber has just boarded his bus. Yes, he said. "When I see an Arab with a package, I say to myself, 'Please don't blow up, please don't blow up.'"

Anyway, this is not about what Israelis think as they ride a bus in Jerusalem. It is what an American thinks, on his first ride. An American watches every new person as he boards, prioritizing his concerns. Old woman, good. Old man, okay. Young, skinny

person in tight clothes, no problem. Fat person: Is his flesh jig-
gling, or might it be something more rigid than protoplasm under
that baggy shirt? Why is no one watching the back door? Someone could slip on, undetected, as a passenger gets off. No one
is watching! Good, a soldier got on. But maybe that isn't good,
maybe it makes us more of a target.

By minute 10, the American is pretty exhausted. But by minute 30, he's let down his guard a little. By minute 40, he has
reached a state where he actually notices the pretty woman in
shorts. Because, really, isn't that what life is about—noticing the
pretty woman in shorts? Isn't that what the human animal does?
Life, as they say, goes on.

IN A PSYCHOLOGICAL experiment in the 1980s, a group of municipal judges were asked to set bail for prisoners in mock criminal
cases. Half of the judges were first told to fill out a questionnaire
about their own mortality. Those judges wound up setting much
higher bails. Contemplating death toughened them. It reduced
their compassion.

Mizrahi had one more place to show me before we said
goodbye. French Hill is an upscale neighborhood in northeast
Jerusalem. Attacks here are frequent; one of the most notorious
occurred in March, when a drive-by shooting by Palestinians
killed a twenty-year-old jogger. The victim, apparently chosen at
random, turned out to be the son of Elias Khoury, an Arab lawyer
who had represented Yasser Arafat himself. Khoury had also lost
his father in 1974 to a terrorist bombing near Zion Square—the
abandoned refrigerator that blew up, back when Mizrahi was a
little boy. Nothing is ever over in Jerusalem.

French Hill is a lick of land, a part of Jordan taken by Israel in
the '67 War. It protrudes into the West Bank like a raised middle
finger. Mizrahi led me to a corner patrolled by Israeli soldiers in

camouflage gear, with assault weapons. I counted seven soldiers in the space of 60 feet. They were stopping everyone, even other soldiers, to demand ID. The center of the street was bisected by metal barriers. That is to slow up any suicide bombers trying to race toward the street corner from the Arab area. That delay will, with luck, buy enough time for the soldiers in the sniper's nest, up above us, to aim and fire.

This is not a war zone, exactly. It is a civilian bus stop.

The soldiers wore bulletproof vests. They were wary. The people waiting at the bus stop were wary. One Muslim woman, in a head scarf, was being detained by the soldiers because her papers were not in order. The woman was apoplectic, shouting that she was in Israel just to shop for new eyeglasses for her daughter. She commanded the embarrassed ten-year-old to show her scratched lenses to the soldiers, to the police, to the journalists, to random passersby. Over the soldiers' radio crackled a command, in Hebrew, to let the woman go. But the soldiers didn't. Twenty minutes had gone by, and it would be another twenty before they released her, so she'd learn from her mistake.

Never in my life had I felt so much ambient mistrust, fear, and hatred in one place at one time.

And suddenly, seemingly from out of nowhere, a shaggy black dog showed up. She was Benji-sized, a little projectile of panting exuberance. She scampered up to everyone in turn, wagging her tail like mad, going person to person, saying howdy, ignoring no one, bursting with enthusiasm and slaphappy joy. For me, it broke the tension, and I found myself grinning. Then the dog wheeled around, raced back the way she had come, and hopped into her cage on the back of a trailer on a military vehicle.

She'd been sniffing for bombs.

———

The dread of evil is a much more forcible principle
of human actions than the prospect of good . . . What
worries you masters you.

—John Locke

RICKI BERNSTEIN IS peeling sweet potatoes. Her husband, David,
is preparing the grill. Their extended family bounces in, one after
another, gathering as is their custom for Shabbat dinner.

This is a family that never should have been. I know because I was at Ricki and David's wedding, thirty-three years
ago in New York. She was eighteen, he was nineteen; out in the
audience, my girlfriend and I agreed it was a shame that these
two good kids were marrying so young—obviously, this union
was doomed. Sensibly, my girlfriend and I waited longer. We're
divorced now.

There is a Yiddish expression, *bashert,* which means that some
things are "meant to be." It would be hard to find a closer family, anywhere, than the Bernsteins of Jerusalem. David—"Bernie"
to his friends—is a history teacher and dean of a Jewish studies
institute. Ricki is a therapist who specializes in the treatment of
trauma—a thriving, if dispiriting, business in this city.

They have four children, whose names suggest the cultural, spiritual, and geographic journey that Ricki and Bernie
have made since he and I were raising hell together on the NYU
newspaper thirty-three years ago. Their oldest, at twenty-seven,
is Jessica. Daughter Ariel is twenty-four. Their older son, Shai,
is twenty-one. Tani, the youngest child, is seventeen. Only Shai
couldn't make it today; he is in the army. That would be the same
Shai who used to lose fights with his older sisters, growing up.
Now he's a member of a combat unit. All Israeli kids serve in the
military.

One day not long ago, Ricki got a text message on her cell
phone from Shai: "It just said, 'I'm okay, I love you,'" she re-

calls. "It took me twenty minutes before I realized what that was about. It came on the news that two soldiers had been killed in an attack in Gaza. He was preparing me, telling me not to worry."

There is a skill to living in Jerusalem, a skill in taming personal terror.

"It's like a head game, a bargain you make with yourself," says Ricki. "It's a kind of denial you have to practice if you believe in living here."

"In my apartment," Jessica says, "the living room faces one of the main roads to the hospital. So I count sirens . . ."

"With a siren," Ricki interjects, "we all say to ourselves, 'It's just a woman in labor, it's just a woman in labor . . .'"

"If you hear one," says Jessica, "you brace yourself, because you don't want to hear two or more. One siren, just one, delivers a sense of relief."

How you respond depends often on what you have seen. Ariel rides city buses, as many as four a day, except in the few harrowing days after a terror attack, when, at her parents' insistence and with their money, she grudgingly takes taxis. Jessica won't ride city buses at all. In 1996, she was in a bus directly behind one of the No. 18s that blew up on Jaffa Road. She remembers it as a dull thud—"it's not like an explosion in the movies."

"I hear about it from the dreams," Ricki says. She is talking about her clients who have been through a bombing, and the memories that plague their sleep. "There's a silence after a bomb, a deathly stillness. The birds have flown away, the air is sucked out of everything. Everyone is frozen. They can't speak."

"Then," she says, "it starts."

"It" is what happens afterward. Each person tends to carry away a specific image, a memory that haunts him. With Jessica, it is the cinders that floated down like sinister black rain. Levi Levine, Ariel's husband, was at the scene moments after Sbarro was bombed, in 2001, trying to help the victims. Many were beyond help.

"My mother takes care of babies," Levi says. "One day, afterward, I was with her, and one of the babies was asleep, and I had to ask her to move the baby's hand, because the baby's palm was in the same position as a baby's palm I saw in Sbarro."

Shai was among the first at the scene at a Friday morning bombing of a supermarket in which three people died, including the teenage female bomber and a security guard who was trying to stop her. That afternoon, at home, Shai became nauseated when Ricki was cooking chicken.

"Olfactory triggers," Ricki says, "are very common."

It's all visceral. Some of it stays visceral and needs help escaping. Disguising details to protect the privacy of the person involved, Ricki tells a story about a client of hers: The patient was a young man experiencing emotional problems, for no apparent reason. Ricki first interviewed the patient's mother and asked for a routine mental health history. Were there any particular traumas in the boy's life? The mother ticked off the usual list: hospitalizations, divorces in the family, death of pets, that sort of thing. Nope, nothing special.

Meanwhile, the patient was delayed in arriving. The mother apologized, saying that he couldn't take the bus. "I almost didn't ask why," Ricki says. It turned out he wouldn't ride a bus because he had been personally affected not by one bus bombing but by four—hearing one happen, losing a relative in another, and so forth.

"You raise your kids to think people are good, because the alternative is too terrible to bear," Ricki says. "You don't want to live in a world like that, where there is evil lurking behind every smile. You don't want to believe in that. And then your children find out on their own."

One ordinary Israeli family. Seven people. Levi, Jessica, and

Shai have each been at the scene of a bombing. Ricki counsels victims. And Bernie? "Two students of mine were killed at the bombing of the cafeteria at the Hebrew University in 2002. A third one was sitting between them, and bent down to get something from a knapsack, and because of that, though she was wounded, she lived." Only Tani, the quiet, handsome boy with the soft eyes, seems not to have a story to tell.

I ask Bernie and Ricki: Why do you still live in this place?

"There has to be a Jewish homeland," Ricki says. "This is not a guaranteed thing. Someone has to do it, and we didn't want to be people who just send money to plant trees."

And so they live, partly in defiance, but mostly, they do what they must to keep their own tree flowering. Bernie, one of the gentlest men I've ever known, owns a pistol. He carries it when he is traveling with his students somewhere. The Israeli Ministry of Education requires armed escorts on class trips.

In the intractability of the current situation, the history teacher hears echoes of the past. "The history of war," Bernie says, "shows us that there is always a demonization of the enemy. You don't know what to believe. In World War I, we were told that the Kaiser was murdering children. That was not true. In World War II, when the Allies said the Germans were killing civilians, it also sounded like propaganda. Now the Palestinians are being told outrageous things. They are being told by their leaders that the Jews are poisoning their wells. They don't know what to believe. They are deprived of a decent life, and they are whipped into a frenzy. I don't think most Palestinians are evil."

It is at this point that Tani speaks out. It turns out he does have a story to tell, after all. "When I was in eighth grade, I had a friend who lived in a settlement. He and another friend skipped school and took a hike down the valley near their home. A Palestinian shepherd killed them with bricks and stones, and dipped his hands in their blood, and wrote things in blood on the wall of a cave. They were beaten so badly they couldn't be identified by dental records. They needed DNA."

An ordinary Israeli family, preparing for Sabbath dinner.

MY TRIP HOME was uneventful. As it happens, there was nothing at all to worry about with the fated, fearful Flight 223. Security was surprisingly light, and we were checked aboard by a Sikh in a turban and a Muslim woman with a head scarf.

There are no more bad rumors about Flight 223, no more delays or cancellations. There used to be a problem, but British Airways has taken care of it. Flight 223 no longer exists. The same plane still flies along the same route at the same time, but it is now called Flight 293.

International air corridors are not Jerusalem. Things are simple, still.

On the way to my house, I asked the cabdriver, as I always do, if anything interesting had happened while I was gone.

Plenty, he said. The government had issued an alert to be on the lookout for seven people suspected of belonging to al Qaeda, possibly planning something bad, though it wasn't clear what, or when, or if they were in this country at all. The government was urging people to go on with their holiday plans, though. The driver said he felt things were getting pretty scary, here.

Then he asked me why I was laughing.

NO ONE KNOWS what terrorism, fueled by new technologies, will unleash on our country in the coming months, or years. In our climate of strategically restrained anxiety, it is considered almost a crime to make predictions. When, shortly after 9/11, the brilliant physicist Stephen Hawking dared to speculate once again that advances in genetic manipulation of biological toxins will make it almost inevitable that mankind will extinguish itself on this planet in the not too distant future, scientific colleagues rose one by one to distance themselves from these terrible, irresponsible thoughts. You probably don't even remember this episode. Good, good.

Will America of the next decade resemble more closely the Jerusalem of today than it will the America of today? Maybe. How scary is that? Plenty. But I'm a little less scared of it than I was before I met my old friend Bernie and his family, surviving with love and dignity and a sense of purpose.

In Israel, I think, the constant grind of terrorism has not only penetrated people's sense of denial, it has sanded it almost completely away. But what it has exposed is not the blind, paralyzing fear that Ernest Becker envisioned in *The Denial of Death*. It is something else altogether.

The Israelis live defiantly, indomitably, with a heightened intensity, as though each day might be their last. After a bomb killed two dozen young people at a Tel Aviv disco a few years ago, Israeli youth refused to be cowed. They resumed a robust nightlife. Today, outside the scene of the bombing, beneath a stone memorial listing the names of the dead, is a single inscription: LO NAFSEEK LIRKOD. It means "We won't stop dancing."

I think Becker got it only partly right. Yes, death is a certainty, and we get by through denial. But would immortality, in a world such as ours, really be better? Becker, in his own bleak way, was too insistent on defining the human as just another animal dumbly fulfilling his Darwinian destiny. With the right frame of mind, denial can be a magnificent ignorance; the possibilities within it are limitless. In the end, those possibilities—not self-delusion—are what make us human and keep us sane.

Just before I left on this trip, my friend Laura gave me a $5 bill. Laura is a journalist, an expert in affairs of the Middle East, and the daughter of a rabbi. The bill, she told me, was "mitzvah money." When someone is heading off on a possibly dangerous journey, it is a Jewish custom to give him money to give to a beggar at his destination. That turns the journey into a good deed. With luck, God will protect you.

The bill is still in my wallet; I'd completely forgotten about it. At first, I felt ashamed. But sometimes, when you focus too intently on your own situation, you miss the big picture. I'm going outside, right now, to give the five bucks to the first homeless person I see. It's all the same world, you know.

Yankee Doodle Danny

Affection is hard to express in writing without seeming like a sap. A good way to do it is through indirection; write of facts, not feelings. But choose the right facts.

July 1, 2001

MY SON WAS named on an airplane over the Gulf of Mexico during the summer of 1978. This was six years before he was born, but his mother and I were already planning a future together, inasmuch as we had just survived simultaneous dysentery in a small Mexican hotel room and still tolerated each other's company, which had to mean something. All that remained were the petty details of getting married and choosing a city to live in and careers to pursue.

These things were still up for grabs in the summer of 1978, but what we knew for sure was that our son would be Danny, and that he would be a Yankees fan. First things first.

So here we were on a Tuesday night six years later, in a hospital delivery room in Miami. Danny was on the way, but I was not happy. I can explain, but not justify, what happened next.

These were the 1980s, the heyday of "natural childbirth," a medical philosophy that rejected the distasteful use of analgesics in favor of a woman's right to writhe in agony for hours on end. It was during this process that I asked my wife, politely, if she could "hold off just a little bit longer."

Silence.

A couple of hours would do the trick, I said.

Silence.

It was important, I said. To me.

My wife shot me a glance that was pregnant with meaning. If I translated the precise meaning here, it would cost me my job.

Danny had announced his impending arrival earlier that evening as my wife was driving home from work. I telephoned my in-laws to ask them to take care of our three-year-old daughter for the night. They weren't home but had left the number of the restaurant at which they'd be.

My father-in-law envied my college education, which I took for granted. I envied his combat experience, which he took for granted. John Reidy had served valiantly as a seaman in the Pacific during World War II, but his only medal was a serpentine scar from an appendectomy performed hastily in the darkness belowdecks during a kamikaze attack. To me, this far outclassed my A-minus in behavioral psych.

I'd missed my war, the one in Southeast Asia. Had I been called to serve, I would have declined at whatever penalty, and I would have told myself it was an act of conscience, not cowardice. In those years, ambiguity clouded many things, particularly the definition of patriotism.

At the end of his war, John turned in his Navy whites for drab green pants and a work shirt, the uniform of a municipal employee. Now he was retired.

I phoned the restaurant and, on impulse, had him paged as "Admiral Reidy." For years afterward, he laughed about how the retired Bridgeport, Connecticut, electrician had strode importantly to the phone past the curious and admiring stares of all those retired West Palm Beach lawyers and doctors.

In the delivery room, the writhing was proceeding pretty much according to schedule when a nurse started looking real hard at a monitor beside the bed. The line that recorded the baby's heartbeat was flattening out. Fetal distress. She suggested a change in position. If this didn't correct itself immediately, she explained, they'd have to do a Caesarean.

My eyes moved from the monitor to the clock. Still too soon! I moved my wife onto her side and prayed for luck.

John believed in luck. He always played the lottery, just a few bucks a week, and kept elaborate charts of winning numbers, convinced there had to be a pattern. Painstakingly, I exploded the illogic of this, using probability and number theory. John listened patiently, and kept drawing his charts. I had facts, he had faith. We disagreed on religion, too.

We disagreed on newspapers. John loved them but felt they were at their least patriotic when they were finding fault with the American government. That, I argued, was when they were at their most patriotic.

John always drank Busch beer and drove American cars, because they were American. I always drank Heineken and drove Japanese cars, because they were better. We had some debates about this, too. In my mind, John always won. He had the scar.

My wife would have no scar. The baby's heartbeat strengthened, the Caesarean was averted, and after dawdling for another hour or two—just long enough—my son finally made his appearance a little after midnight.

As he nursed as an infant, Danny liked to grab a fistful of my wife's hair. It comforted him. John had no hair to offer, so to bottle-feed his grandson in the style to which he was accustomed, he bought a floor mop and wore it on his head.

Gotta love the guy. I did.

John died suddenly of a stroke a few years ago, with none of our little disagreements resolved.

Danny is Dan now. He doesn't give a damn about the Yankees, but has otherwise grown up splendidly. He turns seventeen on Wednesday, the Fourth.

It's a good birthday. The best, in fact. On that, John and I actually agreed.

Pardon My French . . .

People sometimes ask me if I am comfortable doing the sorts of things journalists occasionally must do: embarrass people, invade their privacy, write things that will provoke, disturb, or injure. I answer honestly that I am not comfortable with it at all, but that the Machine is.

The Machine is what I become when working on a story. It is rational, but soulless. It thinks but does not feel. It observes basic rules of fairness but is impervious to emotion; it is a stranger to guilt; it cannot be humiliated. The Machine operates always under a single rule: Within the limits of human decency, it always does what is necessary to get the best possible story.

This story was assigned at a time when the French government was—zut alors!—daring to insinuate that the U.S. invasion of Iraq was unjustified. The mood in America was hostile. Diplomatically, both countries were walking on eggshells. My job was to head over there in hobnail boots.

To carry this off, I had to behave like a complete jackass. And, yes, I had a problem with that. Fortunately, the Machine did not.

September 7, 2003

T HE FRENCH MINISTER of agriculture politely awaited my
question. We were seated in the study of his ministry in
the heart of Paris, overlooking a garden with ancient statuary. At forty-three, Hervé Gaymard is already a member of the
national cabinet, custodian of nothing less formidable than the
French wine industry. Sandy-haired, lithe, urbanely handsome
like Paul Henreid in *Casablanca*, the minister was in shirtsleeves,
slacks, and—as became apparent when he crossed his legs—
loafers sans socks. He looked effortlessly fabulous, of course. He
is French.

This interview almost didn't happen. I had requested an audience with the highest French official available, on the subject
of the strained relations between our two nations over the war in
Iraq. The French Embassy initially seemed reluctant, at which
point I observed that it would be a pity if, to secure an official audience with a French dignitary, I had to seek out Jean-Marie Le
Pen. That would be the race-baiting cryptofascist whose stunning
showing in the last presidential elections threatened to create an
international embarrassment for the French of a magnitude unseen since a swastika flapped beneath the Arc de Triomphe.

Soon afterward, Monsieur Gaymard was made available.

This was a delicate situation. If I was not representing all of
America, I was surely representing the American media, blamed
by many for taking an awkward situation and, in search of spicy
headlines, gleefully making it worse.

I began by assuring M. Gaymard that confrontation and
controversy were the last things on my mind; that my role was
conciliatory; that my questions were designed to elicit an open
and frank exchange of views, so vital to the healing process. The
minister inclined his head graciously, and I began.

"I think we can both agree that the diplomatic situation between our two nations is both regrettable and unnecessary . . . Perhaps the worst part is that it has resurrected in the United States some ugly, unfair, inaccurate, and totally unsupportable stereotypes about the French. You know: that you are elitist, that you are rude, that you are cowards, that you have an insufferable air of superiority, that your fashion shows are nothing more than elaborate parades of clown costumes . . ."

The minister waited for translation.

". . . that your movies are long and boring and unbearably pretentious, that you lack personal hygiene and let your dogs poop all over the streets, and indeed, that your national pet, the poodle, is a ridiculous life form better never to have survived the evolutionary process."

The minister shifted slightly in his chair.

"I will not insult you, or dignify these preposterous, obviously untrue stereotypes by asking you to respond to them. But I was just wondering if the French have any equally preposterous and obviously untrue stereotypes about Americans that you might enumerate here for the purpose of my not dignifying them with a response."

As I awaited his answer, it occurred to me that, yes, diplomacy is a difficult and subtle art. But one must try to do one's part.

IN FRANCE, THE president of the United States is widely perceived to be a squinty-eyed bully, a cowboy given to shooting first and asking questions later. Worse, he is seen by the sophisticated French as something of a yokel—uncultured, unschooled, inarticulate, anti-intellectual, dangerously shallow—elected and supported by a populace too fearful of terrorist attacks, an electorate that values too much the blunt, common touch and too little the more complex virtues of the Renaissance man. For his part, the prez isn't so crazy about the French, either. Small wonder, then, that a relatively minor dispute would lead to intemperate words and a serious crisis in diplomacy.

We are talking, of course, about . . . 1834. The man in the White House was Andrew Jackson, hero of the Indian campaigns, our first cowboy president. Sorry, you have been hoodwinked by the oldest journalistic trick in the book, the ironic time-frame switcheroo. You stupid, gullible, non-European, linear-thinking, literal-minded American.

Yes, that is a stereotype. But this is all about stereotypes, and journalism, and the rhythms of history.

It is often said that the French republic is our oldest continuous ally, and this is inarguable. The American Revolution might never have succeeded without the support of the French; it is immaterial that their real goal was sticking it to their superpower rival, England. It is likewise immaterial if that initial alliance was a hypocritical marriage of convenience between our fledgling democracy and a country that was at the time a despotic state more suffocating than the one against which we'd just rebelled. The fact is, the French were there for us when we needed them the most.

And yet, conventional wisdom aside, relations between the United States and the French republic have never gone smoothly. The *Washington Post* library is full of yellowed newspaper clippings, beginning in 1898 and resurfacing every fifteen years or so, breathlessly reporting the latest rupture or repair in Franco-American relations. Franco-American relations freeze and thaw and warm right back up like a plate of SpaghettiOs.

We are now facing a time of chill, with repercussions both silly ("freedom fries") and substantial (tourism and commerce in both directions have taken a hit). There is a great deal of hand-wringing about it on both sides of the Atlantic. No one seems quite certain how to deal with it—least of all the French, who thought it a swell idea to enlist Woody Allen to tell us, as a specialist in ethics, how we are being unfair to France.

As usual, it falls to a journalist to make things right. This has happened before. Back in 1834, during the Jackson administration, the French-American rift was trivial, really—largely a matter of bookkeeping: We sought reparations for damage done to American shipping during the Napoleonic Wars, and France was stiffing us. The whole matter was easily resolvable, but President Jackson was given to gruff, obliquely threatening pronouncements—"bring 'em on" kind of stuff—and before you knew it, France had recalled its Washington ambassador and invited ours to leave Paris. There was muffled talk of war.

At that precise moment, a young French writer named Alexis de Tocqueville published a book about the national character of America, gleaned from a nine-month visit here. *Democracy in America* proved an instant balm to global tensions, not because it was entirely complimentary—it wasn't—but because it was entirely honest. It confronted openly the differences between Americans and the French, and found much for the French to like and admire. War reparations were paid and cultural exchanges began again between the two countries, with young Tocqueville himself in the middle of it—an ambassador without portfolio.

Tocqueville had nine months, but he probably dillydallied. You know the French. I figured six days should do it.

In preparation for my trip, I tried to cleanse myself of the many prejudices we Americans hold against the French. Unfortunately, the French kept doing stereotypically French things. When Marseille found itself in the middle of a trash collectors' strike, with tons of garbage rotting in the streets, the French government leapt into action. It sprayed the garbage with perfume.

This was also the time of the great Parisian fashion shows. The main *New York Times* photo featured a male model striding purposefully down the runway in a Louis Vuitton ensemble consisting, in its entirety, of a nice sports jacket, a striped shirt, a bow tie, dress shoes, white socks, and what appeared to be underpants.

To purge myself of negativity, I decided to consult experts who liked and admired the French—the authors of two excellent cultural guidebooks: *French or Foe?* by Polly Platt, and *Sixty Million Frenchmen Can't Be Wrong* by Jean-Benoit Nadeau and Julie Barlow. From them, I concluded that France is a splendid place, though visiting it can be like visiting a beloved but eccentric maiden aunt of sensibilities as fragile as Limoges: One must be careful at all times not to offend, and to adhere to her rules of decorum, however peculiar. And so I learned that one must never ask personal questions, for although the French will opine volubly on any and all subjects of public discourse, they will bridle if asked their name or occupation or anything at all about their personal lives. I learned that, in greeting, one must not say merely, "Bonjour," but "Bonjour, madame" or "Bonjour, monsieur," lest one appear impolite. I learned that before addressing strangers, one must apologize profusely for intruding on their time, using a French sentence that must be memorized precisely and may not vary by even a syllable. I learned that the French have no precise word for "friendly." The authors warned that the locals can be somewhat prideful and protective about their culture, wary of accepting strangers into their fraternity.

How wary, I asked Jean-Benoit Nadeau.

Oh, very, he said.

Well, I speculated, let's say I went to France, and decided I loved it so much I could not bear to return to the comparatively odious United States. So I quit my job, bought a château in Lyon, adopted a French child, and spent the remainder of my life writing influential articles in prestigious international publications about the splendors of France and its superiority to any other place on Earth. By the time I was eighty and toothless, might the French be willing to accept me as one of them?

Silence. Finally: "They would have reservations."

The most surprising thing I learned, from Polly Platt, was that when visiting France, one must not smile at strangers. The French do not condone the casual smile, she reported. They think it a sign of untoward familiarity.

I brought this matter up at lunch with Nathalie Loiseau, the capable press officer at the French Embassy in Washington. Loiseau is in the business of bringing people together; she is inclined to regard the current French-American rift in optimistic terms, convinced our two peoples have far more in common than what divides them. But what about the smiling thing? Can this be true?

Not really, she said. The French like to smile.

Whew.

Then the French diplomat paused, diplomatically.

What? What?

"They just don't like the American smile," she said. "It is too commercial and . . ." She searched for the word.

"Insincere?" I suggested.

Yes, she said. Precisely.

It was shortly afterward that I stepped off the plane in Paris, scowling balefully, hoping for acceptance.

DAY ONE

"BONJOUR, MONSIEUR," I say, careful to remember the "monsieur." The news dealer looks up from his kiosk. *"Excusez-moi de vous déranger,"* I say, careful to remember the precise words and syntax of the sentence necessary to assure the French person to whom you are speaking that you are a miserable insect requesting the honor of a moment of his time. Unfortunately, my next words, in English, are, "Do you speak English?" and that gets a shake and a shrug. So I have to wait until I am joined by my photographer and translator, Jérôme De Perlinghi.

The news dealer, Guinot Fabrice, is literally surrounded by anti-American, I-Told-You-So sentiment: headlines reporting the latest squirmy bit of buck-passing by a U.S. government facing the growing likelihood that there are no Iraqi weapons of mass destruction, never were, and that the stated purpose of the war may well have been a cynical pretext. I chose this place for my first interview on the theory that if one is to defuse a prejudice, one must first confront it. So I ask Fabrice what he thinks about Americans.

"They are nicer than the French."

C'est what?

Certainement, he says. But, I protest, Americans malign the French mercilessly. We say the most impolite things, such as that the French are rude.

Fabrice shrugs. "That is probably because the French are rude. We complain about everything. We will get the best room in a hotel, and still complain about this and that." Americans, he says, are fine. "It is the French who can be . . ."

. . . And then he uses a French word that, were it an English word, would rhyme with "glass bowls."

Jérôme and I decide that Fabrice must not be typical enough. So we walk to the Frenchiest place in all of Paris, Les Deux Magots, a famous Left Bank café that caters to an idle class of clientele the French call boulevardiers. (There is no easy English equivalent for the term, though, in a neat accident of transliteration, the name of the café offers a clue.) It is at Les Deux Magots that we spot our perfect Frenchman. He is a man of middle age and impossibly erect bearing, bald as a thumb, seated alone outside, dressed in midmorning in a jacket and tie, smoking a cigar, reading *Le Monde*, his mustache waxed just so.

Here is where we could begin to explore the nature of stereotype. This man would dislike America, would be positively eager to explain why, but above all would be fiercely protective of his privacy, reluctant to disclose any personal facts. We approach gingerly and ask his opinions of Americans. He answers instantly in English.

"I spend sree years in ze United States, and I cannot find ze woman to put in ze bed! In France I am married four times and have twelve women in ze bed!"

Vincent de Kerempenec, fifty-seven, describes himself as "an aristocrat from an old family, with a pack of hounds for the hunt and a small castle in the Dordogne." He doesn't seem to have much problem with privacy. He also doesn't seem to have much problem with Americans, except for his lamentable difficulty in the boudoir, which he ascribes to the fact that American women suspect a man of his appearance and bearing to be gay. This, he says, is a monstrous injustice, but what can one do? American men cannot bed French women, either, he says with dignity.

And so it goes throughout the day. The French people are open, not suspicious. They are self-deprecating, not arrogant. They are almost gallant in their treatment of a stranger. They are defying stereotype.

They are being contrarian. How damnably French of them.

When I am inwardly troubled, I often consult the dead. And so, toward day's end I find myself shuffling alone through historic Montparnasse Cemetery, contemplating the puzzlement that is France. How can I explain this in Tocquevillian terms? The whole country seems paradoxical. The French do not spend money on air-conditioning—in mid-July, Paris is a sweatbox, indoors and out—yet their underground parking garages pipe in classical music. They are famously resistant to American cultural influences, yet *Charlie's Angels* is their current big movie, and in the subways Hulk Hogan sells Internet service. The French are famously artistic and creative, yet, by indisputable evidence on the radio, they still haven't figured out how to write a competent rock song.

It is, perhaps, a historical thing. The French have always considered themselves the most sophisticated people on Earth, and yet at the fin de siècle a century ago, the most popular performer in France was a man billed as Le Pétomane, whose entire act consisted of farting.

At this moment, I see before me three elderly women on a cemetery bench, chatting intently. Those eccentric old aunts I am seeking, perhaps, with Limoges sensibilities. Here is a chance to be treated with classic Gallic disdain, particularly because I am without Jérôme and, exactly as I suspect, they speak no English. Pressing one's English upon a Frenchman is supposed to be like pressing one's tongue upon a wall socket. But the ladies just listen politely as I ask them about their feelings toward Americans. They chatter to one another in French, hands flying. Clearly, the American wants something, but what?

Finally, one of them stands up and crooks a finger. Follow me.

I start to protest, but she takes my hand. We walk perhaps 100 feet, and finally she points triumphantly at the ground. It is the grave of Jean-Paul Sartre.

I stand there contemplating the tombstone of France's most famous existentialist, and then contemplating the woman contemplating me contemplating the tombstone of France's most famous existentialist. She is smiling and nodding.

What is the meaning of this?

Can it be that . . . it has no meaning?

Sartre's grave offers nothingness. Dates of birth and death only. But on the footstone are little scraps of paper that mourners have left, weighted with pebbles. They are in French, but some I can decipher. One says simply, "You make us proud. Thank you."

And suddenly I understand.

"You make us proud"—that simple phrase tells me what I need to know. I have been asking the wrong question. Or rather, I have been asking the right question the wrong way. I now know what I have to do. It won't be nice, but it is necessary.

DAY TWO

JÉRÔME AND I are at Le Bec Rouge, an excellent Alsatian restaurant in south-central Paris. It is still morning, and the place is not yet open for business. The dapper owner and head chef, Jean-Luc Maurice, graciously comes out from the kitchen to meet us. Maurice is dressed in crisp chef's whites and carries himself with an air of self-confidence authorized by years of training under the tutelage of the great chef Paul Bocuse.

Yes, yes, Maurice likes Americans. They are like all people, he says—there are good, there are bad . . .

Right, right, right.

"I was just wondering," I ask slowly, "why portions in French restaurants are so small."

Maurice gives a wary answer, something about quality being paramount.

"Well, we like big portions back in the States," I say, patting my tummy. "I was wondering if you agree that American chefs are better than French chefs because they give you more food."

Maurice listens to the translation. There is a moment of silence. And then he begins to speak very rapidly.

"He says French chefs make love to their food . . ." Jérôme translates.

And American chefs? I ask.

Now Maurice is really elocutionizing. His hands are flying. He appears to be pointing to . . . his derriere. I don't really have to wait for the translation, but when it arrives, it does not disappoint.

American chefs, he says, make love to the food, too. But in a most unnatural and deviant way.

Voilà.

Here is what I had failed to understand. The French are quite willing to admit that they are quintessentially French, for good or bad. They will cop to being terribly Gallicly rude, or too Gallicly refined and continental to land ze American chick, and they will confess to a prejudice for logic over spirituality—"We French are Cartesians, after all," explained Anne-Marie Leveque, a woman I had met in the cemetery and with whom I was discussing God.

Sartre makes them proud. Descartes makes them proud. This is the key. If one is in France and one wishes to roil within the French the deepest, muddiest waters of prejudice and stereotype, one must be prepared to belittle their Frenchness.

In short, you have to be prepared to show a little . . . gall.

I am on a bridge overlooking the Seine. Below me is one of the odder sights available to an American in Paris—a pipsqueak Statue of Liberty. It is identical to the one that illuminates New York Harbor, but 50 feet tall, tops. It's a prototype model produced by sculptor Frédéric-Auguste Bartholdi before he tackled the big one. The very subordinate scale of this statue is what gives it power—modestly yielding grandeur to the one France gave to a nation it considered an undying friend. It's hard to look upon this restrained work and not feel some depth of emotion.

Hard, but not impossible.

"How come yours is so small?"

Sophie Martins is twenty-four, an auditor for a French company. She is taking in the exquisite summer day, comely in a sleeveless black top and white slacks.

Small?

"Yeah, in the States we have a much bigger one. Are you embarrassed this one is so puny, compared to ours?"

Martins remains pleasant. "We do not need a large statue,

because we have the Eiffel Tower," she says—pointing proudly down the Seine to the magnificent filigreed monolith.

"Actually, in the States, we have office buildings bigger than that," I say. She blinks.

"Also, why is it just brown? Don't you think you guys should paint it?"

"Yes, it is true, everything is bigger in the United States," Martins says dryly. "When you go to the supermarket, all the food is sold in very large quantities." American women, she says, are always buying large volumes of food.

French women do not?

She fixes me with a steely stare. "French women like to be slim."

Aboard the Métro, heading back to my hotel. The news today is good for the French—a Frenchman has briefly taken the lead over American Lance Armstrong in the revered Tour de France. I observe to the man next to me that the Tour de France is swell and everything, but it could be better. Alain Bequer is a mechanic and, as it happens, a bicycle enthusiast. His English is passable, and he seems most affable. How, he asks, could the Tour be better?

"Motorcycles."

Motorcycles?

"Sure. That would get more Americans to come watch it. You could use our business, if you know what I mean. In the States, we like things fast and loud."

"Yes, you do," Bequer says. "Guns, zey are fast and loud. And Americans like to shoot people and kill people wees guns, no?"

DAY THREE

DESPITE OUR PROGRESS, Jérôme and I are once again doubting the quality of our science. Are we losing our Tocquevillian objectivity? We have found the classic French rudeness, but only by coercion and sabotage. Plus, by limiting ourselves to Parisians, are we not also creating a geographical bias? One would come away with a decidedly skewed view of Americans if one confined one's inquiries to, say, New York City, or Provo, Utah. Tocqueville traveled far and wide. So we decide to go on a road trip, to the place most likely to embrace us.

Opera house executive Laurent Bondi lives in the small dairy village of Argueil in the heart of Normandy. It is there we meet Daniel Foucret, Bondi's next-door neighbor. The retired restorer of fine art is seventy-five, a character, plopping down at Bondi's picnic table and demanding a whiskey—at noon.

Foucret was a sixteen-year-old in Paris on August 25, 1944. That was the day the American army marched in, the final day of a four-year German occupation under which there had been no liquor, no sports, no jobs, no fun. Foucret's father, a steel merchant, was permitted only one client: the Nazi army. This client did not pay.

So when the Americans arrived, Foucret went to watch them. He took his girlfriend along. She was sixteen also, Foucret says, wistfully tracing an hourglass in the air with his hands. So, did he run to greet the Americans?

No, he says. But she did.

Ah.

No hard feelings, though. Foucret's affection for Americans may be laced with a certain Gallic flavor—one example he gives of our worth as a people is that we are intelligent and refined enough to admire French impressionist painters—but it's surely genuine. Just don't get him started on our president.

It is impossible to overstate the French antipathy for the current American head of state. A successful Parisian stage play, now in its fifth month, is titled *George W. Bush, or God's Sad Cowboy,* a farce about how Dubya wants to create a "United States of the World." The exterior of the theater is splattered with faux blood.

Back at Les Deux Magots, the fox-hunting Vincent de Ker-empenec had called Bush "a very large liar." This theme has been repeated and repackaged by people of all ages and backgrounds: America, good. American leadership, bad. Americans, nice. President Bush, glass bowl.

"Doubleyou Boosh," Foucret calls him in a sort of curse. The socially liberal French detest Bush on almost every level, from the predictable—his adventurism in Iraq, his enthusiasm for the death penalty and handgun ownership, his aggressive malapropisms and other perceived lack of refinement—to the more surprising. Though predominantly Roman Catholic, the French demand secularism in government and find Bush's very public trumpeting of his Christian faith to be naked sanctimony.

Interestingly, the French prefer our previous president. His zipper weakness not only doesn't bother them; it seems to be a humanizing point in his favor. They like Hillary, too. Foucret begins to tell of a time that the first couple was out driving, and it is only when he is halfway through that you realize it is a joke. Bill and Hill stop at a gas station, and Hillary gets out to hug the attendant. When she gets back in the car, Bill asks her who that was, and she answers that it was an old high school boyfriend. "Interesting," Bill says. "Imagine, if things had gone differently, you would have been married to a gas station attendant instead of the president of the United States."

"No," Hillary says. "If things had gone differently, he would have been president of the United States."

We are all laughing and having a great time, and toasting the friendship of our two countries. At precisely that moment, Laurent Bondi's beautiful ten-year-old daughter, Analia, arrives, bounds up to each American in turn, and greets us with innocent European abandon.

Both cheeks still wet from Analia Bondi's kisses, I head off confidently for the Normandy beaches themselves.

Marie Lebourg and David Chesnel are enjoying a day in Dieppe, a resort town on the English Channel. She is as lovely as any woman you or I are ever likely to see in person; he is all man. They look like Aniston and Pitt would look if Aniston and Pitt were French—which is to say, more self-possessed than Aniston and Pitt, and more intelligent and more sophisticated. They are not movie stars, though. They are just ordinary people. Ordinary French people.

(I am feeling good and loved and magnanimous, and thus able to confront some stereotypes with openness and candor. Frank observation No. 1: The French are slimmer and sexier than we are. No, this is not a matter of different cultural norms and attitudes toward body type yadda yadda yadda. Americans are "consumers." By and large, we buy, and are large.)

I have chosen Dieppe for a reason. It is here, in this town, on August 19, 1942, that a dry run took place for the great Allied invasion that would eventually liberate France. Operation Jubilee, as it was grotesquely named, was a massacre. The picturesque white cliffs overlooking the harbor held Germans in machine-gun bunkers, and they picked off Canadian and American soldiers like wharf rats as they stumbled up the rocky beach that was as slick as wet marbles.

The old German bunkers are still there, and so are the slippery and treacherous rocks. But Marie and David seem to be negotiating these imperturbably. It is as though, when one reaches a certain level of beauty and grace, one need not remain obedient to the laws of physics.

(Frank observation No. 2: It is possible to become envious and resentful of the French. One must resist this.)

Jérôme approaches to ask a question on my behalf, but Marie and David wave him off. How friendly of them to take a crack at it in English! I frame my question simply, and speak slowly, as if to children: What do they think of America and Americans?

They whisper together a moment. Was the question too complicated? Finally, Marie speaks in perfect English.

"I am afraid we do not approve of your commercial and ideological imperialism."

(Frank observation No. 3: While envy and resentfulness of the French is unbecoming, a small amount of indignation is, at times, unavoidable.)

She is a student, he works for Renault. They are well traveled, of course, though they are only twenty-four. They are genuinely distressed at having to tell an American of their disappointment in his country, but he has asked, and they are being honest. David explains that hungry French people used to get a baguette and some cheese; now they are likely to visit a McDonald's. From his expression, he may as well be describing a visit to an abattoir.

Marie shakes out her chestnut hair over the top of her sundress. "We perceive this situation," she says, "almost as . . ."

Don't say it.

". . . an invasion."

(Frank observation No. 4: The French are completely intolerable.)

Where is the gratitude? Surely they can find something good to say about America, in this of all places. I actually ask this: What's good about America? They are consulting each other in fevered whispers. They want to throw the American a bone, they really do. There must be something, I hear Marie say. David shrugs massively. She pouts, then looks at me helplessly. She holds up a finger for more time.

Finally, Jérôme intercedes. He needs a picture. So the three of them begin walking off toward a picturesque floral backdrop, which will seem wan and wilted beside Marie's beauty. When they are 50 feet away, I see her suddenly stop, and turn to Jérôme.

She looks triumphant and says something to him. He turns and shouts back to me:

"Pancakes!"

I THINK THIS is the appropriate moment to address, and dispense with once and for all, an oft-repeated and particularly noxious American calumny about the French. Do the French stink?

After many days in France, I have a solid answer to this question. And it reminds me of the old joke about the billionaire who hired a famous architect to build him a new bathroom. Cost was no object. Space was no object. All that mattered to the billionaire was that he had a bathroom designed so it would not stink.

No problem, said the architect, and after six months, for a cool million dollars, he produced the stateliest bathroom anyone had ever seen. It had a library, a lounge, and gold-plated fixtures. The billionaire was delighted, but that night he telephoned the architect in a fury, demanding that he rush right over, which the architect did. "I said I wanted a bathroom that didn't stink! Well, the first time I used it," the billionaire bellowed, "the smell was terrible."

And the architect said, "You *used* it?"

No, the French do not stink. It is only when they fail to bathe regularly—a circumstance occurring with slightly greater frequency than with Americans—that they stink.

DAY FOUR

WE ARE BACK in Paris, at the abattoir. If it so offends the French, I figure it must be truly terrible, but near as I can tell, it is simply a McDonald's. Well, not simply a McDonald's. It doesn't offer supersizing, for some reason. But everything else is pretty much what we know and love, and what's not to like?

As I leave the premises, I can't get over how silly the French are. If they don't want a Quarter Pounder® with Cheese™ they can always walk right across the street to the restaurant at the ancient, five-star Hotel Concorde Saint-Lazare and order from the menu, which today features terrine de poulet confite et foie gras de canard à la sarriette. From the Saint-Lazare, you get a nice view of the McDonald's. It's been installed in an old building with an eighteenth-century Strasbourg feel. Iron Parisian balconies and a mammoth bas-relief monarch adorn the facade. Atop the building is a statue of a pelican and a handsome ancient coat of arms that is still mostly visible behind the enormous plastic Golden Arches™ that dangle above it on a chain from the roof, like a big cartoon tushie. No other object insults the majesty of the building, other than the 30-foot-high tomato-red and banana-yellow McDonald's banner that hangs from top to bottom.

Jérôme and I continue discussing the oversensitivity of the French, their sometimes comical resistance to what they see as cultural rape. You've heard of these things: The custodians of the French dictionary are thin-lipped despots, banning certain English-influenced expressions. The term "e-mail" is forbidden in French government correspondence, replaced by the French *courriel*. French laws require that 40 percent of all playlists on the radio be French songs. Don't they understand how preposterous this makes them look to the rest of the world? Can't they see that times have changed? There is a new global economy, an exchange of ideas and cultures.

It's not all bad. Is it?

I lose track of Jérôme for a minute, but then find him. He is bent over a car, taking a photograph of the rear windshield. I crane my neck to see. It is a yellow plastic sign that reads: "BÉBÉ

À BORD!" Jérôme looks at me, and I look at him, and we keep walking in silence.

We are almost done for the day. All that is left is a photo opportunity. We decide that because this story is about slurs and stereotype, we will seek a visual pun for the cover of this magazine. Jérôme will shoot me with the Eiffel Tower in the background, contemplating a . . . frog.

We simply need to find a live frog. Two hours later, we are still looking. No frog is to be found. In Paris, France.

Finally, we are in a market district, talking to a dealer in reptiles and amphibians. Alain Debouve shrugs. There are strict import laws. It's been some time since you could easily get a frog in France. Even the ones in restaurants don't come from France.

Where do they come from?

"Many come from the United States," he says.

DAY FIVE

IT HAS BEEN quite a while since I left you dangling, my insolent question to French Agriculture Minister Hervé Gaymard as yet unanswered. Your wait is over, because he is now seated in front of me, composing his response.

I did not spring that question out of the blue. I had first asked him about his primary ambit of responsibility, the French wine industry. Would France, I asked, be willing to reach out to the American consumer by converting its cabernets and merlots to twist-top caps?

Gaymard's English is pretty good, but he needed the scroogie concept explained. It was. He opened his mouth to speak, then closed it again. A flicker of a smile. "In a word," he said placidly, "no."

Excellent! He is defying stereotype. To the French politician, stereotypically, nothing is monosyllabic, and nothing is simple: Whereas American politicians are said to be ignorant of history and inclined to regard all situations as having been birthed fully formed the day before, the French are said to be chained to a thousand-year past, turning every issue into a complex geopolitical morass, nursing grudges and flogging old causes.

Now we are ready for the big question: The one about the French being insufferable, elitist, silly, effeminate, filthy-dirty pretentious snots. The one inviting the minister to reciprocate with his own stereotypes of Americans. Will he take the bait? He listens. "Well," he offers at last with a smile, "it is said you eat tasteless food." Good, good! And . . .

He steeples his fingers. "Now, this is not really a stereotype because stereotypes are what the ordinary person believes. But what the European elite holds against Americans . . ."

Remember, he is responding to a question about whether the French are pompous.

". . . is that your country will vacillate between virtuous hegemony and contemptuous retreat."

The minister follows with a lengthy historical dissertation about how American foreign policy has waffled inconsistently between isolationism and humanitarian activism. He nimbly plucks historical antecedents involving Woodrow Wilson, the League of Nations, William Howard Taft, and Charles de Gaulle, moving forward through the abandonment and fall of Dienbienphu in French Indochina in 1954. I stop taking notes midway through the twelfth minute.

It is all extremely instructive, and I have no doubt the minister is correct on all points. I depart chastened and deflated, pretty sure my own country has behaved disgracefully, particularly during the first Eisenhower administration.

———

Bastille Day on the Champs-Élysées, Paris's grand boulevard. I've been told what to expect, but it still comes as a surprise. The French celebration of their day of independence is a hyper-military display, featuring a parade of tanks and other massive armored hardware one would more expect to see in Beijing or at the central square of a consonant-oriented country with a name like Tkczjrkistan.

Before the festivities, Jérôme and I mingle with the march-ers, companies of cadets in their dress finery—with cutlasses in scabbards and swagger sticks and splendiferous, ornate multicol-ored uniforms of a sort that would not be worn by the American military outside of some cruel hazing ritual. Some wear aprons and carry axes. One man wears a hat featuring a dangly, red feather-tufted ball. I want to tell the guy I have seen this precise fashion accessory in a book by the distinguished American author Dr. Seuss, but there are too many cutlasses around.

There are waves of flyovers by Mirage jets, and long columns of treaded vehicles rumbling on the cobblestones, giant amphibi-ous tanks with rear-mounted howitzers, an endless march of businesslike war machines in camouflage green, missile launch-ers and troop transports. For a while it is truly impressive. Then the vehicles begin looking more and more ordinary until we are watching what seem to be military garbage trucks.

The crowd is demonstrating an odd solemnity, at least by our standards. There are no balloons dancing or Frisbees flying—just polite, almost awed, applause. In the ensuing sweltering summer weeks, thousands of elderly French will die alone of heatstroke, victims of an inadequate public health safety net. But at the mo-ment, surrounded by symbols of power, people just seem . . . re-assured.

You don't see this sort of display in the United States, a country that in three minutes could—not to put too fine a point on it—flatten France like a crêpe suzette. We do not flaunt our might in this way. We do not need to. We do not whistle in the dark. Well, except perhaps for our continued dispatches from the War on Terrorism, which we are, needless to say, winning.

DAY SIX

DID I MENTION that when I am troubled I often consult the dead?

I am negotiating once again the walkways of Montparnasse Cemetery, this time with Jérôme. Here is the grave of another great writer beloved by the French. Samuel Beckett, of course, wrote *Waiting for Godot*, but also a lesser-known work called *Happy Days*.

No, it is not about the Fonz. You stupid American. Beckett's *Happy Days* is about a woman who is trapped in a mound of sand up to her waist, but who is perfectly content and finds her life a paradise. By the end of the play, she remains equally optimistic and satisfied, even though she is now buried to her neck. *Happy Days* is said to be about the power of denial.

There's nothing wrong with denial, of course. It's how we get through life without being consumed by the inevitability of our own death. You know, whistling in the dark. It explains a lot of human behavior, things big and small, including the elaborate, xenophobic dance we do to hold on to our pride and self-confidence—denying our own weaknesses by ridiculing others not like us. You know what I mean?

Yesterday, I was in a close-packed, unair-conditioned Parisian bar. It was at the end of a long day, and I couldn't help noticing that stereotypical, telltale body odor of the French. Then I realized it was coming from me.

What's real? What's slander? I am telling Jérôme how confused I am by all this, how the only thing I can count on is that there is not a person walking the streets of France who likes George W. Bush.

"I like George W. Bush," a woman calls out to us, in English.

"I *love* George W. Bush," says her husband.

I pull out my notebook. Why? Tell us why!

"Well, we live only thirty miles from his ranch."

Allan and Arminda Lane of Whitney, Texas, are in Paris on vacation with the kids, Amy, Aaron, and Rachel. Allan is a Baptist minister. He counts himself one of George W. Bush's most ardent supporters. Arminda, too. Their support knows few reservations. But what about those missing WMDs? Allan says he thinks they might still be there, hidden, waiting to be found. I shoot him a skeptical look.

"Well, either that," he says, "or we had to delay so long in dealing with those U.N. resolutions that they snuck them out of the country."

It's *France's* fault!

Maybe it all comes down to this: We're going to believe what we want to believe, if it keeps us feeling good about ourselves. French people love to repeat the well-known idiocy by George W. Bush, a Bushism now famous in France: "The main problem with the French is that they have no word for 'entrepreneur.'" It's a wonderful quote, very revealing, if only he had actually said it. He also never said that "Gruyère cheese is stupid because it has holes." I have heard that one in France, too.

As we all know in the United States, the French are soft on terrorism because they haven't felt its sting the way we have. But here in the cemetery—as well as all over the streets of Paris—you can't help but notice the absence of garbage cans. Instead, there are translucent green plastic bags hanging from metal rings. That's because you can see a terrorist bomb in those. The French were there, long before us.

National prejudices aren't attractive, but there's one thing about them that's hard to deny: They're inextricable from national pride.

You don't have to take my word for it. That was the conclusion of an expert in human and international relations who studied democracy and aristocracy and discovered an essential difference between them:

> Men living in democracies love their country just as they love themselves, and they transfer the habits of their private vanity to their vanity as a nation . . . Moralists are constantly complaining that the ruling vice of the present time is pride . . . I would willingly exchange several of our small virtues for this one vice.

That was Tocqueville, writing in *Democracy in America*.

I would like to end this story here, but I can't do it in good conscience. Tocqueville confronted everything, however distasteful.

Jérôme and I are still standing in the cemetery, and something happens that must be reported.

Jérôme has taken the Lane family of Whitney, Texas, away to be photographed against the cemetery wall. As they are shooting, Allan Lane mentions how much his whole family likes Paris. Really, he says, they have only one complaint. They've had to wait too long for their meal at McDonald's. What's wrong with Paris, he says, is that it needs more McDonaldses, so the lines will be shorter. Also, he says, some Burger Kings would be nice.

Doonesbury's War

The most perilous prejudice a writer can have—the prejudice most likely to sabotage his story—isn't some sort of personal or political antipathy. It's hero worship. When you are writing about someone you admire enormously, you are in serious danger of the sin of adoration. You sometimes have to force yourself to be nitpicking, faultfinding, caviling, hypercritical.

Garry Trudeau pronounces the t in "often." No, you won't see that minor affectation exposed to ridicule in this profile of him. I put it in the story, but my editor deleted it because he said I was grasping at straws. Which I was.

October 22, 2006

IN THE BANQUET room were men who were blind, men with burns, men with gouges, men missing an arm, men missing a leg, men missing an arm and a leg, men missing an arm and both legs, men missing parts of their faces, and a cartoonist from the funny pages. We were just a few blocks from the White House, at Fran O'Brien's Steak House. Fran's was hosting a night out for casualties of the current war, visiting from their hospital wards.

It's hard to know what to say to a grievously injured person, and it's easy to be wrong. You could do what I did, for example. Scrounging for the positive, I cheerfully informed a young man who had lost both legs and his left forearm that at least he's lucky he's a righty. Then he wordlessly showed me his right hand, which is missing fingertips and has limited motion—an articulated claw. That shut things right up, for both of us, and it would have stayed that way, except the cartoonist showed up.

Garry Trudeau, the creator of *Doonesbury*, hunkered right down in front of the soldier, eye-to-eye, introduced himself, and proceeded to ignore every single diplomatic nicety.

"So, when were you hit?" he asked.

"October twenty-third."

Trudeau pivoted his body. "So you took the blast on, what . . . this side?"

"Yeah." .

Brian Anderson, twenty-five, was in shorts, a look favored by most of the amputees, who tend to wear their new prostheses like combat medals. His legs are metal and plastic, blue and knobby at the knee, shin poles culminating abruptly in sneakers.

Trudeau surveyed Brian's intact arm. "You've got dots."

"Yeah." Dots are soldier-speak for little beads of shrapnel buried under the skin. Sometimes they take a lifetime to work their way back to the surface. At this, Brian became fully engaged and animated, smiling and talking about the improvised explosive device that took his vehicle out; about his rescue; his recovery; his plans for the future. Trudeau, it turned out, had given him what he needed.

("In these soldiers' minds," Trudeau will explain afterward, "their whole identity, who they are right now, *is* what happened to them. They *want* to tell the story, they want to be asked about it, and you're honoring them by listening. The more they revisit it, the less power it has over them.")

Trudeau has been talking to injured vets for a couple of years now. It's partly compassionate support for people he has a genuine regard for, and it's part journalism—the damnedest sort of reporting, for a professional cartoonist.

This was April 25. On the comics pages that day, Dagwood fixed himself an absolutely *enormous* sandwich; Garfield kicked Odie off the table again; and in Beetle Bailey, the only military-themed comic strip, Lt. Fuzz accidentally dropped a glass of water and cussed in funny cartoon hieroglyphics.

In *Doonesbury*, this was the story: B.D., the football coach and Vietnam vet who went to Iraq with the National Guard and lost a leg in a rocket-grenade attack near Fallujah, has been shamed into entering therapy for posttraumatic stress disorder because he overheard his little girl, Sam, tell a friend that she'd become afraid of her daddy. On this day, B.D. will begin to relive the battlefield event he has repressed, the one that made him a moody, alcoholic paranoiac and that torments him with guilt and shame that he does not understand. Through the rest of the week, B.D. will retell what happened when his armored vehicle came under attack from insurgents and—desperate to escape and save himself and his men—he gave the order to flee through a crowded marketplace, mowing down civilians.

Not many of the injured vets in Fran O'Brien's were where B.D. was yet. Their deepest wounds, like the dots, had not yet surfaced. On that day they were jovial, mostly, and indomitable, all of them, stolid and impervious, more so than the moms, wives, and girlfriends who hovered at their elbows, lovingly kneading shoulders, patting thighs, holding on, looking bravely upbeat and just a little overwhelmed.

Trudeau bellied up to another vet.

"So, when were you hit?"

———

IF YOU DON'T know much about Garry Trudeau, and you probably don't, it's because he has done his best to keep it that way.
With the exception of the time in 1980 when his island wedding to America's Sweetheart, TV personality Jane Pauley, turned
him into a sullen bridegroom hounded by paparazzi in boats and
helicopters, Trudeau, now fifty-eight, has managed to remain
comfortably obscure. Aside from a couple of semirecent TV interviews, he's had almost no public presence for three decades.
Considering the extraordinary reach of his comic strip, and the
role it has had over the years in analyzing, reflecting, and even
helping shape American culture, he may be the most famous unknown person in the country today.

———————

IT'S AN ODD type of fame, one that attaches hungrily to what you
do but not at all to who you are. Take this woman here, at a lunch
counter in the Dallas/Fort Worth airport. Her name is Connie
Dubois. A candlemaker, Connie lives in Ethel, Louisiana, population 2,000, a fleck on the map of East Feliciana Parish, which
itself contains only two traffic lights. Connie, who is fifty, has just
flown on a plane for the first time in her life, heading to a trade
show for candlemakers.

"Do you know what *Doonesbury* is?" I ask her.

"Sure," she says, putting down her sandwich. "It's a cartoon.
In the paper. Been around a long time. It's a little off-center and
radical, and I like that."

"Do you know the name of the guy who draws it?"

Dubois scrunches up her face, thinking.

"Nope. No idea."

Dubois says she wouldn't know the cartoonist if she saw him,
which is undeniable, since at the moment Trudeau is sitting 4
feet away. He is head-down, digging into his Caesar salad, doing
his best to disappear. He *hates* things like this.

Trudeau is so viscerally averse to self-promotion that he once threw up before a scheduled interview for a *Time* magazine cover story, then canceled it. (*Time* wrote the story anyway.)

I'm at Trudeau's elbow on a trip out West because I'm doing the first extensive profile of him in the thirty-six years since he began the comic strip that became an American icon. That's reason enough, but the fact is, something astonishing has happened to *Doonesbury* in the last two and a half years, after the United States invaded Iraq and Trudeau made the startling, uncartoonish decision to mutilate one of his characters.

It was not just any character. B.D. had been a Doonesbury fixture since Day One. Literally. On the day the strip debuted in twenty-eight newspapers nationwide—October 26, 1970—B.D. was alone in the opening panel, sitting in his dorm room on the first day of school, football helmet inexplicably on his head, wondering what kind of roommate he'd get. To his everlasting annoyance, it turned out to be Michael Doonesbury.

That was so many years ago—a generation and a half, really—that the strip has outlasted even its original cultural references. Does anyone remember that "B.D." were the initials of Brian Dowling, the hotshot quarterback at Yale when Trudeau was there in the late sixties? Or that in the eastern prep-school lexicon of the time, a "doone" was something of a doofus?

It's *Doonesbury* that survived and metamorphosed over the years into what is essentially an episodic comic novel, with so many active characters that Trudeau himself has been known to confuse them. *Doonesbury* has always remained topical, often controversial. Unapologetically liberal and almost religiously antiestablishment, Trudeau has been denounced by presidents and potentates and condemned on the floor of the U.S. Senate. He's also been described as America's greatest living satirist, mentioned in the same breath as Mark Twain and Ambrose Bierce.

But for simple dramatic impact and deft complexity of

humor, nothing else in *Doonesbury* has ever approached the story line of B.D.'s injury and convalescence. It hasn't been political at all, really, unless you contend that acknowledging the suffering of a war is a political statement. What it has been is remarkably poignant and surprisingly funny at the same time. In what Trudeau calls a "rolling experiment in naturalism," he has managed every few weeks to spoon out a story of war, loss, and psychological turmoil in four-panel episodes, each with a crisp punch line.

Here's one:

It is a cliché, and it is also true, that humor springs from existential pain—from a need to blunt the awareness that life is essentially a fatal disease of unpredictable symptoms and unknown duration. Usually, though, the laughter comes through indirection—acknowledging that death awaits us all, for example, by joking about memory loss as we age. But there's been nothing comfortably oblique in these episodes of *Doonesbury,* no comic exaggeration, no use of metaphor. There is no distance whatever between the pain and the humor.

Over the years, *Doonesbury* has been remarkably consistent in its quality, if not universally beloved. Republicans can make a reasonable case that Trudeau's lefty politics sometimes make him seem a water boy for Democrats. He is not above the occasional cheap shot, such as when he devoted an entire week in 1991 to a felon's unsubstantiated charges that Vice President Quayle had been a pothead. At times, he has seemed to lapse unattractively from political satire to political advocacy—lending his characters' support to John Anderson in 1980 and Howard Dean in 2004. Some feel he has occasionally been tone-deaf to popular culture—buying too readily, for example, into the notion of a slacker Generation Y. Undeniably, the strip's edge dulled a little in the mid-1990s, when a Democratic ascendancy left him without a meaty political issue to lampoon. But there aren't many people—especially among experts who read and critique comics for a living—who are calling the continuing saga of B.D. anything other than genius. "What it is," says comics historian R. C. Harvey, "is breathtaking. Just a stunning body of work."

So, WHO IS Trudeau, really?

It turns out he's not afraid of publicity so much as he's horrified at being perceived as the kind of person who wants publicity. He treasures his literary license to kill but feels a twinge of guilt that it isn't really a fair fight. He's a genuinely humble know-it-all. His regard for injured soldiers is sincere, his knowledge of their lingo profound, almost as if he's one of them; watching this, you can't help but hear faint, soul-rattling echoes of Vietnam, which he escaped, like many sons of privilege, by gaming the system. He's got the greatest job on Earth—no boss, his own hours, enormous clout, public adulation, a seven-figure income, absolute creative freedom—but he speaks with longing about a different career altogether, one that the huge success of *Doonesbury* ensured he'd never have.

Also, he's a smartass.

But you knew that.

IT'S MONDAY NIGHT out for the meatheads, as they call themselves. These are Trudeau and some of his best friends, who assemble irregularly on weeknights in Manhattan to attend excellently terrible movies their wives won't see with them. Today's choice is *Poseidon*. They're pumped for a real stinker.

"A lot of research goes into this," Trudeau explains, "so we don't make many mistakes. We get these movies when they're dying, so we have the theater to ourselves. We like to talk to the screen."

"And throw popcorn."

This is David Levinthal, fifty-seven, who looks like the manager of a Jiffy Lube but is an acclaimed modern artist. Levinthal's medium is plastic toys: He arranges them in unusual ways, photographs them in intriguing lighting, and sells the pictures for thousands of dollars. Not long ago he had a show entirely of made-in-Japan erotic dolls.

Levinthal is not the most unusual guy here. That would probably be Fred Newman, fifty-three, who is, at this very moment, barking like a dog. It's the best imitation bark you'll ever hear. Newman's a professional sound-effects man, author of a popular how-to book called *MouthSounds*, and is a regular whistle, boing, and honk man for Garrison Keillor's *A Prairie Home Companion*. When you're doing a woof, Newman is saying, the rookie error is to blow out. You've got to suck in.

We're sitting outdoors at an East Side Manhattan burrito joint, so Newman is entertaining more than just our table. He once taught Meryl Streep how to convince a radio audience that she was lighting a cigarette and blowing out the match, which isn't as easy as it sounds.

The guy with the graying ponytail is David Stanford, who handles the elaborate Doonesbury.com Web site and edits Trudeau's *Doonesbury* books.

Trudeau is the normal one. He "travels incognito," as Levinthal says. It's true. The guy could blend into a room of waiters. He dresses with an elaborate lack of vanity. He is a millionaire many times over, but Jane cuts his hair.

Dinner over, the meatheads assemble in the second row of a mostly empty downtown Manhattan theater as the credits for *Poseidon* are beginning to roll. The meatheads are hoping this one will be a lot worse than the last film they saw, *Good Night, and Good Luck*, which turned out to have some disappointingly redeeming qualities. The best worst recent choice was a Lou Diamond Phillips flick where a car exploded and then, in a later scene, the same car drove off a cliff.

In the opening minutes of *Poseidon*, as the characters are being introduced, Trudeau and his friends start to loudly handicap who will live and who will drown. "You think Kurt Russell will live?"

"No, he'll die, because the kids are the future."

"Okay, right, he'll die, but he'll die *saving* people."

Popcorn is definitely being flung.

"The nasty guy's gonna die in a really bad way."

Fred is making excellent glub-glub noises.

"Richard Dreyfuss is suicidal? If he wants to die, then he won't die."

"Right, he needs to learn that *life is a gift*."

If you've seen the movie, you know the meatheads were right about everything.

LIKE ANY SATIRIST whose work endures, Trudeau has been right about a lot of things. From the moment that hippie college deejay Mark Slackmeyer looked at the reader and gleefully declared that an indicted former Attorney General John Mitchell was "Guilty! Guilty! Guilty!" Trudeau has shown a world-class instinct for piercing a babble of crosstalk and nailing the truth. He was right about Vietnam. (When a conservative columnist said that he saw "a light at the end of a tunnel," Michael asked him: "When you've dug yourself into a hole, why do you always insist on calling it a tunnel?") Trudeau was right about the greed of eighties big business, about the cynicism of the marketing industry, about Bill Clinton's flippy-flop, polls-based approach to governance (*Doonesbury* regularly portrayed Clinton as a greasy waffle).

At times, his prescience seemed more clairvoyant than calculated: During the waning years of the Reagan administration, Trudeau sent his trench-coated TV newsman, Roland Hedley, into the president's brain, where he confronted a desolate, soupy wasteland of fizzling synapses. It seemed funny then, if mean-spirited; if you look at those strips now, they're chilling.

Most recently, Trudeau was right about Iraq. As the invasion began amid optimistic forecasts of a quick and decisive victory, before mandatory re-ups became routine, National Guardsman B.D. matter-of-factly informed his stunned wife, Boopsie, that he'd see her again "in five to seven years."

Surely, after three decades of being right, the man is bound to be a little smug. I went searching for signs of this in his studio, an airy fourth-floor walkup in the East 70s. Though the walls are covered with original classic comic art—Saul Steinberg, Jeff MacNelly, George Herriman's *Krazy Kat*, and Winsor McCay's *Little Nemo in Slumberland*—there is no *Doonesbury* visible anywhere. Just . . . nothing. "Why would I have my own art up?" Trudeau asks. "I want to show the work of people I admire."

The quality of Trudeau's drawing has been a matter of some

debate in the cartooning world since the strip's debut. Back then, a common joke was that Trudeau had "made the comics pages safe for bad art," which was, in a sense, true. Before there were *Dilbert* and *Pearls Before Swine* and other strips drawn with meticulous infantilism, there was *Doonesbury*, which resembled, in its early years, the sort of thing someone's moderately talented kid brother scribbled into the flyleaf of his textbook.

There was nothing meticulous about it. Trudeau was consciously trying to imitate Jules Feiffer's sparsely sophisticated style, but he didn't progress much past sparse. Sometimes he just didn't bother giving his characters mouths. They *never* had feet—their legs would just flutter off the page in mid-calf. Heads would swivel in physiologically irreproducible ways.

Over time—particularly after Trudeau's famed twenty-month hiatus in 1983 and 1984, when he allowed his characters to ripen into reluctant adulthood off the page—he seemed to learn the fundamentals of cartooning, and then some. The art in *Doonesbury* became far more professional, with inventive angles, cinematic shading, even intimations of an occasional foot. This led to a widespread suspicion that Trudeau was getting major help from the man who ostensibly just did his inking—a suspicion nudged into an assumption a few years ago when *Entertainment Weekly* stated flatly that Trudeau wasn't drawing it himself.

"For years," he says, laughing, "I was blamed for my art, and then I couldn't get credit for it."

For the record, the art is his. I'm looking right now at Trudeau's pencil drawings of a recent week of *Doonesbury*s before they were sent to the inker. They are rich in detail, identical to the finished version, and every line is Trudeau's, even the lettering.

"It's serviceable, is the best I can say about it," Trudeau demurs. "I will say this: It's a signature style. It doesn't look like anyone else's." Even this modest bit of immodesty does not go immediately unpunished.

"But my stuff's amateur hour compared to this."

Trudeau is pulling open a drawer. Inside are a few originals drawn by the great Walt Kelly, whose *Pogo* strips of the 1940s and '50s were among the first to mine politics for humor. Kelly was a masterful artist. "Look at this—this one's pure motion," Trudeau says. "And look at this detail; look at the bugs." It was a single-panel Sunday strip of the *Pogo* characters poling a raft through their swamp. Even the tiniest characters—insects a few millimeters high—had expressive faces.

Eventually, I did find some Doonesiana displayed in Trudeau's studio. There were nine framed covers of major magazines—*Time, Newsweek, Rolling Stone, Mother Jones*, etc., spanning thirty years, all either drawn by Trudeau or about him. And yes, Trudeau's got 'em right up there, framed, on a wall, plain as day, inside a closet where he stores pushpins and computer paper.

ON THE MORNING of April 19, 2004, newspaper readers were served something startling with their morning coffee. The first panel of *Doonesbury* was completely black, except for the word "Hey!" Then, framed by the smoke of war, a soldier's face. It's Ray Hightower, B.D.'s buddy. He's sweating, looking scared. He calls for a medic. Then black again, as though someone is drifting in and out of consciousness. The gut-punch line comes at the end, with a shouted name. "B.D.?"

And here is the image people saw two days later:

It was shocking for obvious reasons, but in another way as well: B.D. had never been seen without his helmet. It was as if Trudeau was declaring that something fundamentally and forever had changed.

Ask creative people where they get their ideas, and they will roll their eyes. It's the most common question, but it's also a bad one because the answer is inevitably disappointing. From the inside, creativity seems like an arduous task, often involving plebeian, imperfect choices, driven less by inspiration than by deadline. And Trudeau is a deadline junkie, always pushing it to the limit. ("Once a week," he says, "I am a very desperate man.")

So when you ask him why he decided to take B.D.'s leg, the answer isn't very satisfying. Trudeau doesn't regard his characters in romanticized terms, or even as people; *Doonesbury* has always been more about ideas than personalities, so Trudeau thinks of Mike and B.D. and Zonker and Joanie as puppets. He pulls the appropriate ones out of the closet when he has a point he wants to make. In this case, he says, he wanted to make a statement about the suffering in this war.

Originally, he was going to kill Ray, but Ray got spared when Trudeau decided that a death would not leave much of a storyline to pursue. So, with a bit of sang-froid, he amputated B.D.'s left leg, on the theory that he'd . . . think of something.

What happened next was unusual, to say the least. Within a day or two of B.D. lying broken on that stretcher, Garry Trudeau, bane of every presidential administration since Nixon's (particularly the current one, which he has absolutely lacerated), got a call from the Pentagon. The brass was offering to help him figure out where to go next.

THE TYPICAL DAILY newspaper comic strip has a degenerative arc. The cartoonist's best years come early, when the ideas are fresh, the gimmick is still a novelty, and the grind of daily deadlines has not yet taken its toll on creativity. Three years of excellence is a pretty good run before the inevitable decline, as the cartoonist runs out of new things to say and becomes content to imitate himself. It's easy to forget, but many of today's formulaic, intellectually listless strips, such as *B.C.*, *Cathy*, and *Dennis the Menace*, were once lively and daring and different. They're still around because their bland familiarity becomes a sort of comfort food, and newspaper editors are loath to drop them.

"Having a successful daily comic strip," Trudeau says wryly, "is the closest thing to tenure that popular culture offers. But it doesn't seem to have freed up creativity any more than tenure for professors has. It's been an open invitation for complacency."

Doonesbury has never become complacent, partly because Trudeau is no ordinary creative talent but also because the strip feeds continually off the culture it lampoons. Trudeau is very much a reporter—what *Newsweek*'s Jonathan Alter once called "an investigative cartoonist." When two of his principal characters were homeless, Trudeau spent time working in shelters. When *Doonesbury* accompanied President Ford to China, so did Trudeau. When B.D. served in the Persian Gulf War, Trudeau briefly went to Kuwait. So when the new invitation came from the Pentagon—essentially, carte blanche to visit injured vets— the investigative cartoonist leapt at it, not sure what he would find.

The very first person he spoke to was a twenty-seven-year-old MP named Danielle Green. She had been a college basketball star, a left-handed point guard at Notre Dame. Green had just lost that hand in Iraq. She'd been on the roof of a police station, behind sandbags, trying to defend it from enemy fire, when she took a direct hit from a rocket-propelled grenade.

"This was an elite athlete, and she'd lost her whole professional identity," Trudeau said, "but that's not what she wanted to talk about. What she wanted to talk about was how her buddies carried her down, put her on the hood of a Humvee, where they stopped the bleeding, then went back up to the roof, against orders, and found her hand buried under sandbags. They took off her wedding ring and gave it to her. She's telling me this with a million-dollar smile. This was not about bitterness or loss. It was about gratitude."

And so Trudeau started taking notes.

———————

DOONESBURY HAS DEALT with emotional subjects before, most notably when gay lawyer Andy Lippincott died of AIDS in 1990, wisecracking to the end. Trudeau was never entirely satisfied with that sequence, because Andy was two-dimensional—literally *and* figuratively. He became a bravely noble funnyman dying with bravely noble humor.

"Andy handled it with more grace and humility than any human would," Trudeau says. The problem was, Trudeau hadn't known people with AIDS.

The access he has had to injured vets has given him a sure-handedness he didn't have then; the B.D. storyline has shown extraordinary emotional complexity.

At a VA program for posttraumatic stress disorder in Menlo Park, California, Trudeau was allowed to sit in on the treatment of a forty-year-old military truck driver who had been delivering a weapons system to Baghdad Airport when his convoy came under fire. He had to flee through a crowd—just as Trudeau would later have B.D. do.

"The guy was back home, living with his parents, isolated with his TV, his PC, and his alcohol," Trudeau says, consulting his notes. "He hated public places and would only go shopping at night at twenty-four-hour stores, when no one was around. He told us he was late for a job interview, but he had an hour, and it wasn't an hour away. It turned out he had to go by back roads, because he would not drive under an overpass. Overpasses freaked him out." Overpasses could give snipers cover.

"He was a computer expert, but he decided to take a $10-an-hour job over a $25-an-hour job," Trudeau said, "because he wanted to work at a nursery, with plants. It was only when he talked about working with plants that his face softened."

HE'S GARRY, NOT Gary, because his given name is Garretson. Trudeau is a blueblood, albeit one of a strange sort. The boring summary is that he's the end-of-the-line son of four generations of physicians. But to leave it there would be a grave disservice to the narrative arts.

Trudeau's great-great-grandfather, James de Berty Trudeau, was a friend of John James Audubon, for whom he shot birds. He lived in the wilds with the Osage Indians in the Louisiana territories. Oh, and he was a medical doctor in nineteenth-century New York City who ran afoul of his peers over his hobby of sculpting amusing figurines of the most dignified medical men of his era. To this they did not take kindly, drumming him out of polite society and down to New Orleans.

During the Civil War, he was made a brigadier general in the Confederate Army, apparently more for his status as a gentleman than for his military prowess. In short order, he assisted in the mismanagement of not one but two enormous Confederate defeats—Shiloh, a turning point of the war, and the battle of Island No. 10, which left the Mississippi undefended clear to Vicksburg. Who knows how many more miserable, crushing losses he would have helped midwife had he not been captured, held under house arrest, and released to continue his medical practice?

Meanwhile, the general's wife had left him and headed for Paris, where their son—Trudeau's great-grandfather, a lad of just ten or so—distinguished himself by whapping the Confederate ambassador in the back with a pellet from a slingshot. ("Actually, I see a lot of myself in him," Trudeau laughs.)

Tuberculosis ravaged the family, which brought the next generations of Trudeau doctors to the fresh air of Saranac Lake, New York, in the Adirondacks, where they set up the nation's first TB research sanitorium. Garry's father, Francis Trudeau, was the town's family physician, a man with grave responsibilities and appropriately sober mien. He once informed his son: "Life is not something to be enjoyed, so just get on with it," a statement so splendid and outrageous it would eventually find its way into *Doonesbury*.

Francis Trudeau was dignified and reserved, and a father figure to an entire city. "I would hear him leave the house at four A.M., sometimes in snowshoes. I knew even then that the sense of mission was too big for me to take on."

Eleven years ago, Francis called his son into his den, handed him a medical book, and asked him to read an entry on a relatively rare illness called amyloidosis. "Now," Francis said, "as you can see from the prognosis at the bottom of the page . . ." That is the way Garry learned his father was dying.

We're sitting on the roof deck of Trudeau's studio, talking about the cartoonist's famous aversion to publicity. The conversation goes right to his father.

"Late in his career, he was sued by a patient. He didn't share it with me for three years. It was nothing, just a nuisance suit that was thrown out, but it shattered him to have his integrity challenged in a public forum. I grew up in a household where reputation was placed above all else."

So?

"So it helped me when fame was introduced into the mix."

There's a difference between reputation and image, Trudeau explains. "These get confused in people's minds," he says, but one involves character, the other public relations.

"I just refused to get entangled by issues of image maintenance that fame implied. I made a deliberate retreat from a publicly visible life."

What resulted was an unusual guy with a wall between his public and private selves, a guy who is intellectually fearless but so personally unassuming, Jane Pauley says, "that he's afraid to return a shirt that's the wrong size."

"Inside Garry, there's a little boy and a man," Pauley says. "And the little boy is secretive and vulnerable, and the man isn't. It would hurt him if I made a joke at his expense, but if the president of the United States says something negative about him, he puts it on the cover of his book."

———————

"SUFFICE IT TO say that I hold him in utter contempt."

This is John McCain, the former prisoner of war, speaking about Trudeau on the floor of the U.S. Senate in 1995. He was angered by a *Doonesbury* strip suggesting that presidential candidate Bob Dole was exploiting his war injury for political gain. That was then. This past year, it was McCain who wrote the introduction to Trudeau's *Long Road Home,* a for-charity book compiling the strips about B.D.'s injury and recovery.

A curious thing has happened to Trudeau's image as a result of the B.D. subplot—nothing the cartoonist could have predicted. The predictable, in fact, happened almost immediately: Calling Trudeau a "committed leftist," Fox News Channel host Bill O'Reilly wrote in an online column that "a case can be made that Trudeau is attempting to sap the morale of Americans vis-à-vis Iraq by using a long-running, somewhat beloved cartoon character to create pathos."

O'Reilly doesn't talk about Trudeau anymore. He can't, really.

We're in Tucson, at the National Leadership Conference of the Vietnam Veterans of America, where Trudeau is about to take the stage to receive the group's award for excellence in the arts. These are fifty- and sixtysomething guys, many with ponytails, tattoos, ample guts, and an attitude. They weren't treated right; they want better for new vets, returning home scarred.

This is a potentially tricky audience for Trudeau's acceptance speech. As they've aged, their politics have moved rightward, and many of them have a lingering distaste for antiwar talk, particularly from people they might consider draft dodgers. (Back in 1970, Trudeau pulled a disastrously low draft-lottery number—27, which he later bestowed on his slacker surfer-dude character, Zonker, in the strip. Trudeau wound up getting a medical deferment because of old stomach ulcers that hadn't given him trouble for years, and haven't since. His dad the doctor suggested he try that.)

As apolitical as the B.D. story is, elsewhere in the strip Trudeau regularly unleashes his disgust for the Iraq War and the man who is waging it. Trudeau's time at Yale overlapped with George W. Bush's—he knew him slightly and disliked him even then, largely for what he saw as a sense of smug entitlement ("all noblesse and no oblige"). In the strip, often on Sundays, with maximum readership, Trudeau just *kills* Bush. One Sunday this year, Michael Doonesbury and his old friend Bernie were discussing the Iraq War and wondering whether it keeps the president awake at night because of its enormous human toll. In the final panel, Trudeau cuts to a signature exterior nighttime view of the White House. From inside come two dialogue balloons: "What's wrong, dear?" And: "It's the stem cells. I hear their cries."

So is Trudeau going to play it safe in this speech and stay away from politics? I'm apparently not the only one wondering. The instant the cartoonist rises to take the mike, a large American flag behind him suddenly and inexplicably crashes to the ground. From a group of organizers near me comes a whisper, "Oh shit, not a good sign."

The speech starts benignly, praising the courage of the soldiers he had met, but here's how Trudeau wraps it up:

> When I talk to wounded veterans, I usually don't ask them what they think the mission was. I don't presume, because their lives are wrenching enough without the suggestion that their sacrifices may have been without meaning. Moreover, if that is so, it will become apparent to them soon enough . . . The young men and women who we've repeatedly put in harm's way are paying the price for this misbegotten mission, and as long as it continues, I, like so many of our countrymen, must walk this strange line between hating the war but honoring the warrior. I don't know how long we can keep it up . . .

He finishes to a standing ovation.

If there had been any lingering antipathy to Trudeau in this crowd, the story of B.D. appears to have wiped it out. It's as though he's been in the jungle with these guys.

THE TUCSON HEAT has dropped all the way to 90 degrees at night. In a patio outside the convention hotel, Vietnam veterans are slow-dancing with their wives, in a mournful shuffle, to a live band's version of "A Whiter Shade of Pale."

> *She said, There is no reason, and the truth is plain to*
> *see . . .*

If there is one thing this convention has made plain, it's that plenty of Vietnam vets still live with the madness of that war, still suffer from PTSD. You can hear it in their stories, read it in their eyes. It won't be different in this war. B.D.'s story is fiction, but it is true.

Inside at the bar, Trudeau and I have taken shelter from the heat. We're discussing whether he believes in God ("Why should I? Is there anything in the last five years in particular that suggests to you a divine purpose to life?") and whether he thinks Bush is evil or just stupid. ("I think he is smart but willfully ignorant, and he uses his ignorance for strategic advantage, which is appalling. He substitutes belief for thought. It protects you from self-doubt.") The only fact marring the sepulchral seriousness of this conversation is that it is occurring as we sit side by side on full-size western saddles, mounted on poles, facing the bar. There's an enthusiastic cowboy theme here. You can take only so much of that, so we grab our drinks, dismount and mosey on over to a table.

Trudeau claims that he never thinks about *Doonesbury* unless he is actually drawing it; it may be true, but it's misleading. He's a born listener, and, in a sense, he is always thinking about *Doonesbury* and filing things away.

At the table is a filmmaker named Chuck Lacy, who just produced a documentary called *The War Tapes,* which followed three National Guardsmen to Iraq and back home. Lacy is saying there is something about this war unlike any other in history. The Internet has made it possible for soldiers to be in country, in a theater of war, but still communicate daily with their families, in real time, sometimes with video.

Is that good or bad? Trudeau asks.

Both, says Lacy: The soldiers say it's their lifeline, but it's also a terrible drain on their emotions; they're dealing not only with their own anxieties but also with the anxieties of their families 6,000 miles away. It can be surreal. They'll come back from a firefight and then try to resolve a mortgage problem.

A few weeks after returning from Tucson, I opened the newspaper to *Doonesbury* and saw this.

It was Day One of what would be a funny, oddly disturbing week of the strip, in which Ray tries to stay alive while placating his wife and stepson back at the home front. I immediately e-mailed Trudeau. Until I told him, he said, he hadn't remembered exactly where the idea came from.

———

"CLINTON MADE A mistake in letting 'Don't ask, don't tell' be the defining issue of his first month in office, to be followed by the health-care disaster. He should have gone directly to welfare reform. It was intellectually dishonest to say the existing system was working. If welfare had been his biggest priority . . ."

We are on the plane heading back to New York, and Trudeau

is in his geek-drone mode. He is a highly opinionated public policy wonk, and this sort of thing just happens from time to time. When he reads a book, he edits in the margins, correcting errors of grammar, syntax, or cloudy thinking.

Bingo. Trudeau's a nerd! It's no big deal, but I'll take it. Negative assessments are important when you write profiles, but with this guy they've been hard to come by. He's generous with his time, gracious to everyone, and shrewd with me. I tried to bait him, asking where a dillweed like him gets off having the nerve to date Candice Bergen (he did, way back when) and then marry America's Sweetheart? I was hoping for an unattractive defense of his virility, but Trudeau wouldn't bite.

Finally, in desperation, I decided to get help from America's greatest living satirist. What would Trudeau ridicule, if the subject were himself?

Basically, he says, though not in so many words—he's a bully.

"Occasionally, people accuse me of courage," he says. "And that's wrong. I'm sitting on a perch of safety. Cartoonists have a tar-baby immunity. The more people react to us, and the more angrily they react, the better it is for us. So we're invulnerable. It just doesn't seem fair."

The first George Bush learned that the hard way. When *Doonesbury* accused him of having "put his manhood in a blind trust" after becoming vice president and changing his politics to match Reagan's, Bush repeatedly lashed out at the cartoonist— at least five times between 1984 and 1988. ("Garry Trudeau is coming out of deep left field. The American people are going to be speaking out, and we are going to see whether they side with *Doonesbury* or the Reagan-Bush message." "He speaks for a bunch of brie-tasting, Chardonnay-sipping elitists.") This blowback further elevated Trudeau's stature and made Bush seem like a petulant, humorless old fud.

As the plane begins its descent to LaGuardia, Trudeau remembers something interesting, something from his teens, when he had a summer job working at *Time* magazine.

"As I was walking out the building one day on my lunch break, two-thirds of a block away this spectacularly beautiful young woman in a very short miniskirt was walking toward me . . ."

Not sure where this is going, but I'm taking notes as fast as I can.

"She was in her early twenties. I was sixteen and looked all of twelve. You could feel it in the air, her coming at you. Her presence was destabilizing the street for a one-block radius. Guys were gawking, cars were slowing. This woman was a menace. She was walking in a confident way, with a swing to her hips. I was geeky and shy, too shy to make eye contact. I wouldn't even have known what to *do* with eye contact. My discomfort must have been obvious because, as she passes me, she leans over, her breath is warm, and she softly . . . *growls* in my ear."

Wow.

"I thought to myself: I've just been handed the most extraordinary gift. She showed such wisdom, with such a generous use of power. She just changed the life of a young boy. I thought, Anything is possible."

Trudeau sits back in his seat, smiles. "So I guess you could connect the dots to Jane, actually."

Or you could extrapolate it to the entirety of his life, the whole improbable arc of it, the combination of a fundamental humility and humanity empowered by an otherwise inexplicable, blazing self-confidence. You could find, in one moment from a man's teens, the entire key to who he is and the unlikely, monumental achievement of his professional life.

I vocalize some of this. Trudeau just looks at me.

Okay, we'll just stick with connecting the dots to Jane.

———

TRUDEAU IS A Yankees fan, so we're catching a Sunday afternoon game at Yankee Stadium against the White Sox. Some people's lives just seem to be charmed, and so it's not surprising that this afternoon turns out to be historic—Yankees great Mariano Rivera comes in with a 6-4 lead and closes out the last two innings for the 400th save of his career.

At one point, Trudeau's attentions turn to the ballpark itself—specifically, the facing of the mezzanine deck, a long, narrow strip that, as in many modern stadiums, is used as an electronic crowd-hooching display board. "The dimensions are about one to twenty," Trudeau says, "but see how much they get out of it, how much they say with just a suggestion? That's great use of design."

Trudeau's got a master's degree in graphic design. It was his first career choice until *Doonesbury*—a success right from his college newspaper days—made everything else moot. Design remains, to this day, the thing Trudeau longs to be doing. In all the time we'd spent together, the only artwork of his that he'd shown me with any particular pride were *Doonesbury*-themed coasters, cups, T-shirts, and figurines that he had designed for free. They wound up raising $1 million for a Starbucks-sponsored reading charity. It was a subtle piece of work, marrying the Starbucks corporate logos and design with the *Doonesbury* characters.

"I had more flow as a designer," Trudeau explains. "I could just drop down into the zone and stay there for hours. With cartooning, I'm constantly coming up for air, procrastinating, looking for reasons not to be doing it. I spend all day granting myself special dispensation, with 'creative process' as my cover story. Carpenters and deli countermen can't do that, so I think they may feel better about themselves at the end of the day."

Midway through the game, Trudeau's younger son shows up. Tommy, twenty, a student at Brown, has a summer job in the Yankees' front office. He gets to fraternize with the players and play pickup softball games with coworkers in the outfield, from which he's hit balls into the upper deck. Not bad, for a summer job.

Pauley and Trudeau's two other children, twins Ross and Rickie, are twenty-two. Ross graduated from Brown and is heading off on a teaching career; his sister, a Yalie, wants to be a pop singer, which worries Trudeau more than a little.

He played me an audio file of Rickie singing Alicia Keys's "If I Ain't Got You." Kid's definitely got the voice. It's all personality. Trudeau knows this but also knows the odds against success in that business. "I want her to follow her passion," he says, "but I just hope she's sturdy enough."

It's an interesting worry for a guy who could easily have been a doctor in a long-established family practice, but chose cartooning despite certain initial practical obstacles, such as a basic inability to draw. Being a father inspires a completely different risk-aversion calculus.

As we leave the stadium, the three of us are joined at the subway by Ross, who was sitting elsewhere with friends. The camaraderie between father and sons is effortless and unencumbered. The whole family thing seems almost comic-strippy perfect, like Dagwood and Blondie and Cookie and Alexander. Only this is a real family, not to mention a *Doonesbury* family, so you know you're going to have some complexity, somewhere.

JANE PAULEY IS still beautiful, at fifty-five, and she still projects frank vulnerability, or vulnerable frankness, or whatever is that subtle combination of qualities that made her America's preeminent morning-show host in the 1980s. We're meeting for breakfast because there is something Trudeau wouldn't really talk about, and Pauley will.

In 2001, Pauley nearly lost her mind. After receiving steroids to control a case of the hives, she began doing oddly intense things. How intense? She bought a house one day, for no good reason, on impulse, from an ad on the Web. Misdiagnosed with depression, she was hospitalized under an assumed name, to protect her privacy. Eventually, she was found to have a bipolar disorder—triggered but not caused by the steroids—for which she is still undergoing treatment. Pauley chronicled her struggle in a 2004 memoir, *Skywriting*.

Trudeau was largely absent from *Skywriting*, and he had been guarded with me about the effect of Pauley's illness on him and the family. He volunteered only two things: "I was told by a doctor that forty percent of marriages just don't survive it, so from the beginning I knew we were up against something really significant"; and, "The disease subverts your basic survival instinct in the sense that the people who you need to help you survive are the same people you are attacking."

So that's what I ask Pauley about.

"Yes," she says dryly, "there is a free-floating anger that needs a target and *will* find one."

For a year or so, Pauley says, before her symptoms were under control, Trudeau and the family lived with her irrational rages. The twins were hunting for colleges, Trudeau was pressed by deadline after deadline, and Mom was a fulminating piece of work—demanding, histrionic, impossible. "It was just incredible torment for them," Pauley says. "Garry was keeping the house together. It has to have been the most painful part of his life."

Pauley has recovered with the help of lithium, a drug she says she will be on for the rest of her life. Things are mostly fine, she says, except for some side effects, such as a persistent tremor to the hands. She looks murderously at her coffee cup, which the waiter has overfilled, almost to the brim.

"For example, I can't risk trying to pick that up."

Pauley thinks the story of B.D. has been something special, the best work Trudeau has ever done. And then she says,

"I don't think he's consciously aware that it has anything to do with me."

With . . . her?

Pauley smiles. "Garry's mind is very compartmentalized. The department doing the strip in his brain is not directly connected to the husband part, but . . ."

Pauley takes a forkful of scrambled eggs.

". . . it defies credulity that on some level it is not present in his work. What is he writing about, really? He's writing about mental illness, and how it's possible to find a way out of it, with help. It's very hopeful."

I start to say that Trudeau has never made that connection to me, in fact denies that his private life ever intrudes into the strip. But Pauley is ahead of me.

"He'll want to say no, but it's hard to argue with. Isn't it?"

TRUDEAU'S GREATEST WORK is coming at a time when *Doonesbury* is fading a bit from the national consciousness. He's still in six hundred newspapers, but that number has been higher; there simply aren't as many newspapers as there once were, and their readership is dwindling. Young adults who know *Doonesbury* today are mostly picking it up haphazardly from the Web. The *Doonesbury* compilation books are not selling the way they used to.

Trudeau is considering experimenting with sophisticated animation, for *Doonesbury* online. He's just finished a screenplay, a comedy about a teenager who is elected mayor of a small town. His newest *Doonesbury* compilation—*The War Within*, about B.D. dealing with his mental health issues—has just hit the bookstores, and a second compilation, *Heckuva Job, Bushie!*, is due out this month.

Since I last saw him, the investigative cartoonist traveled

to New Orleans to see the hurricane desolation firsthand. This past September 11, as politicians on both sides sought political traction in a battle of coordinated outrage and strategic shows of grief, the meatheads took in pro wrestling at Madison Square Garden. (In the main event, Vince McMahon defeated Triple H with the help of a folding chair.)

And week after week in the newspapers, the quite remarkable story of B.D. continues. Check out this one.

Let's see what's going on here. B.D. appears to be considering cheating on Boopsie. It's surprising, but maybe not that surprising. From the swiftness and specificity of Celeste's reaction, it's clear that she—the secretary at the vets' clinic—has seen this sort of behavior before. Can it be that many vets who've lost a limb might well be tempted to assert their manhood in unwise ways? But see how nimbly Celeste deals with it, in what one might call a generous use of power? She redirects B.D.'s attention to what's really important, reproaching him for hitting on her, but in a way that leaves his vulnerable dignity intact.

There are many types of therapy, and it's not all dispensed by licensed professionals.

Four panels. Forty-eight words. Funny, too.

Meanwhile, the same day, in *Blondie*, Dagwood and Herb go fishing, but Dagwood is so hungry he eats the bait!

You Go, Girl

This story is the truth, but every single emotion I pretend to have in it is a lie.

September 12, 1999

S OME PEOPLE GET all weepy when their children leave home for college, but not me. Children are supposed to grow up and move away. It's no big deal.

So I shed no tears on the final week of summer vacation when I drove my daughter, Molly, to the University of Pennsylvania, where she and a roommate will live. Their dorm room would fit two Volkswagens and a wheelbarrow. The air inside is suffocating. The decor is Kmart. The carpet is septic. The place reminds you of those hotel rooms in the movies where stubbled gangsters in ribbed undershirts and fedoras hide from the fuzz while a neon sign blinks outside. Molly's walls are a shade of paint that Sherwin-Williams could market as "Dingy Yellow." Or "You'll-Never-Take-Me-Alive Copper."

Molly took one look around and was giddily happy.

So I am happy. That is the way it is supposed to work, and it is working fine, in my case.

Molly's roommate is from Chicago. Within minutes of meeting, the two women were bouncing around campus, their lives already jubilantly intertwined. It seems odd to use this term, women. I know it is the accepted designation for eighteen-year-old human females, the legally correct word, a word sanctioned by the restroom doors at some of the nation's finest institutions of higher education. But until a few days ago, or so it seems, I was wiping strained prunes off this woman's chin.

I am disoriented but not dismayed. The whole point of being a parent is to reach this moment. You spend eighteen years encouraging your daughter to be independent, even headstrong, and when she strides away confidently on her own, you should feel good. And I do.

The University of Pennsylvania is in Philadelphia, and on the day I arrived, the local newspapers reported that a sicko was stalking the streets. He is believed to have raped several women and killed at least one. Molly is unworried; when you choose to live in a big city, she informs me, you must accept certain risks.

Molly chose this city, and worked hard for it, and got it. My daughter usually does what she needs to get what she wants. When she began to drive, she angled for a deal: We would allow her to come and go as she pleased, within reason, so long as she used good judgment, never lied about her whereabouts, and maintained high grades. She did all those things, and a deal was a deal. So there was many a night when Molly came home after our bedtime, and that was okay with me. I was comfortable and confident as I lay there downstairs on the couch, inches from the door, beneath an old clock ticking loudly in the stillness, awaiting her step on the stair. I am also comfortable and confident about her safety in Philadelphia.

I have not told Molly to be careful out there, because she already knows it, and besides, no one tells Molly what to do. To use the ladies' room at her dorm, she must walk down a long hall and up a flight of stairs. There is a bathroom right across from her room, but it is labeled for use by men only. Instantly, Molly announced that she would regard this designation to be optional.

For the last two years, Molly has volunteered at a firehouse, dressed in a baggy blue uniform, riding the ambulances. She wants to be a doctor, and at the youngest allowable age she became a licensed emergency medical technician. One night she came home from work with blood on her, and a story: A car had hit a bridge abutment at high speed, and people were gravely injured. Molly had been ordered to ride to the hospital with a man whose leg was snapped in two at the thigh; her job was to be a human traction splint, tugging his bones into place as he moaned and whimpered.

She was not yet seventeen. Her mother and I hugged her and asked if she was okay.

"*Okay?*" she said. "This was the greatest day of my life."

Molly is small and pretty, and from time to time she took some crap from the guys at the fire station, the usual bawdy banter and good-natured lechery. But when Montgomery County mounted an official investigation into alleged sexual harassment there, she declined to be interviewed. I asked her why. "It's a *firehouse,* Dad," she said, rolling her eyes.

Her eyes are slightly blue but mostly gray, precisely the color of the door of van Gogh's bedroom at Arles. A reproduction of that painting hangs on the wall of Molly's bedroom, which I am pacing right now. The room almost echoes. It is half empty, and tidy for the first time in my memory because her mother spent hours after Molly left fanatically cleaning and recleaning it, explaining all the while how she, too, is untroubled by Molly's departure. It's no big deal, we agreed.

I notice that Molly has not taken her baseball glove. The stitching is frayed, the knots are undone, and part of the heel has been gnawed by our dog. I kept offering to buy her a new one, but she refused, explaining that a glove is supposed to be old and weathered.

Molly never cared much for sports until a few years ago, when she and I began watching Yankees games together. In the beginning she understood only the rudiments, but it's gotten so she can tell you the best pitch on which to execute a hit and run with a lefty at the plate and one out.

Molly thinks certain rules of baseball should be changed to make the game better. She calls her new, improved version "Mol-lyball," and here is how it works: When a fielder makes a valiant lunge at a ball, even if he misses, or when a player runs really hard to first base, even if he is out, he is awarded a point for effort. If you accumulate enough points, your team gets an extra run. Also, if a player slides and gets his uniform dirty, he is afforded reasonable time to go to the clubhouse and change. Also, really handsome players like Derek Jeter get an extra strike. Also, there are trees in the outfield. Because they look nice.

Playing catch with me in the back yard, Molly learned to snare anything within her reach. She has a good, strong arm. As we slung the ball back and forth, I invented bases-loaded-bottom-of-the-ninth clutch fielding scenarios, the way fathers and sons have done forever. Molly got into it, or pretended to for my sake.

I always felt Molly and I were particularly close, but she kept me guessing, right from the get-go. When she uttered her first word, she pointed at me and said "da-da." I was elated. A few seconds later, she said "da-da" again and pointed at the toilet.

It is that way with children. You never really know what they are thinking. You try to give them no reason not to love you, and hope for the best.

Molly and I haven't played catch for a while, because she was preparing to leave for college and had friends to visit and things to do. Experts will tell you that a child about to leave the home will sometimes become cold and detached, and even precipitate fights with her parents. No malice is intended; they are unconsciously trying to create a distance that will make the leaving easier. Molly did this. Like everything she does, she did it magnificently.

When I kissed her goodbye at school, I told her to take care and she told me to take care, and that was that.

Back home, I picked up a baseball and her ratty old glove and went out in the back yard. It was starting to drizzle, which was good because we needed the rain. I began to play catch with myself, underhanding the ball and basketing it like Willie Mays.

Each time, I threw it harder, and when I could get the ball no higher, I began throwing overhand, again and again, stupidly hard, trying for greater and greater height even after my shoulder began to ache. I was grunting with each throw, and finally the ball was so slick with rain that I lost control of it and it sailed away and came down in the middle of a thick stand of bamboo on the edge of my property. The treetops are dense with foliage, and the ball was swallowed up. It didn't hit the ground. It probably caught on something: a latticework of branches, maybe, or a squirrel's empty nest.

It must still be up there. I never found it. It's no big deal.

None of the Above

Years ago, as an election approached, I wrote a humor column proposing the formation of a "Non-voters Party." My theory was that, since they'd represent fully 50 percent of the U.S. population, the Nonvoters Party would instantly become a political powerhouse, the largest voting bloc in history. Yes, the theory has a certain logical flaw, which the column cheerfully and pointedly ignored.

The basic idea stuck with me, though: Who are these tens of millions of people who are so comfortable with their laziness, ignorance, and apathy?

By the end of my visit with Ted Prus, I had to rethink almost every assumption I'd made about the American nonvoter.

October 31, 2004

ON THE MORNING of Monday, September 13, a white Ford truck with a grouchy engine pulled out of a garage in Muskegon, Michigan, and headed toward the airport. Many other vehicles were going in the same direction—cars and vans and caravans of buses chartered for the day. Up in the sky, somewhere to the east, an airplane was en route as well, carrying the president of the United States.

In just an hour or so, the airport would play host to some grass-roots politics at its grassiest—a presidential appearance in a key region of a battleground state in an election some think will be too close to call.

Muskegon is a hurtin' place. Its downtown is desolate, the most impressive landmark being a pair of enormous sand dunes, six stories high, in an empty lot right across from the tattoo parlor. They're pulverized concrete, all that remains of a downtown mall that was returned into dust after the businesses fled for the burbs.

The city needed a boost, and the president needed a forum that mattered; hence, this convergence at the airport. If the heady populism of the day was tempered a bit by elitist logistics—attendance was invitation-only, invitations only going to the Republican faithful—few of the invitees seemed to mind. Two thousand Bush supporters, faces beaming, were trundling toward the airport in all those vehicles.

The face in the cab of the old white truck, however, was not beaming. It was resolute. Its eyes were flinty and business-like. The truck was a coughing, irascible mess. If this had been a movie, the music would have swelled ominously, because, from a cinematic perspective, the man at the wheel looked less like a presidential supporter than like a presidential assassin.

This was real life, however, and at the last minute, the truck turned harmlessly west, away from the airport, down a residential lane and into a driveway. Out walked Ted Prus, masonry worker, with a hammer in his hand. Ted's job for the day was to help turn a big old hole in the ground into someone's garage.

The president's job for the day was to deliver a speech on health care, a subject on which Ted might well have taken an interest. Ted is thirty-seven and makes $15 an hour, unless it rains, in which case he makes nothing. His main experience with health care is not having it—a situation that, despite his youthful appearance, is not exactly irrelevant.

Twice in the last few years, Ted had seizures that left him unconscious. Once, it happened on the banks of a river he was fishing; had his best friend, Brian, not been there to drag him out of the water, he likely would have drowned. Ted could barely scrape together the $400 a doctor charged him to tell him that she didn't know what was wrong with him and that he'd have to see a specialist. The specialist was out of the question, financially, so Ted just keeps his fingers crossed and worries about those frequent headaches.

Ted also has no dental insurance. This, too, is not irrelevant. A few years ago, when a balky molar began to bark, Ted did not see a dentist. Instead, he says, he sat in his kitchen, loosened the tooth with a pocket knife and then yanked it out with pliers from his tackle box.

The presidential appearance had been all over the news in Muskegon for more than a week, but Ted hadn't heard about it until the day before, and only because someone told him. He doesn't read the papers much, except for NASCAR results and sometimes the classifieds. On TV, he watches the Weather Channel or the farm reports.

It was a nice day. As Ted wielded his hammer, something amazing happened, something that a hack writer—an abuser of clichés searching for a perfect moment soaked in irony and pregnant with meaning—would not dare make up. *Air Force One* roared directly overhead.

Ted didn't even look up. Because, when it comes to politics, as Ted will tell you himself, he just doesn't give a rat's ass.

MOST AMERICANS WHO are eligible to vote, don't. It may be hard to believe, and harder to accept, but the numbers are inescapable.

In recent presidential elections—the quadrennial events that are the pinnacle for voter turnout—roughly half the potential voting population chose not to exercise its franchise. For some off-year elections, barely a quarter of eligible voters show up. Even this year's ballyhooed spike in registration is considered unlikely to boost turnout to 60 percent, or anywhere near.

In short, there is no political force more to be reckoned with, no constituency potentially more influential, no voting bloc potentially mightier, than those who are too lazy or indifferent or disaffected or angry to go to the polls. The candidate of a Nonvoters Party would win in a cakewalk. You know, theoretically.

The voice of their silence is deafening. It may be, as some studies suggest, that their political preferences would mirror those of voters, anyway. But the sheer number of nonvoters is so great that, in a close election, even the most minuscule difference in their pattern of preference could be decisive. If only they would vote.

Nonvoting is, many say, a national disgrace. The United States is practically first among world democracies in voter apathy: Only Switzerland has lower turnout in elections to choose its leaders, but Switzerland is a case unto itself. The Swiss don't care all that much about who governs them, because, in a sense, they govern themselves: Almost every significant issue of public policy is put to a plebiscite.

There's no such ready explanation for what happens here; in fact, it defies intuition. Over the last half-century, many of the historical impediments to voting have been lifted—educational opportunities have improved among all demographics; Jim Crow laws that disenfranchised southern blacks have been taken off the books; complicated registration procedures have been streamlined. And yet, since 1960, voting rates have been steadily declining.

Political scientists point to several reasons, among them the ascendancy of negative campaigning, which tends to sour voters on the candidates and on politics in general. Some cite the fact that, in the era of cable TV, we have too many choices of where we obtain our information, making it easier to ignore politics in favor of entertainment. Actually, politics used to *provide* entertainment; historians have observed that in other eras, people felt about their parties much as they do today about their sports teams. Turn-of-the-century urban political clubs sponsored neighborhood athletic teams, and their meeting houses served as social clubs. That sort of generations-long loyalty and blind partisan devotion is gone, even among the politically astute. Involvement in all civic areas has declined.

Most political experts see low voter turnout as a problem to be fixed. Earnest citizen-advocacy literature—the sort of things passed out at polling places and party headquarters—makes the passionate argument that every vote counts. Those documents tend to include long, familiar lists of important matters decided by one vote (Thomas Jefferson wins the presidency; Texas enters the Union; France becomes a republic). Unfortunately, such examples, while well intentioned, are bogus. All of the "elections" cited are not popular votes but votes within legislatures, where one-vote majorities are not only commonplace but typically are illusory—the deliberate result of leadership compromises on issues.

Every vote, to be impolitic, does *not* count and never has. In America, no presidential election, no gubernatorial election, no U.S. senatorial election has ever been decided by a single vote at the polls.

All of this raises a valid, if impertinent question: When it comes to voting or not voting, why should any individual give a rat's ass?

One of the more intriguing books about nonvoting, *To Vote or Not to Vote,* actually begins by wondering why anyone votes at all. Author André Blais tries to answer this question by applying the modern economist's favorite scientific model, the Rational Choice Theory. Rational Choice analyzes human decision-making based on a fairly simple mathematical cost-benefit ratio. Blais, who is a Rational Choice acolyte, winds up basically throwing up his hands. The costs of voting (registering, going to the polls, waiting in line, etc.) so outweigh any palpable benefits (no vote is ever likely to directly influence anything) that the model essentially falls apart.

Can it be that those who don't vote are the most rational among us? If a single vote is without influence, isn't casting one illogical?

Mathematically speaking, sure. Even in Florida, even in 2000, the breathtakingly narrow margin in the official vote tally was hundreds of times larger than one person's vote.

But there is something profoundly unsettling about the idea that voting is, basically, senseless. That may be because mathematical logic is not the only type of rigorous reasoning. Moral and political philosophers have spent centuries mulling civic duties and obligations. Perhaps that's the place to look for guidance, because deciding whether to vote is not so much a question of math as a matter of morals.

Immanuel Kant, the eighteenth-century German philosopher, lived in an era of monarchy; his works never directly addressed the issue of voting. But he addressed, at great length, issues of moral responsibility. In his treatise on the Categorical Imperative, Kant concluded that all human actions, if moral, must be taken not to achieve what is best for you, or even to accomplish a particular result you desire. The moral act, he said, is the one which, if universalized, would result in the greatest good. In other words, in a given situation, minor or momentous, the moral person acts the way he would want everyone to act if they were faced with a similar choice.

What would happen if, literally, not a single person voted? Jefferson's Grand Experiment ends in ignominy. Anarchy reigns. Regional warlords rise to power in a return to a feudal state. There are medieval codes of honor, indentured servitude, after-dinner floggings.

Hence, Kant would argue, the only moral choice is to vote.

Implicitly, we understand this. In a totalitarian state, voting is a distant dream; in a democracy, it is a civic obligation. But that still leaves the United States with low voter turnout, for which we have no ready explanation.

All we have are more questions: Since nonvoters tend to be less politically knowledgeable than voters—all polls confirm this—might it not be worse if these particular people cast an ignorant ballot? Who needs them?

And: If voting is a matter of morals, and America practically leads the world in nonvoting, are we an amoral country? Is something else in play?

To help find the answers, we decided to talk to a typical non-voter. Unfortunately, since half of America doesn't vote, it's no more possible to find a "typical" nonvoter than it would be to find a "typical" woman. So, instead, this is what we did.

We asked the *Washington Post* pollsters to generate a list of people who, when telephoned in the last few months for their political views, had identified themselves as nonvoters. This was basically a list of discarded calls; no one conducting political preference polls particularly cares what nonvoters think. We did.

We took a list of ninety-odd names, eliminated those people who were not from battleground states (we wanted people with *resonant* nonvotes), and then started telephoning. To eliminate any bias in our choice, we decided to profile the very first person who agreed. The first name on the list, as it happens, was Ted Prus. Here is how the call went.

"Hi. This is the *Washington Post*. Are you registered to vote?"

"No."

"Are you planning on voting?"

"No."

"We'd like to write a long story about you. Would you be interested? It would make you famous."

"You mean a famous idiot?"

"Actually, we're not sure. There's no guarantee one way or the other."

"Sounds good."

TED IS IN his truck and I am following in my rental car. We are driving to a restaurant of his choosing for a dinner on the *Washington Post*; price is no object. Muskegon is not renowned as a mecca of haute cuisine, but the Sardine Room does offer a robust $26 filet mignon, and for $49.99 you can get two lobster tails at Dockers Waterfront Cafe. Ted, however, has chosen Famous Dave's Bar-B-Que.

Ted's preferences are simple. He drinks Bud Light because he likes it; the importeds cost too much and taste skunky to him, anyway. He smokes Basics, which are generic cigarettes that don't jack up their price for fancy packaging or slick ad campaigns. He likes the Steve Miller Band because he can make out the damn words. He can do fancy, decorative stonemasonry—fireplaces and things like that—but it's a painstaking process, and he's impatient, so he prefers flatwork, which means pouring garages and sidewalks.

With Ted in the cab is Kim Miller, the woman with whom he has been living for nine years but whom he never married because neither of them sees any good reason to jump through that hoop. Between them is their six-year-old son, Slate, who got his name because it's unconventional and Ted wants his boy to be his own man, and because it's a construction material Ted respects for its hardness, and Ted wants his boy to grow up strong.

The truck pulls into the restaurant parking lot, then jerks to a stop. Ted bounces out of the cab and nods sourly toward the restaurant entrance, around which a few parties of three and four congregate. "Sorry," he explains, "I don't wait in lines."

He heads back to the truck. "It's okay. I know another place."

So we're off again, snaking through the residential streets of suburban Muskegon. We make a left, and then a right, and then a few more lefts and rights, until it becomes apparent that this trip won't be over anytime soon. Ted drives friskily. The scenery passes in a blur, including all the Kerry and Bush signs that dot the tidy front lawns but which go as unnoticed as crabgrass.

Finally, we arrive at a Chili's restaurant. The trip has taken exactly 19½ minutes, probably longer than the wait for a table at Dave's. But this place is half empty, and we can plop right down. Ted is happy. Me, too. Here is my first real sit-down chance to try to figure out Ted's politics, or lack thereof.

The first hypothesis to be explored was proposed by no less influential a political observer than columnist George Will, the bow-tied, sesquipedalian voice of American conservatism. Will and others have opined that low voter turnout is in some ways a *good* thing, that it prevents fickle swings in national policy since the least committed and knowledgeable voters tend to be more inflamed by momentary passions. More to the point, they say, it implies "good government"—a general satisfaction with how the country is going and how its leaders are doing.

Me: "Is America doing okay?"
Ted: "For the rich, maybe."
Me: "Well, what's the problem?"
Ted: "The guys in charge."
Me: "You like the other guys better?"
Ted: "No. All politicians are liars."

So much for George Will.

A Northwestern University study of people who do not vote—compiled into a 1999 book, *Nonvoters: America's No-Shows,* by Jack C. Doppelt and Ellen Shearer—confirms some intuitive impressions about the group. Interestingly, Ted seems to be remarkably typical. So does Kim. She doesn't vote, either, and for a lot of the same reasons.

Like the majority of nonvoters, Ted and Kim are between the ages of eighteen and forty-four, are white, have below-average incomes and high school educations. Moreover, they seem to fit into not just one but three of the five categories of nonvoter that the book identifies: They are "irritables" because they don't like the way most things in the country are going. They are "alienateds" because they mistrust and disbelieve politicians. And they are "unpluggeds" because they tune out the news.

> Me: "What have you heard about the presidential
>   campaign?"
> Ted: "When I was watching the farm report on TV
>   this morning, they mentioned something
>   about it."
> Me: "What was that?"
> Ted: "I don't know. I went to the bathroom to brush
>   my teeth."
> Me: "Why don't you guys watch the news?"
> Kim: "Too much war and crap."
> Ted: "It's too depressing. They're always talking about
>   everything bad."
> Kim: "Like whose head got chopped off."
> Ted: "If something's good, it doesn't make the news."

Ted takes a bite of the fried-onion appetizer: "They usually get the weather wrong, too."

Ted has a likable laugh, a heh-heh bark, punctuation to acknowledge irony.

Slate is winsome, an Opie Taylor type just shedding the last traces of a little-kid lithp. Kim, a green-eyed blonde, is disarmingly straightforward and friendly. Of the three, Ted is the most reserved. He is wiry-handsome, and with the baseball caps he favors, he's got the look of a veteran middle reliever, down to the stoic demeanor and the requisite mustache-and-goatee combo.

Many weeks, Ted pulls in less than $500, and Kim—who used to manage a video store—hasn't worked steadily since Slate was born. During times when construction work is light, they sometimes subsist on what Ted brings home from fishing and hunting and scavenging for wild mushrooms. The fungal forays are often done with Slate in tow because, being low to the ground, he's a better morel hunter.

It's a rule of thumb that mushrooms with insects crawling on them are the safe ones to eat. In Ted's world, that's just one of those homely facts of life you accept and live with if you're a survivor. Another is that life isn't always fair.

Ted and Kim live in Twin Lake, a blue-collar Muskegon suburb of 1,600. Until recently, their home was an apartment above John's Market, right under the big wooden sign advertising CHOICE MEATS COLD BEER WINE LIQUOR. Some months ago, the store got a new owner. John's is now owned by Deedar. Deedar Singh.

"Foreign guy," says Ted. He does an excellent imitation of the voice of Apu, the Indian convenience-store proprietor from *The Simpsons*.

Ted is not altogether happy with the influx of foreigners into the United States. He's heard that they don't even have to pay taxes for the first five years they live in this country. He's not sure where he heard it, but he's pretty sure it's true, and it just doesn't seem right.

No, it's not true, but Ted doesn't seem convinced. He is not easily shaken from his view of the world as an uneven playing field, and things keep happening to confirm it. Pretty quickly, Ted got into a rent dispute with Singh. It wound up in court, and Ted and Kim had to move.

To Ted, life is something that happens to you; sometimes it's good, sometimes not. And, as it happens, this turned out fine. Ted and Kim wound up buying a house together a few blocks away. Kim was married before, but this is the first home she's ever owned. Ted, too. It's a humble starter house—a two-bedroom, one-bath bungalow, less than 1,000 square feet, all told. The price came to $72,000, counting closing costs. The thing Ted remembers most about the closing is that when it was over, he got a check for $497. "They gave me money to buy my house!"

Ted doesn't know much about the intricacies of home financing, or cash-back transactions, and he never asked about this sudden bounty. It was just one of those things that happen.

The house may be small, but it's cozy, and the back yard is big—nearly an acre. So they've gotten themselves a pup, a friendly chow mix named Buddy. "We bought Slate a video game, but it's stayed on the shelf ever since we moved," Ted says. At first, it sounds like he is grumping about Slate's ingratitude. But then he says, matter-of-factly, "My son has a back yard now." Ted doesn't readily show emotion, even pride.

It's hard for me not to like Ted and Kim; they seem almost entirely without pretension.

The Chili's waitress delivers our entrees. They're still sizzling, served in cast-iron skillets, the handles of which are sheathed by cheerful little potholder sleeves.

"Look at those," Kim says. "That's a great idea. We could use those things on our frying pans."

I observe that Chili's is a big company and probably wouldn't mind losing a couple of those cheap little thingies.

Ted looks at Kim. Kim looks at Slate.

Probably happens all the time, I say. They probably just throw them out when they get dirty, anyway.

"No," Kim says.

"It's not worth feeling bad all the way home," Ted says.

"I can make us some," Kim decides.

As we leave, they ask me what my story is going to be about. I tell them I'm not really sure, that it's getting a little complicated.

Sunday morning, six-thirty. Ted and I meet to go fishing.

Other than his family, fishing is Ted's life. The rivers and creeks around Muskegon are churning with tasty life—trout, salmon, and walleye, mostly. Ted was born around here, in Hesperia, and he's been fishing since he was Slate's age. The area is still pretty much Prusville—driving around, Ted points out one home after another belonging to uncles and cousins and boyhood friends. You grow up here, you hunt and fish.

A few years ago, one of Ted's friends shot a 300-pound bear. He brought it home and skinned it, but he couldn't eat it, because lying there, naked, it looked like a big fat man. Worse: Bear hunting is illegal; someone ratted him out, and he got popped. State agents came to the door. Ted adopts an official-sounding voice: "We know you got a bear in there, sir." They took his hunting license for five years, so for five years, the poor guy would go out in the woods and watch Ted hunt.

After high school, Ted left for the Army and worked his hitch in Europe as a mechanic. When he came back, he moved to Tennessee, got married, had a son. Allen is now twelve and living with his mom in Tennessee, who remarried after the divorce. Allen visits Kim and Ted from time to time. When the boy's schoolwork began to slip, Ted refused to let him come until he improved. "He's in advanced math now," Ted says laconically in that same prideless tone that is full of pride.

We set out in the dark for Ted's secret fishing spot. Ted is happy to talk about politics, but he just frankly doesn't have all that much to say. If someone frog-marched him into a voting booth with a gun to his head, he says, he'd probably go for John Kerry over George Bush. That's because, as Ted sees it, Bush got where he is strictly on account of his father. It's just another example of the world being stacked in favor of the haves. "It's the same with NASCAR drivers," he says. "Just 'cause your dad was good at something doesn't mean you're good at it. Other people could do better, but the son gets the shot." Ted is no particular fan of Dale Earnhardt, Jr.

I point out that if Ted favors Kerry but doesn't vote, he's really voting for Bush. Ted doesn't see it that way. The way he sees it, a vote for either man is a vote for a liar, a member of the privileged class who will promise whatever it takes to get your vote and then do whatever it takes to keep the country safe for the privileged class. Screw 'em all.

What about voting as a moral issue? The only moral issue, Ted says, is the immorality of the guys asking for our votes: "I feel fine about myself. I can look at myself in the mirror and not feel bad about not voting."

I ask Ted if there are any circumstances under which he'd actually cast a ballot. Let's say, for example, that one of the candidates for governor of Michigan was a pantywaist animal rights activist who wanted to outlaw fishing. Would that, at last, bring Ted Prus to the polls?

Ted considers this: "No, because I wouldn't have to worry about that guy. Michigan wouldn't vote for him in the first place, because there's too much tourism based on fishing." If he'd lose anyway, Ted figures, why bother to vote against him?

And if, somehow, he won, and made good on his promise to ban fishing?

"I'd fish anyway." Heh-heh.

We stop for coffee and fishing tackle at a Twin Lake gas station owned by a friend of Ted's. On the shelves are Zig-Zag cigarette papers, which I've seen plenty of, and Zig-Zag tobacco, which I'm stunned to discover actually exists. A lot of people here roll their own. It's more economical.

The gas station seems to sell everything but gas. The pumps are closed. After we leave, Ted explains: Some months ago, the owner got into a price dispute with his gasoline supplier, and rather than cave in, he just turned off his pumps. He may be losing some money, but he sure got satisfaction.

Ted likes Twin Lake. He likes the people, especially.

Ted once actually tried voting. It was 1992, and he liked what he heard from Ross Perot. Perot seemed to be the only guy who was a straight shooter. So Ted registered, but when he got in the voting booth, he got confused. "The way they got it set up, with all kinds of levers and buttons, I'm not even sure who I voted for. And I didn't know half the names."

Didn't voting make him feel powerful, in a way?

"No, it made me feel stupid. I don't consider myself a stupid person, but I felt stupid."

We've left the blacktop and are jouncing over rutted paths on the back roads. I ask Ted what is the worst thing that ever happened to him.

"When my mom passed away. I was twenty-six."

Ted takes a sip of coffee.

"She shot herself."

It's quiet, out here in the woods. Only the shuddering of the truck over the ruts in the road. "She didn't die right away. She blinded herself. Afterwards my dad set up ropes from the sliding door on the back of the house to the lake, so she could still fish. She liked to fish, and that was one of the few things she could still do. She died a few months later."

Why did she do it?

"She was an alcoholic, and she was taking Prozac, and they don't mix."

That's all he knows. His mother wrote a suicide note, but Ted never saw it. Ted says he asked, but the cops said no, and he accepted that.

Ted's father has remarried; he still lives in the area. I ask Ted how his father took his mother's death.

"I don't know. We never really talked about it."

And Ted? How does he feel about it?

"I try to wipe it out of my memory."

We pull into Ted's secret fishing spot. It's getting light now.

"So, yeah, I guess that's the worst thing that ever happened to me," he says, grabbing the fishing gear from the bed of the truck.

———————

As WE WALK along the bank of the salmon stream, Ted's eyes are reading the water. They're a lot busier, his eyes, than when he was reading the menu at Chili's.

"You see that eddy over there?"

"Where?"

"There."

I see water.

"You see that dark spot?"

"Where?"

"There. The dark area where the rapids and the still water meet."

I see water.

"It's cold and deep. Something is hiding in there."

Ted baits my hook with a lure, helps me cast. As instructed, I reel it in, slowly. I cast again, reel it in. Again. One more time. Then Ted baits his hook and casts. The lure plops squarely into the area Ted was eyeballing.

All conversation has stopped. Ted is slowly drawing the lure back, the way I was, but a little faster and with more purpose. Also, he's holding his fishing line away from the rod, in his left hand, the line resting lightly against his fingertips, which are splayed as though he were playing a C chord on a guitar. He's feeling for nibbles at the other end.

Then he tenses, whips up on the rod, and zzzzzzzzzz, the reel starts spinning. Ted whoops and starts bringing in his catch. It fights tenaciously. He's breathing heavily by the time he draws it up onto the bank and into a net. She's a 32-inch, 10-pound salmon, so gravid her eggs are literally spilling out of her.

We fish for a while more, without luck, and Ted decides we've taken what this part of the stream has to offer. He heads farther downstream. He's carrying more than I am, but it's hard to keep up. Ted is uncannily sure-footed on the muddy riverbank.

As we are walking, I ask him if he has any thoughts on what happens to us after we die.

"After we die?" he says, not breaking stride.

"Right," I say. "What's after death?"

"Well, I am gonna be . . . what do they call it—incinerated?"

"Cremated?"

"Right, cremated. I'm going to be cremated after I die."

Apparently, that's all Ted has to say on the topic.

In a while, we find ourselves at another spot, beneath a bridge. Once again, I make a few futile casts. Then Ted tries. The ripples from the lure hitting the water haven't yet subsided when Ted gets a bite. Another whoop, another fight, another big fat salmon, 31 inches, this one male.

For the rest of the day, when passersby ask us how the fishing is, Ted impassively shows them the two monsters in the cooler in the back of the truck. He anticipates compliments and deflects them, simply reporting that he was using 25-pound test line and a Hottentot-type lure, as if that explains it. Out here in the woods, there is nothing confused or tentative about Ted. Magnanimously, he informs everyone that I, also, almost caught a fish, which is a mighty considerate lie.

Ted spends a lot of weekends here, alone or with friends. Sometimes, if he's feeling bad, he doesn't even fish. "I'll just dangle my foot in the crick. It's real cold, spring-fed, and I'll just relax and drink a beer, and the bad day goes away. I consider myself lucky, really. I got two healthy sons, and I get to hunt and fish." As he walks, Ted bends to pick up someone's discarded snack food wrapper. His truck is full of other people's garbage. He'd rather it be there than in the woods.

I ask him if he has any particular dream for the future. He says he'd love to be an outdoor guide, charging people money to take them hunting and fishing. He knows a man who makes $350 a day doing that, a figure he relates with near disbelief. Three hundred and fifty dollars a day, just to hunt and fish! But that requires a boat, which Ted can't afford, and it takes clientele, which he's not sure how to go out and get. Plus, Ted says, characteristically blunt, he's just not certain he's got the kind of swallow-hard-and-risk-it-all nerve to try something like that.

Ted's happy enough with the job he has. His dad has urged him to consider factory work, because it pays better and often has benefits. But factory jobs—"shop jobs," Ted calls them—keep you indoors, and he finds that asphyxiating. So he's holding fast at $15 an hour. He's pretty much living paycheck to paycheck and worries about meeting his $550 mortgage payment. That's just how it is, and Ted concedes it isn't likely to change very soon.

After the fishing is done, Ted takes me to a small dam in Hesperia, the town in which he grew up. He used to come here all the time back when he was a kid, and he still visits now and again. The dam is Hesperia's claim to fame.

It's quite a sight, actually. The dam controls the flow of the White River, which is the same river we'd been fishing downstream. Just a few feet past the dam wall, there's a two-foot-high concrete step over which the released water cascades. If you wait here long enough, on this far side of the dam, you're apt to see a sight most people never see in their lives.

We're standing and waiting, and there it is. It happens a couple of times. Salmon, swimming upstream to spawn, ignited by instinct and powered by unimaginable determination, will every so often make a run at the concrete step. In an instant, they flash out of the water and fling themselves up over the top of it.

It's glorious. But their triumph lasts only seconds. In front of them now is the dam wall, which no leap can surmount. So they just wash back over the step, plopping futilely down into the puddling river.

ON THIS SUNDAY evening, like many Sunday evenings, there's a party at Ted and Kim's house. Guests start arriving midafternoon, bearing beer and potluck dishes. Today, the main course will be fish—walleye that Ted caught the week before, and the two salmon he pulled out of the White River this morning. Cooking is usually a family affair; Kim prepares the side dishes, Ted bakes the fish, which Slate seasons with gusto.

The decor in their home mostly reflects Kim's tastes, which mostly reflect Kim: They are cheerful knickknacks and curios, unapologetically hokey—smiling trolls and lamps in the shape of owls and squirrels. Ted's touch is the plastic clock on the wall; it's got a picture of star NASCAR driver Mark Martin. Martin is an older guy who claims he once got cheated out of a lot of money by a sponsor; he failed, then came back strong.

Both Ted and Kim are NASCAR fans. Recently, they packed up a motor home and drove to Brooklyn, Michigan, for a NAS-CAR event with their friends Anna and John and Patty and Mike. Someone sneaked under the motor home and affixed a cardboard sign to the chassis that flapped down when it got jostled by the rumble of the road. It said HONK IF YOU'RE HORNY. Ted and Kim thought it was the darnedest thing how many people were waving and honking at them, until they figured it out. Some people might have been angry, but there isn't a touch of self-importance to Ted and Kim. They stopped and took a picture.

Patty and Mike are here tonight, and Anna and John, and Ted's brother, Tony, and their families. Kids are running around. The talk is loud and merry, and, because of me, there's some good-natured teasing going on. Someone prompts: "Tell him why you registered to vote, Ted."

Whoa. Ted *registered to vote?*

Yes, he concedes. Two weeks before, at NASCAR.

"Tell him why!"

Ted produces a T-shirt he says he got for free from Rock the Vote, in return for registering.

"That's not why!"

Kim agrees. The shirt was a different freebie. "Tell him!"

Ted is just laughing.

Anna taunts him, nanny-nanny-boo-boo style:

"Ted registered for earplugs."

Ted grins sheepishly. Yeah. He registered to vote, at NAS-CAR, so he could get free foam earplugs.

"Here's another nonvoter!" This is how Ted's friend, Troy Ropp, announces his arrival. Troy is thirty-seven, with flaming red hair and a backwoods beard. Troy used to work at a Herman Miller furniture factory, but he rose so far he got a semimanagement position, and he found it too distasteful to boss people around. So he runs his own tree service now.

I ask him about the election. Troy thinks President Bush made a bad mistake going into Iraq the way he did. There were other ways of solving the Saddam Hussein problem, he says. "They could have took Saddam out with a fifty-caliber at five hundred yards." Nods all around. A brief discussion of firearms ensues.

Troy seems to have given the issues of the day more thought than either Ted or Kim. It occurs to me that what we have here might be a statistical anomaly—a well-informed nonvoter. I press him on why he's not voting.

"Because I don't think my vote will matter." Plus, he says, politicians are all alike. "Bush is just like . . ." Troy pauses.

". . . like that guy he's running against."

"You mean Kerry?"

"Yeah."

I look at him, he looks at me. He laughs.

"I would have thought of it if you'd gave me a little time."

On an end table in the living room is a framed picture of a pretty brunette. It's Kim's best friend, Linda, who died last December, suddenly, of a brain aneurysm. Kim can't talk about Linda without tearing up. She'd feel even worse if she weren't sure that Linda is coming back, and she'll meet up with her some day. Some people come back as people, and some people come back as ghosts, Kim says. She knows because she's seen them.

"My old lady sees ghosts," Ted had told me out in the woods. I hadn't realized he meant it literally.

Kim knows it sounds kooky, but she sees what she sees. She thinks they could be visible to anyone, but you have to have your mind open to them or they'll float right past. Kim saw her first ghost up close about fifteen years ago—a Victorian-era school-girl in high-buttoned shoes. The ghosts are people who died in the houses that they haunt, she believes. Some are mischievous; sometimes they'll move Slate's toys or Kim's cigarettes. Kim says she's never been afraid of the ghosts, and in some way even finds them comforting; they are a sign, after all, of a sort of afterworld, that this life isn't all there is. Nothing is final, not even Linda's death.

Ted doesn't see the ghosts, and it wouldn't be fair to say that he humors Kim about it; he simply accepts it as he accepts many things—good-naturedly and without question. If it makes Kim happy, he says, it's fine with him. He sounds almost envious, the way agnostics sometimes talk about the devout.

The women stay inside, and most of the men repair to the back yard for more beer and horseshoes and shooting the bull. Ted tells the others how I took a salmon egg right out of the fish's butt and plopped it in my mouth. This meets with some incredulity. I explain that in big-city Japanese restaurants, ten or twelve of those suckers on a piece of seaweed will sell for $4. There's some derisive laughter at the expense of big-city idiots.

Ted's friends then start ragging on him, teasing him because he's going to be famous. The cover of a magazine! Ted says the only time he's ever contemplated being on the cover of a magazine was when he was in Tennessee. Down in Gatlinburg, there was this novelty store that would take a picture of you and then put you on the cover of *Sports Illustrated*.

Ted takes all the banter with good grace. Then someone says, "Tell him about how you're afraid of the dark." Ted smiles and nods, but he's got something to attend to in the kitchen.

Afraid of the dark?

It's true, Kim says, laughing. The same guy who isn't scared to yank his tooth out with pliers won't walk into a dark room. At night, she says, if he stays up watching TV, he'll leave the TV and all the lights on, so his path into the bedroom is lit.

And once he's in bed?

"He'll go to bed in the dark if I'm with him. If not, he'll sleep with the lights on."

MONDAY MORNING. IT'S a workday. Ted meets his coworkers at the small Muskegon garage that serves as headquarters for Brown

Concrete Construction, Inc. It's a bare-bones, guy kind of place, the only splashes of color being the obligatory 1970s-era pinup posters. One is of a woman wearing only big hair and what appears to be a frilly whalebone corset. There are also a couple of back seats from cars, propped up on the ground, which provide passable couches for slouching.

With Ted are the rest of his team—Joe McCann, Mike Anderson, and Randy Baker. Randy is telling a story about the weekend: He just moved into a nice new neighborhood, and during a meet-the-neighbors night, someone asked him whether he had any particular plans for the back yard. Randy said he was "thinkin' of getting a couple of hogs." All conversation stopped. Randy explained that it was a funny joke, but the wife disagreed, and now Randy's in the doghouse.

Andy Brown, the owner, arrives. Ted is not always great about taking orders from others, but he and Andy get along fine. Andy likes Ted because he's a good, reliable worker, and Ted likes Andy because, even though he's younger and has more money, he's not stuck up. Andy works side by side with his men. "If I've got a shovel in my hand," Ted says appreciatively, "Andy's next to me with a shovel in his."

Fifteen minutes later, Andy and his crew have driven past those Republican cars and buses heading for the airport, and arrived at the big hole in the ground that is to become a garage.

What happens next is mesmerizing. This team of five guys has been working together for so long, there's no need for much gab. They just know what to do. While Ted and the others are breaking down the metal braces that support the newly hardened walls of the garage, Andy is driving a Skidster earth mover, flattening out the dirt floor. Joe runs a plastic drainage tube from the center of the floor through the dirt and out into a gully. Now Mike is pounding stakes into the ground to the level of a string line that Ted and Randy are holding taut, from marks on opposing walls. These are puddle stakes, leveling markers that will tell the men exactly how high the cement should be poured. Things seem to be happening very quickly, and on a split-second schedule. They finish moments before the cement mixers arrive.

The owner of the property has race cars, and this is to be a giant garage—room for four cars at least. The floor is going to require two mixers, each filled to its capacity of nine cubic yards of cement. The whole nine yards.

The whole nine yards. I've lived fifty-three years and used that expression dozens of times, and this was the first time I had any idea where it might have come from or what it might mean. It's interesting how things that seem to make no sense can suddenly come into focus.

Take Ted's financial troubles. For several days, something was bothering me, and then it hit me. A couple of phone calls to the federal government confirmed what I suspected. As a U.S. Army veteran with an honorable discharge, Ted is eligible for a lifetime of medical care. His income is well below the cutoff point for need.

It's not a handout for which he need feel ashamed—it's his right, same as anyone else who served his country. Most medical services, from simple doctor's visits to that MRI that will tell Ted if he's got a problem with his brain, are available to veterans for the price of a few dollars' copayment. Ted's been eligible ever since his discharge in 1988.

When I told Ted this, he was thunderstruck. "It just never crossed my mind," he said.

Here is what crossed my mind.

Like all people who don't vote, Ted has distanced himself to some degree from the society in which he lives. It's symptomatic, I think, of a larger choice he has made. He has willed himself into a certain protective ignorance about the way life works. This intellectual callus might make some things easier to bear, but

I'll bet it comes at a cost. The world must be a more terrifying place when you don't know all you can about why things happen the way they do, and why people do what they do, and whether there's anything out there that can leap out at you from the dark.

Still, in some ways I envy Ted. When it comes right down to it, there is something to be said for keeping it simple. There isn't much moral ambiguity, for example, in the birth of a garage. Nothing is abstract. Everything is, you know . . . concrete.

Here come the cement trucks, with their whole nine yards. Andy's work crew has changed into knee boots, and what will follow seems almost a choreographed work, an odd ballet performed by hairy guys in T-shirts and overalls.

The mixer, with a long delivery chute, moves in like a lumbering elephant, its trunk swaying left and right, depositing wet cement. Randy, Ted, and Andy work expertly around it, wading through the goo, each with a 2-by-4, smoothing the cement into place, precisely to the level of those puddle stakes and, somehow, not a millimeter higher.

A mile away, George Bush strides to the lectern, to thunderous applause. He urges the Republican crowd to get everyone out to vote for him, for a safer America. This wasn't billed as a campaign event, exactly, but nobody seems to mind. "Step one," says the president, "is to remind your friends and neighbors that we have an obligation in a free society to participate."

The elephant-truck slowly backs away as the men continue to smooth the cement in place; as they work, an interesting alchemy plays out: The pebbly pieces begin to flatten and sink, so what first resembled wet gravel turns into oatmeal and then, slowly, into a surface as smooth as a table top.

The men are working quickly; they have to.

Across town, Bush is busy mispronouncing the name of his "friend," the local Republican congressman, Peter Hoekstra. No matter. The crowd loves him. "Four more years! Four more years!"

The second truck is gone now, and the finishing work begins. Mike whacks the puddle stakes down into the cement, so there's no sign they were ever there. With big flat hoes on 20-foot handles, Ted and Joe stand at the periphery, beyond the walls, and begin smoothing the surface even more, testing it with practiced hands, feeling for the right moment for the final cosmetic step.

Bush is mostly steering clear of the declared topic of the day, health care. It's a complicated, nuanced issue—no match for the sexier topics of national security and tax relief, which is where the president mostly stays. We are winning the war on terror, he says, and the place goes wild. The economy is strengthening, he proclaims, with dubious authority but to raucous applause. One Republican stalwart stands to say he's mad at the president. Deadpan, Bush asks him why. Because America didn't get to enjoy his great policies over the last thirty years, the man says, and everyone cracks up in bonhomie.

With pads for their knees, Ted, Randy, Andy, Joe, and Mike cautiously step onto the surface. It's just right; unyielding, but still chalky atop. They work purposefully, squatting down, buffing the surface with steel trowels, evening out any little pocks or lines. This is the final touch, and when they are done, they have turned what was a pit of dirt two hours ago into a garage floor with a surface as slick as a hockey rink. It's simply perfect.

Fatal Distraction

An actor who is frightened or angry or embarrassed is often encouraged not to stifle that emotion but to capture it and transform it into something useful. Emotion is too valuable an asset to throw away. This holds true for writing as well.

When my editor called me to tell me that yet another baby had been found dead inside a parked car—accidentally left there by his father—I felt a familiar surge of nausea, followed by a familiar sense of dread. It happens every time I hear about one of these cases, which occur with grisly regularity several times a year somewhere in the United States. This new case was local. I knew right away that I had to write about it, whether I wanted to or not.

A quarter-century ago, I almost did this to my baby daughter. The only reason Molly is alive today is that, at a critical moment, as I was parking my car outside my newspaper office in the searing heat of a Miami summer, having totally forgotten I had my two-year-old in the car . . . she woke up and said something.

The incident stayed with me as a private horror. I never told anyone, not even my wife. She learned of it only recently, as I was reporting this story, when

I needed to explain why I kept waking in the middle
of the night in a cold sweat.

    When I finally screwed up the nerve to tell Molly
about the tragedy that never happened, twenty-five
years after the day no harm was done, I couldn't look
her in the eye.

The editor of this anthology, the mother of a baby boy, asks me to
caution parents with infants that they may find what follows ex-
tremely disturbing. She's right.

March 8, 2009

THE DEFENDANT WAS an immense man, well over 300 pounds, but in the gravity of his sorrow and shame he seemed larger still. He hunched forward in the sturdy wooden armchair that barely contained him, sobbing softly into tissue after tissue, a leg bouncing nervously under the table. In the first pew of spectators sat his wife, looking stricken, absently twisting her wedding band.

The room was a sepulcher. Witnesses spoke softly of events so painful that many lost their composure. When a hospital emergency room nurse described how the defendant had behaved after the police first brought him in, she wept. He was virtually catatonic, she remembered, his eyes shut tight, rocking back and forth, locked away in some unfathomable private torment. He would not speak at all for the longest time, not until the nurse sank down beside him and held his hand. It was only then that the patient began to open up, and what he said was that he didn't want any sedation, that he didn't deserve a respite from pain, that he wanted to feel it all, and then to die.

The charge in the courtroom was manslaughter, brought by

the Commonwealth of Virginia. No significant facts were in dispute. Miles Harrison, forty-nine, was an amiable person, a diligent businessman and a doting, conscientious father until the day last summer—beset by problems at work, making call after call on his cell phone—he forgot to drop his son, Chase, at day care. The toddler slowly sweltered to death, strapped into a car seat for nearly nine hours in an office parking lot in Herndon in the blistering heat of July. It was an inexplicable, inexcusable mistake, but was it a crime? That was the question for a judge to decide.

At one point, during a recess, Harrison rose unsteadily to his feet, turned to leave the courtroom, and saw, as if for the first time, that there were people witnessing his disgrace. The big man's eyes lowered. He swayed a little until someone steadied him, and then he gasped out in a keening falsetto: "My poor baby!"

A group of middle-schoolers filed into the room for a scheduled class trip to the courthouse. The teacher clearly hadn't expected this; within a few minutes, the wide-eyed kids were hustled back out.

The trial would last three days. Sitting through it, side by side in the rear of the courtroom, were two women who had traveled hours to get there. Unlike almost everyone else on the spectator benches, they were not relatives or coworkers or close friends of the accused.

". . . the lower portion of the body was red to red-purple . . ."

As the most excruciating of the evidence came out, from the medical examiner, the women in the back drew closer together, leaning in to each other.

". . . a green discoloration of the abdomen . . . autolysis of the organs . . . what we call skin slippage . . . the core body temperature reaches a hundred eight degrees when death ensues."

Mary—the older, shorter one—trembled. Lyn—the younger one with the long, strawberry-blond hair—gathered her in, one arm around the shoulder, the other across their bodies, holding hands.

When the trial ended, Lyn Balfour and Mary Parks left quietly, drawing no attention. They hadn't wanted to be there, but they'd felt a duty, both to the defendant and, in a much more complicated way, to themselves.

It was unusual, to say the least: three people together in one place, sharing the same heartbreaking history. All three had accidentally killed their babies in the identical, incomprehensible, modern way.

"DEATH BY HYPERTHERMIA" is the official designation. When it happens to young children, the facts are often the same: An otherwise loving and attentive parent one day gets busy, or distracted, or upset, or confused by a change in his or her daily routine, and just . . . forgets a child is in the car. It happens that way somewhere in the United States fifteen to twenty-five times a year, parceled out through the spring, summer, and early fall. The season is almost upon us.

Two decades ago, this was relatively rare. But in the early 1990s, car-safety experts declared that passenger-side front airbags could kill children, and they recommended that child seats be moved to the back of the car; then, for even more safety for the very young, that the baby seats be pivoted to face the rear. If few foresaw the tragic consequence of the lessened visibility of the child . . . well, who can blame them? What kind of person forgets a baby?

The wealthy do, it turns out. And the poor, and the middle class. Parents of all ages and ethnicities do it. Mothers are just as likely to do it as fathers. It happens to the chronically absent-minded and to the fanatically organized, to the college-educated and to the marginally literate. In the last ten years, it has happened to a dentist. A postal clerk. A social worker. A police officer. An accountant. A soldier. A paralegal. An electrician. A Protestant clergyman. A rabbinical student. A nurse. A construction worker. An assistant principal. It happened to a mental health counselor, a college professor, and a pizza chef. It happened to a pediatrician. It happened to a rocket scientist.

Last year it happened three times in one day, the worst day so far in the worst year so far in a phenomenon that gives no sign of abating.

The facts in each case differ a little, but always there is the terrible moment when the parent realizes what he or she has done, often through a phone call from a spouse or caregiver, wondering about the child. This is followed by a frantic sprint to the car. What awaits there is the worst thing in the world.

Each instance has its own macabre signature. One father had parked his car next to the grounds of a county fair; as he discovered his son's body, a calliope tootled merrily beside him. Another man, wanting to end things quickly, tried to wrestle a gun from a police officer at the scene. Several people, including Mary Parks of Blacksburg, Virginia, have driven from their workplace to the day-care center to pick up the child they'd thought they'd dropped off, never noticing the corpse in the back seat.

Then there is the Chattanooga, Tennessee, business executive who must live with this: His motion-detector car alarm went off, three separate times, out there in the broiling sun. But when he looked out, he couldn't see anyone tampering with the car. So he remotely deactivated the alarm and went calmly back to work.

THERE MAY BE no act of human failing that more fundamentally challenges our society's views about crime, punishment, justice, and mercy. According to statistics compiled by a national child-safety advocacy group, in about 40 percent of these cases authorities examine the evidence, determine that the death was a terrible accident—a mistake of memory that delivers a lifelong sentence of guilt far greater than any a judge or jury could mete out—and file no charges. In the other 60 percent, parsing essentially identical facts and applying them to essentially identical laws, authorities decide that the negligence was so great and the injury so grievous that it must be called a felony, and it must be aggressively pursued.

As it happens, just five days before Miles Harrison forgot his toddler son in the parking lot of the Herndon corporate-relocation business where he worked, a similar event had occurred a few hundred miles southeast. After a long shift at work, a Portsmouth, Virginia, sanitation department electrician named Andrew Culpepper picked up his toddler son from his parents, drove home, went into the house and then fell asleep, forgetting he'd had the boy in the car, leaving him to bake to death outside.

Harrison was charged with a crime. Culpepper was not. In each case, the decision fell to one person.

With Harrison, it was Ray Morrogh, the Fairfax commonwealth's attorney. In an interview a few days after he brought the charge of involuntary manslaughter, Morrogh explained why.

"There is a lot to be said for reaffirming people's obligations to protect their children," he said. "When you have children, you have responsibilities. I am very strong in the defense of children's safety."

Morrogh has two kids himself, ages twelve and fourteen. He was asked if he could imagine this ever having happened to him. The question seemed to take him aback. He went on to another subject, and then, ten minutes later, made up his mind:

"I have to say no, it couldn't have happened to me. I am a watchful father."

In Portsmouth, the decision not to charge Culpepper, forty, was made by Commonwealth's Attorney Earle Mobley. As tragic as the child's death was, Mobley says, a police investigation showed that there was no crime because there was no intent: Culpepper wasn't callously gambling with the child's life—he had forgotten the child was there.

"The easy thing in a case like this is to dump it on a jury, but that is not the right thing to do," Mobley says. A prosecutor's responsibility, he says, is to achieve justice, not to settle some sort of score.

"I'm not pretty sure I made the right decision," he says. "I'm *positive* I made the right decision."

There may be no clear right or wrong in deciding how to handle cases such as these; in each case, a public servant is trying to do his best with a Solomonic dilemma. But public servants are also human beings, and they will inevitably bring to their judgment the full weight of that complicated fact.

"You know, it's interesting we're talking today," Mobley says.

He has five children. Today, he says, is the birthday of his sixth.

"She died of leukemia in 1993. She was almost three."

Mobley pauses. He doesn't want to create the wrong impression.

He made the decision on the law, he says, "but I also have some idea what it feels like, what it does to you, when you lose a child."

So, after his son's death, Andrew Culpepper was sent home to try to live the remainder of his life with what he had done. After his son's death, Miles Harrison was charged with a felony. His mug shot was in the newspapers and on TV, with the haunted, hunted, naked-eyed look these parents always have, up against the wall. He hired an expensive lawyer. Over months, both sides developed their cases. Witnesses were assembled and interviewed. Efforts at a plea bargain failed. The trial began.

THE COURT HEARD how Harrison and his wife had been a midlife childless couple desperately wanting to become parents, and how they'd made three visits to Moscow, setting out each time on a grueling ten-hour railroad trip to the Russian hinterlands to find and adopt their eighteen-month-old son from an orphanage bed he'd seldom been allowed to leave. Harrison's next-door neighbor testified how she'd watched the new father giddily frolic on the lawn with his son. Harrison's sister testified how she had worked with her brother and sister-in-law for weeks to find the ideal day-care situation for the boy, who would need special attention to recover from the effects of his painfully austere beginnings.

From the witness stand, Harrison's mother defiantly declared that Miles had been a fine son and a perfect, loving father. Distraught but composed, Harrison's wife, Carol, described the phone call that her husband had made to her right after he'd discovered what he'd done, the phone call she'd fielded on a bus coming home from work. It was, she said, unintelligible screaming.

In the end, Fairfax County Circuit Court Judge R. Terrence Ney found Miles Harrison not guilty. There was no crime, he said, citing the identical legal reasons Earle Mobley had cited for not charging Andrew Culpepper in the first place.

At the verdict, Harrison gasped, sobbed, then tried to stand, but the man had nothing left. His legs buckled, and he crashed pathetically to his knees.

So, IF IT'S not manslaughter, what is it? An accident?

"No, that's an imperfect word."

This is Mark Warschauer, an internationally acclaimed expert in language learning and technology, professor of education at the University of California at Irvine. "The word 'accident' makes it sound like it can't be prevented," Warschauer says, "but 'incident' makes it sound trivial. And it is not trivial."

Warschauer is a Fulbright scholar, specializing in the use of laptops to spread literacy to children. In the summer of 2003, he returned to his office from lunch to find a crowd surrounding a car in the parking lot. Police had smashed the window open with a crowbar. Only as he got closer did Warschauer realize it was his car. That was his first clue that he'd forgotten to drop his ten-month-old son, Mikey, at day care that morning. Mikey was dead.

Warschauer wasn't charged with a crime, but for months afterward he contemplated suicide. Gradually, he says, the urge subsided, if not the grief and guilt.

"We lack a term for what this is," Warschauer says. And also, he says, we need an understanding of why it happens to the people it happens to.

DAVID DIAMOND is picking at his breakfast at a Washington hotel, trying to explain.

"Memory is a machine," he says, "and it is not flawless. Our conscious mind prioritizes things by importance, but on a cellular level, our memory does not. If you're capable of forgetting your cell phone, you are potentially capable of forgetting your child."

Diamond is a professor of molecular physiology at the University of South Florida and a consultant to the veterans hospital in Tampa. He's here for a national science conference to give a speech about his research, which involves the intersection of emotion, stress, and memory. What he's found is that under some circumstances, the most sophisticated part of our thought-processing center can be held hostage to a competing memory system, a primitive portion of the brain that is—by a design as old as the dinosaur's—inattentive, pigheaded, nonanalytical, stupid.

Diamond is the memory expert with a lousy memory, the one who recently realized, while driving to the mall, that his infant granddaughter was asleep in the back of the car. He remembered only because his wife, sitting beside him, mentioned the baby. He understands what could have happened had he been alone with the child. Almost worse, he understands exactly why.

The human brain, he says, is a magnificent but jury-rigged device in which newer and more sophisticated structures sit atop a junk heap of prototype brains still used by lower species. At the top of the device are the smartest and most nimble parts: the prefrontal cortex, which thinks and analyzes, and the hippocampus, which makes and holds on to our immediate memories. At the bottom is the basal ganglia, nearly identical to the brains of lizards, controlling voluntary but barely conscious actions.

Diamond says that in situations involving familiar, routine motor skills, the human animal presses the basal ganglia into service as a sort of auxiliary autopilot. When our prefrontal cortex and hippocampus are planning our day on the way to work, the ignorant but efficient basal ganglia is operating the car; that's why you'll sometimes find yourself having driven from point A to point B without a clear recollection of the route you took, the turns you made, or the scenery you saw.

Ordinarily, says Diamond, this delegation of duty "works beautifully, like a symphony. But sometimes, it turns into the *1812* Overture. The cannons take over and overwhelm."

By experimentally exposing rats to the presence of cats, and then recording electrochemical changes in the rodents' brains, Diamond has found that stress—either sudden or chronic—can weaken the brain's higher-functioning centers, making them more susceptible to bullying from the basal ganglia. He's seen the same sort of thing play out in cases he's followed involving infant deaths in cars.

"The quality of prior parental care seems to be irrelevant," he said. "The important factors that keep showing up involve a combination of stress, emotion, lack of sleep, and change in routine, where the basal ganglia is trying to do what it's supposed to do, and the conscious mind is too weakened to resist. What happens is that the memory circuits in a vulnerable hippocampus literally get overwritten, like with a computer program. Unless the memory circuit is rebooted—such as if the child cries, or, you know, if the wife mentions the child in the back—it can entirely disappear."

Diamond stops.

"There is a case in Virginia where this is exactly what happened, the whole set of stress factors. I was consulted on it a couple of years ago. It was a woman named, ah . . ."

He puts down his fork, searches the ceiling, the wall, the floor, then shakes his head. He's been stressing over his conference speech, he says, and his memory retrieval is shot. He can't summon the name.

Lyn Balfour?

"Yeah, Lyn Balfour! The perfect storm."

––––––––––

It's mid-October. Lyn Balfour is on her cell phone, ordering a replacement strap for a bouncy seat for the new baby and simultaneously trying to arrange for an emergency sitter, because she has to get to the fertility clinic, pronto, because she just got lab results back, and she's ovulating, and her husband's in Iraq, and she wants to get artificially inseminated with his sperm, like right now, but, crap, the sitter is busy, so she grabs the kid and the keys and the diaper bag and is out the door and in the car and gone. But now the baby is fussing, so she's reaching back to give him a bottle of juice, one eye on him and the other on a seemingly endless series of hairpin turns that she negotiates adroitly.

"Actually," she laughs, "I'm getting better about not doing too much at once. I've been simplifying my life a lot."

Raelyn Balfour is what is commonly called a type-A personality. She is the first to admit that her temperament contributed to the death of her son, Bryce, two years ago. It happened on March 30, 2007, the day she accidentally left the nine-month-old in the parking lot of the Charlottesville judge advocate general's office, where she worked as a transportation administrator. The high temperature that day was only in the 60s, but the biometrics and thermodynamics of babies and cars combine mercilessly: Young children have lousy thermostats, and heat builds quickly in a closed vehicle in the sun. The temperature in Balfour's car that day topped 110 degrees.

There's a dismayingly cartoonish expression for what happened to Lyn Balfour that day. In 1990, British psychologist James Reason coined the term the "Swiss Cheese Model" to explain through analogy why catastrophic failures can occur in organizations despite multiple layers of defense. Reason likens the layers to slices of Swiss cheese, piled upon each other, five or six deep. The holes represent small, potentially insignificant weaknesses. Things will totally collapse only rarely, he says, but when they do, it is by coincidence—when all the holes happen to align so that there is a breach through the entire system.

On the day Balfour forgot Bryce in the car, she had been up much of the night, first babysitting for a friend who had to take her dog to an emergency vet clinic, then caring for Bryce, who was cranky with a cold. Because the baby was also tired, he uncharacteristically dozed in the car, so he made no noise. Because Balfour was planning to bring Bryce's usual car seat to the fire station to be professionally installed, Bryce was positioned in a different car seat that day, not behind the passenger but behind the driver, and was thus not visible in the rearview mirror. Because the family's second car was on loan to a relative, Balfour drove her husband to work that day, meaning the diaper bag was in the back, not on the passenger seat, as usual, where she could see it. Because of a phone conversation with a young relative in trouble, and another with her boss about a crisis at work, Balfour spent most of the trip on her cell, stressed, solving other people's problems. Because the babysitter had a new phone, it didn't yet contain Balfour's office phone number, only her cell number, meaning that when the sitter phoned to wonder why Balfour hadn't dropped Bryce off that morning, it rang unheard in Balfour's pocketbook.

The holes, all of them, aligned.

There is no consistent character profile of the parent who does this to his or her child. The thirteen who agreed to be interviewed for this story include the introverted and extroverted; the sweet, the sullen, the stoic, and the terribly fragile. None of those descriptions exactly fits Lyn Balfour, a thirty-seven-year-old Army reservist who has served in combat zones and who seems to remain—at least on the subject of the death of her son—in battle.

"I don't feel I need to forgive myself," she says plainly, "because what I did was not intentional."

Balfour is tall and stands taller, moving with a purposeful, swinging stride. She's got a weak chin but a strong mouth that she uses without much editing. She's funny and brassy and in your face, the sort of person you either like or don't like, right away.

It had been Balfour's idea to go to the trial of Miles Harrison, and it was she who walked up to Harrison in the hallway during a break, pushed past a crowd, and threw her arms around his neck, pulling him close. For almost a full minute, she whispered in his ear. His eyes grew wider, and then he wept into her shoulder like a baby. What she had told him was who she was and that she knew he'd been a good, loving father, and he must not be ashamed.

Balfour grew up medium-poor in Michigan. There was a man she'd been told was her father and a close family friend who, she later learned, was actually her father. Her two sets of grandparents wound up divorcing each other, then switching partners.

There was alcoholism, divorce, a battle for custody. When Balfour turned eighteen, she was ready for the discipline of the Army.

She served in Bosnia and twice in Iraq, where she specialized in intelligence analysis and construction management, and where she discovered a skill at juggling a dozen things at once. She won a Bronze Star for managing $47 million in projects without mislaying a penny. She got married, had a son, divorced, met Jarrett Balfour and within a month decided this handsome, younger man would be her husband. Eighteen months later, he was. Bryce was their first child together. Braiden, conceived with Jarrett's sperm when he was in Iraq, is their second. Today, in the same way, they're trying for a third.

Balfour has stopped at the fertility clinic for her procedure, and she's now driving to the school of the Judge Advocate General Corps to demonstrate where and how her son's death happened. Down the road to the right is where she dropped Jarrett off at work, which was not customary, and which she theorizes put a subconscious check mark in her brain: Delivery made. Now she's pointing out the house of the babysitter she'd driven obliviously past as she talked to her boss about a scheduling snafu and to her nephew about helping to pay his gambling debts. And here is the parking lot of the JAG School, on the University of Virginia campus. She's pulling into the same spot she was parked in that day, the place where Bryce died.

"It was like this, except these two spots next to us were empty," she notes blandly as she gets out of the car, gathers her keys, and leans in to get the diaper bag.

There is an almost pugnacious matter-of-factness about Lyn Balfour that can seem disconcerting, particularly if you have a preconception about how a person in her circumstances is supposed to face the world.

You might expect, for example, that she has gotten another car. But this black Honda Pilot with the pink Tinkerbell steering wheel cover is the same car Bryce died in, just inches from where Balfour is bending over Braiden to unstrap him.

"It didn't make financial sense to get a new car," she says.

Balfour's eyes are impassive. Her attitude is clear:

You got a problem with that?

NOT ALL CASES of infant hyperthermia in cars are like the ones this article is about: simple if bewildering lapses of memory by an otherwise apparently good parent. In other types of cases, there is a history of neglect, or evidence of substance abuse. Sometimes, the parent knowingly left the child in the car, despite the obvious peril. In one particularly egregious instance, a mother used her locked car as an inexpensive substitute for day care. When hyperthermia deaths are treated as crimes, these are the ones that tend to result in prison sentences.

Cases like Lyn Balfour's, when prosecuted, typically end in some sort of compromise: a plea to a reduced charge, sometimes with probation and a suspended sentence, sometimes with community service. Going all the way to trial is a relative rarity.

What happened to Balfour was even rarer. She was charged not with manslaughter, but with second-degree murder, carrying a possible prison sentence of up to forty years. And as a condition of remaining free on bond, the court prohibited her from being alone with any minors, including her own teenage son.

So Balfour hired John Zwerling, a top-gun criminal defense lawyer from Alexandria. That meant that Jarrett Balfour, an employee of a civilian military contractor, had no choice but to take an assignment in Iraq. The extra combat pay would be needed for legal expenses. Lyn Balfour would have to face this alone.

That is when she began to move past grief and guilt and paralyzing self-doubt to a very specific, very focused anger.

JOHN ZWERLING PRESENTS a passable version of Nero Wolfe, Rex Stout's portly, eccentric genius hero of detective fiction. Zwerling's law offices are in a handsome Old Town townhouse with dark walnut molding and dark wooden shutters. The boss is the guy with the Santa beard sitting in the chair with a hole in the leather, in jeans and a shirt with a big stain, the front buttons laboring mightily to do their job.

Zwerling's first task, he says, was to make the case that second-degree murder was a preposterous charge in a case lacking even the faintest whisper of intent. That, he did. After a preliminary hearing, the charge was reduced to involuntary manslaughter. Zwerling's second and more daunting job was to craft a defense for a case that was being prosecuted with what at times seemed like theatrical zeal.

Here is how Assistant Commonwealth's Attorney Elizabeth Killeen would sum it up before the jury: "This little boy's life did not have to end this way, on a hospital gurney. Deceased. Dead. His life squandered, and gone forever."

In the end, Zwerling had one key decision to make. In criminal cases, jurors want to hear from the defendant. Zwerling liked and respected Balfour, but should he put her on the stand?

"Have you met her?" he asks.

Yes.

"Then you've seen that mental girdle she puts on, the protective armor against the world, how she closes up and becomes a soldier. It helps her survive, but it can seem off-putting if you're someone who wants to see how crushed she is."

Zwerling decided not to risk it.

"I wound up putting her on the stand in a different way," he says, "so people could see the real Lyn—vulnerable, with no guile, no posturing."

What Zwerling did was play two audiotapes for the jury. One was Balfour's interrogation by police in the hospital about an hour after Bryce's death; her answers are immeasurably sad, almost unintelligible, half sob, half whisper: "I killed my baby," she says tremulously. "Oh, God, I'm so sorry."

The second tape was a call to 911 made by a passerby, in those first few seconds after Balfour discovered the body and beseeched a stranger to summon help.

Zwerling swivels to his computer, punches up an audio file. "Want to hear it?"

BALFOUR HAS LEFT her car, carrying Braiden, and is reenacting her movements from that day after work, the day Bryce died. She walks from her cubicle in room 153A of the JAG School, out to the front of the building. By midafternoon, she had finally checked her cell and discovered she'd missed an early morning call from her babysitter. She called back, but got only voice mail. It didn't worry her. She and the babysitter were friends, and they talked often about all sorts of things. Balfour left a message asking for a callback.

It came when she was standing where she is now, on a spacious stone patio in front of the JAG School, heading toward the parking lot. As it happens, there is a Civil War–era cannon that is aimed, with unsettling irony, exactly where she stands.

The babysitter asked Balfour where Bryce was. Balfour said: "What do you mean? He's with you."

It is 60 feet to the end of the patio, then a stairwell with eleven steps down, then two steps across, then a second stairwell, twelve steps down, one more off the curb and then a thirty-foot sprint to the car. Balfour estimates the whole thing took half a minute or less. She knew it was too late when, through the window, she saw Bryce's limp hand, and then his face, unmarked but lifeless and shiny, Balfour says, "like a porcelain doll."

It was seconds later that the passerby called 911.

THE TAPE IS unendurable. Mostly, you hear a woman's voice, tense but precise, explaining to a police dispatcher what she is seeing. Initially, there's nothing in the background. Then Balfour howls at the top of her lungs, "OH, MY GOD, NOOOO!"

Then, for a few seconds, nothing.

Then a deafening shriek: *"NO, NO, PLEASE, NO!!!"*

Three more seconds, then: *"PLEASE, GOD, NO, PLEASE!!!"*

What is happening is that Balfour is administering CPR. At that moment, she recalls, she felt like two people occupying one body: Lyn, the crisply efficient certified combat lifesaver, and Lyn, the incompetent mother who would never again know happiness. Breathe, compress, breathe, compress. Each time that she came up for air, she lost it. Then, back to the patient.

After hearing this tape, the jury deliberated for all of ninety minutes, including time for lunch. Not guilty.

"I DIDN'T FEEL this case should ever have been brought," says juror Colin Rosse, a retired radio executive. "It may have been negligence, but it was an honest mistake."

Jury foreman James Schlothauer, an inspections official for the county government, doesn't fault the prosecution; Balfour's case was complex, he says, and the facts needed an airing. But the facts, he says, also made the verdict a slam dunk. It was "a big doggone accident," he says, that might have happened to anyone.

To anyone?

Schlothauer hesitates.

"Well, it happened to me."

The results were not catastrophic, Schlothauer says, but the underlying malfunction was similar: Busy and stressed, he and his wife once got their responsibilities confused, and neither stopped at day care for their daughter at the end of the day.

"We both got home, and it was, 'Wait, where's Lily?' 'I thought you got her!' 'I thought *you* got her!' "

What if that mix-up had happened at the beginning of the day?

"To anyone," Schlothauer says.

THERE IS NO national clearinghouse for cases of infant hyperthermia, no government agency charged with data collection and oversight. The closest thing is in the basement office of a comfortable home in suburban Kansas City, Kansas, where a former sales and marketing executive named Janette Fennell runs a nonprofit organization called Kids and Cars. Kids and Cars lobbies for increased car safety for children, and as such maintains one of the saddest databases in America.

Fennell is on a sofa, her bare feet tucked under her, leafing through files. Amber, her college intern, walks up and plops a fax of a new wire service story on the table.

"Frontover," Amber says. "Parking lot, North Carolina."

There's a grisly terminology to this business. "Backovers" happen when you look in the rearview mirror and fail to see the child behind the car, or never look at all. "Frontovers" occur almost exclusively with pickups and SUVs, where the driver sits high off the ground. There are "power window strangulations" and "cars put in motion by child" and, finally, "hyperthermia."

In a collage on Fennell's wall are snapshots of dozens of infants and toddlers, some proudly holding up fingers, as if saying, "I'm two!" Or "I'm three!" The photos, typically, are from their final birthdays.

Fennell has met or talked with many of the parents in the hyperthermia cases, and some now work with her organization. She doesn't seek them out. They find her name, often late at night, sleeplessly searching the Web for some sign that there are others who have lived in the same hell and survived. There is a general misconception, Fennell says, about who these people are: "They tend to be the doting parents, the kind who buy baby locks and safety gates." These cases, she says, are failures of memory, not of love.

Fennell has an expression that's half smile, half wince. She uses it often.

"Some people think, 'Okay, I can see forgetting a child for two minutes, but not eight hours.' What they don't understand is that the parent in his or her mind has dropped off the baby at day care and thinks the baby is happy and well taken care of. Once that's in your brain, there is no reason to worry or check on the baby for the rest of the day."

Fennell believes that prosecuting parents in this type of case is both cruel and pointless: It's not as though the fear of a prison sentence is what will keep a parent from doing this. The answer to the problem, Fennell believes, lies in improved car safety features and in increased public awareness that this can happen, that the results of a momentary lapse of memory can be horrifying.

What is the worst case she knows of?

"I don't really like to . . ." she says.

She looks away. She won't hold eye contact for this.

"The child pulled all her hair out before she died."

For years, Fennell has been lobbying for a law requiring back-seat sensors in new cars, sensors that would sound an alarm if a child's weight remained in the seat after the ignition is turned off. Last year, she almost succeeded. The 2008 Cameron Gulbransen Kids' Transportation Safety Act—which requires safety improvements in power windows and in rear visibility, and protections against a child accidentally setting a car in motion—originally had a rear-seat sensor requirement, too. It never made the final bill; sponsors withdrew it, fearing they couldn't get it past a powerful auto manufacturers' lobby.

There are a few aftermarket products that alert a parent if a child remains in a car that has been turned off. These products are not huge sellers. They have likely run up against the same marketing problem that confronted three NASA engineers a few years ago.

In 2000, Chris Edwards, Terry Mack, and Edward Modlin began to work on just such a product after one of their colleagues, Kevin Shelton, accidentally left his nine-month-old son to die in the parking lot of NASA Langley Research Center in Hampton, Virginia. The inventors patented a device with weight sensors and a keychain alarm. Based on aerospace technology, it was easy to use; it was relatively cheap, and it worked.

Janette Fennell had high hopes for this product: The dramatic narrative behind it, she felt, and the fact that it came from NASA, created a likelihood of widespread publicity and public acceptance.

That was five years ago. The device still isn't on the shelves. The inventors could not find a commercial partner willing to manufacture it. One big problem was liability. If you made it, you could face enormous lawsuits if it malfunctioned and a child died. But another big problem was psychological: Marketing studies suggested it wouldn't sell well.

The problem is this simple: People think this could never happen to them.

———————

"I WAS THAT guy, before. I'd read the stories, and I'd go, 'What were those parents thinking?'"

Mikey Terry is a contractor from Maypearl, Texas, a big man with soft eyes. At the moment he realized what he'd done, he was in the cab of a truck and his six-month-old daughter, Mika, was in a closed vehicle in the broiling Texas sun in a parking lot 40 miles away. So his frantic sprint to the car was conducted at 100 miles an hour in a 30-foot gooseneck trailer hauling thousands of pounds of lumber the size of telephone poles.

On that day in June 2005, Terry had been recently laid off, and he'd taken a day job building a wall in the auditorium of a Catholic church just outside of town. He'd remembered to drop his older daughter at day care, but as he was driving the baby to a different day-care location, he got a call about a new permanent job. This really caught his attention. It was a fatal distraction.

Terry, thirty-five, wasn't charged with a crime. His punishment has been more subtle.

The Terrys are Southern Baptists. Before Mika's death, Mikey Terry says, church used to be every Sunday, all day Sunday, morning Bible study through evening meal. He and his wife, Michele, don't go much anymore. It's too confusing, he says.

"I feel guilty about everyone in church talking about how blessed we all are. I don't feel blessed anymore. I feel I have been wronged by God. And that I have wronged God. And I don't know how to deal with that."

Four years have passed, but he still won't go near the Catholic church he'd been working at that day. As his daughter died outside, he was inside, building a wall on which would hang an enormous crucifix.

"THIS IS A case of pure evil negligence of the worse kind . . . He deserves the death sentence."

"I wonder if this was his way of telling his wife that he didn't really want a kid."

"He was too busy chasing after real estate commissions. This shows how morally corrupt people in real estate-related professions are."

These were readers' online comments to the *Washington Post* news article of July 10, 2008, reporting the circumstances of the death of Miles Harrison's son. These comments were typical of many others, and they are typical of what happens again and again, year after year in community after community, when these cases arise. A substantial proportion of the public reacts not merely with anger, but with frothing vitriol.

Ed Hickling believes he knows why. Hickling is a clinical psychologist from Albany, New York, who has studied the effects of fatal auto accidents on the drivers who survive them. He says these people are often judged with disproportionate harshness by the public, even when it was clearly an accident, and even when it was indisputably not their fault. Humans, Hickling said, have a fundamental need to create and maintain a narrative for their lives in which the universe is not implacable and heartless, that terrible things do not happen at random, and that catastrophe can be avoided if you are vigilant and responsible.

In hyperthermia cases, he believes, the parents are demonized for much the same reasons. "We are vulnerable, but we don't want to be reminded of that. We want to believe that the world is understandable and controllable and unthreatening, that if we follow the rules, we'll be okay. So, when this kind of thing happens to other people, we need to put them in a different category from us. We don't want to resemble them, and the fact that we might is too terrifying to deal with. So, they have to be monsters."

After Lyn Balfour's acquittal, this comment appeared on the *Charlottesville News* Web site: "If she had too many things on her mind then she should have kept her legs closed and not had any kids. They should lock her in a car during a hot day and see what happens."

LYN BALFOUR'S RUCKERSVILLE home is fragrant with spice candles and the faintly sweet feel of kitsch. Braiden boings happily in a baby bouncer, the same one Bryce had, and crawls on a patchwork comforter that had been Bryce's, too. As Balfour is text-messaging Jarrett in Iraq, she's checking out Braiden's diaper, multitasking as always.

"People say I'm a strong woman," Balfour says, "but I'm not. It's just that when I grieve, I grieve alone . . ."

The pacifier pops out of Braiden's mouth. Balfour rinses it, pops it back in.

". . . because deep down I feel I don't have the right to grieve in front of others."

Balfour says she has carefully crafted the face she shows the world.

"I would like to disappear, to move someplace where no one knows who I am and what I did. I would do that in a heartbeat, but I can't. I have to say my name. I'm the lady who killed her child, and I have to be that lady because I promised Bryce."

The promise, she says, came as she held her son's body in the hospital. "I kissed him for the last time, and I told him how sorry I was, and I said I would do everything in my power to make sure this will never happen to another child."

Balfour has done this in a way suited to her personality; she has become a modern, maternal version of the Ancient Mariner, brazenly bellying up to strangers in places such as Sam's Club and starting a conversation about children, so she can tell them what she did to one of hers. An in-your-face cautionary tale.

Unlike most parents to whom this has happened, Balfour will talk to the media, anytime. She works with Kids and Cars, telling her story repeatedly. Her point is always consistent, always resolute, always tinged with a little anger, always a little self-serving, sometimes a bit abrasive: *This can happen to anyone. This is a mistake, not a crime, and should not be prosecuted. Cars need safety devices to prevent this.* She seldom seems in doubt or in particular anguish. No one sees her cry.

"The truth is," she says, "the pain never gets less. It's never dulled. I just put it away for a while, until I'm in private."

Balfour doesn't like to think about Bryce's final ordeal. A kindly doctor once told her that her son probably didn't suffer a great deal, and she clings to this resolutely. In her mind, Bryce died unafraid, surrounded by consoling angels. The deity Balfour believes in loves us unconditionally and takes a direct hand in our lives; this delivers comfort, but also doubt.

"When I was sixteen in high school," she says, "I was date-raped. I had an abortion. I never told anyone, not my friends and not my mother. As the abortion was happening, I prayed to God and asked Him to take the baby back, and give him back to me when I could take care of him."

So . . . ?

"So, I do wonder, sometimes . . ."

Balfour wipes a tear.

". . . It's there in the back of my mind, that what happened to me is punishment from God. I killed a child, and then I had one ripped away from me at the peak of my happiness."

On the floor, Braiden is entranced by an Elmo doll.

"Sometimes," Balfour says, "I wish I had died in childbirth with him . . ."

She's weeping now. For the moment, there's no soldier left.

". . . that way, Jarrett could have Braiden, and I could be with Bryce."

———————

MILES HARRISON IS in a Leesburg Starbucks, seated next to the condiment station, pulling napkin after napkin to dry his eyes.

"I hurt my wife so much," he says, "and by the grace of whatever wonderful quality is within her, she has forgiven me. And that makes me feel even worse. Because I can't forgive me."

In the months after he was acquitted in the death of his son, Harrison's public agony continued. His mug shot was back in the newspapers after the Russian Foreign Ministry officially protested his acquittal and threatened to halt the country's adoption program with Americans. It was something of an international incident.

For months, Harrison declined to speak for this article, but in early February, he said he was ready.

"I pray for forgiveness from the Russian people," he said. "There are good people in this country who deserve children, and there are children in Russia who need parents. Please don't punish everyone for my mistake."

Harrison is a Roman Catholic. Weeks after Chase's death, he returned to his local church, where priest and parishioners left him to grieve in solitude. Afterward, the priest embraced him and whispered in his ear: "I will always be here for you."

The church is St. Francis de Sales in Purcellville. The priest was Father Michael Kelly. On New Year's Eve, on a windswept road after a heavy rain, as Father Michael stopped to move a tree that had fallen across the road, he was struck by another falling tree and killed.

Harrison doesn't know what to make of this; nothing entirely holds together anymore, except, to his astonishment, his marriage.

In their home, Carol and Miles Harrison have kept Chase's nursery exactly as it was, and the child's photos are all over. "Sometimes we'll look at a picture together," Harrison says, "and I will see Carol cry. She tries not to let me see, but I see, and I feel such guilt and hurt."

Harrison says he knows it is unlikely he and Carol will be allowed to adopt again.

He leans forward, his voice breaking into a sobbing falsetto, as it did in the courtroom at his worst moment of shame.

"I have cheated her out of being a mother."

In Starbucks, heads turn.

"She would be the best mother in the world."

THE FIRST TIME, someone answers the phone but doesn't say anything. There is just the sound of a TV turned up way too loud, and after a little while, the phone clicks dead. A few days later, he answers, but the TV is not lowered. Call back later, he says. On the third day, he takes the call.

Are you doing okay?

"I don't even know. Tryin' to take it day by day."

Andrew Culpepper's voice is a flat monotone, like a man in a trance. His sentences are short and truncated. This is the sanitation department electrician in Portsmouth, the lucky one. He was the man who wasn't criminally charged when Miles Harrison was. He never had to legally defend himself.

Are you alone now?

"Yeah."

She left you?

"Yeah. She's hurt and stuff. Dealing with it her way, I guess."

Are you thankful you weren't prosecuted?

No answer.

Andrew?

"Not for myself, for my parents. Doesn't matter what they do to me. Nothing I don't do to myself every day."

Are you sure you're okay?

"I try to take my mind off it. When I start thinking about it, I get like . . ."

Like what?

A long silence.

"Like this."

AS PART OF her plan to simplify her life, Lyn Balfour has quit her job. It's going to get a little more complicated soon, because she's pregnant again: The insemination that she had on that day in October was successful. The baby is due in July.

Balfour's lawyers petitioned the court to get the record of her prosecution expunged. Such a request is usually unopposed after an acquittal, in recognition that a legally innocent person has a right to start again with a legally clean slate. But in this case, Commonwealth's Attorney Dave Chapman challenged it and, unusually, argued the relatively small legal battle himself.

Outside the courthouse, Chapman explained: "It's very rare to oppose expungement. But we are, because of the enormity of this case, because it is the sole public record of the death of a completely defenseless and helpless infant."

After a half-day hearing, the judge ruled for the Commonwealth, saying Balfour had failed to prove that she would suffer a "manifest injustice" if the court records remained unsealed.

Afterward, Balfour calmly answered questions from the news media, as always. She was unemotional, unapologetic, on message. She will consider an appeal. She will continue to speak out for greater public awareness of the dangers of leaving children alone in cars. She sounded, as always, just a little bit cold.

Jarrett Balfour finally made it home, after eighteen months in Iraq, where his job was to analyze seized explosive devices made by insurgents and try to identify their technology and trace their origin. He extended his tour of duty twice, as the legal bills kept mounting.

Jarrett is thirty. He's tall, lanky, and strikingly handsome, with sandy hair brushed straight back. He looks like a man leaning into a strong wind.

Initially after he got home, Jarrett says, things were awkward, with "hiccups" in communication. He would make an innocuous statement about something Braiden was doing, and Lyn would overreact, as if he were second-guessing her parenting skills. It's getting better, he says.

Braiden is nine and a half months old, exactly the age Bryce was when he died. Lyn has been having nightmares again.

Just before the tragedy, she had two dreams that seem to her, in retrospect, like foreboding. In one, she accidentally drowned Bryce; in the other, it was death by fire. Balfour believes these dreams were sent by God to help prepare her for what she was about to endure.

Recently, she dreamed she lost control of Braiden's stroller, and it rolled out into traffic. No, she doesn't think it's the same thing happening again.

"I couldn't take it again," Jarrett says quietly.

So, there are tensions. They are working it out. Both of them say they are confident this marriage will last.

After Jarrett leaves for work, Lyn talks about how much the presence of Braiden has helped them heal. She considers her family blessed because they've been able to have other children: "Can you imagine losing your only child and not having a hope of having another? Can you imagine that despair?"

That's why, she says, she's made a decision. She's checked it out, and it would be legal. There would be no way for any authority to stop it because it would fall into the class of a private adoption. She'd need a sperm donor and an egg donor, because she wouldn't want to use her own egg. That would make it too personal.

What is she saying, exactly?

Miles and Carol Harrison deserve another child, Balfour explains. They would be wonderful parents.

This is the woman you either like or don't like, right away. She is brassy and strong-willed and, depending on your viewpoint, refreshingly open or abrasively forward. Above all, she is decisive.

Balfour says she's made up her mind. If Miles and Carol Harrison are denied another adoption, if they exhaust all their options and are still without a baby, she will offer to carry one for them, as a gift.

An Honorable Affair

Monica Lewinsky should have lied.

I believed that at the time. Still do. She should have said that she'd made it all up, that it had all been some childish fantasy she'd giggled out to a girl-friend, not knowing she was being recorded, not re-alizing her little self-aggrandizing lie would become such a big deal.

Everyone would have suspected, of course. The feds might have tried to nail her for perjury. She would have gone through hell, but she'd have also transformed herself into a romantic heroine for the ages.

Her silence would have been an eloquent dec-laration that some things are, and must remain, private—beyond the reach of politics, the media, and sometimes even the law. Above all, she would have saved us from the vulgar, endless spectacle that played out in front of a mortified nation.

It was at the height of the whole sordid affair that I learned about the story of Mary Hulbert, the woman who had held her tongue. I don't usu-ally write historical pieces, but this prim, Victorian melodrama seemed positively tailored for the time.

April 18, 1999

IT WAS TO be a simple bribe. Dollars for dirt.

As the lady recalled it many years later, the stranger at the door said his name was Wilson, but soon amended this to Smith. He said he was a patriot, on a mission of national urgency. Gallantly, he inquired after her health. Solicitously, he wondered if her wardrobe was adequate for the winter months. Mightn't she be more comfortable in furs? With gentle disapproval, he surveyed her modest Manhattan hotel room, tut-tutting that a woman of her breeding should surely be able to afford a full suite, with a proper parlor and sitting room.

She was quite comfortable, she assured him.

Still, he said, an extra $250,000 would make a difference in her life.

She arched an eyebrow. Two hundred and fifty thousand was indeed a great deal of money, she agreed.

Or $300,000, he said. Money was no object to the men he represented.

I see, she said.

And she did see. They wanted the letters.

She inclined her head encouragingly. She knew how to keep a gentleman talking. Once, she had been a society hostess to the mighty and the witty, holding forth from beneath great feathered hats, scandalizing genteel society by smoking cigarettes openly and without apology. She traced her ancestry to Colonial New England, in 1636.

On this day in 1916, she was still handsome, but well past the blush of youth. She was fifty-two, already widowed and divorced. Her soft Victorian features had tautened, her coquettish manner replaced by an appealing, mischievous cynicism. Time and troubles had taken their toll. In the moving pictures, she could have played the careworn, rawboned farm family matriarch, ringing the chow bell and mopping her hands on her apron; indeed, she would soon be reduced to auditioning for just such bit roles in Hollywood. The fact is, at the moment she was strapped for cash.

Her mysterious visitor continued: He represented the Republican Party, an emissary for men who had only the best interests of the nation at heart. If she cooperated, he admitted, she might well discover that America would become temporarily inhospitable to her. But he and his friends could see to it that she was well provided for in Europe.

All to what end, she asked. To bring to justice the cad who had used and then jilted her. To bring about, the visitor said, the impeachment of the president of the United States.

The president was Woodrow Wilson. He was, of course, never impeached or even publicly accused of misconduct. His presidency was never imperiled. This first, feeble effort to unseat a president for sexual improprieties never got off the ground. But there are lessons in this tale that are germane to our times.

For Americans sickened by the ongoing national spectacle of presidential sex conducted as sport, of casual gropings and casual betrayal, of stunning indiscretions and ludicrously loose lips, of private matters played out as public pornography, the story of Woodrow Wilson and his alleged lover, Mary Allen Hulbert, provides a charming respite. Theirs may have been the most proper and dignified and discreet and downright *honorable* illicit affair in history.

Hulbert, the woman in the hotel room, was said to have possessed compromising letters that attested to a lengthy extramarital dalliance between her and Wilson. There had long been rumors to that effect. Hulbert and Wilson had long denied them. But now there was, apparently, an offer on the table. And talk—however reckless—of impeachment.

That a nation headed for war would have jettisoned a popular president because of an alleged romantic entanglement is highly unlikely. That a serious sex scandal would have been devastating to Wilson's presidency, and eroded his moral authority at a critical time in history, cannot be doubted. In any case, nothing ever came of it.

Having extracted all she could from her visitor, Mary Hulbert regarded him with contempt. Any letters that might exist, she said icily, would only redound to Mr. Wilson's credit and further burnish his good name.

Furthermore, she said, "I am not that sort of a woman," and asked him to leave.

OF ALL THE presidents, few seem as unlikely a candidate for sexual scandal as Woodrow Wilson, son of a puritanical Presbyterian minister. Proper, prudish, punctilious, famously repressed, Wilson is said to have remained a virgin until his first marriage at twenty-eight. His long, dour face and prim pince-nez spectacles gave him a look of impenetrable rectitude, and the high starched collars and stovepipe hat in which he was frequently photographed suggested Edwardian formality. Striding the world stage beside the dapper, diminutive Lloyd George and the walrus-mustached Clemenceau, Wilson seemed more modern but also more aloof and unapproachable. When rumors of an affair initially surfaced during Wilson's first presidential campaign in 1912, his opponent, Teddy Roosevelt, peremptorily dismissed them: "You can't cast a man as a Romeo when he looks and acts so much like an apothecary's clerk."

Throughout Wilson's eventful eight-year presidency, the gossip about Mary Hulbert—then known by her married name, Mary Peck—persisted. To the wags of the day, Wilson was "Peck's bad boy." But for a half-century, historians gave the talk little credence. In his 1959 Pulitzer Prize–winning biography, Arthur Walworth made it clear he considered the rumors of an affair to be calumny: Wilson and Mary Hulbert, he suggested, were merely fast friends.

And that would have remained the official verdict, but for certain events.

After the death in 1962 of Edith Bolling Wilson, the president's second wife, tens of thousands of his personal papers became available for publication by the Library of Congress. Under the guidance of renowned Wilson scholar Arthur S. Link, a team of historians began the arduous task of copying and cataloguing them. The collection included papers that Hulbert had sold to an official biographer, long after Wilson's death, as well as voluminous correspondence between Woodrow and Edith. Over the years, as researchers descended on the Wilson Papers and focused on the matter of Mary Hulbert, a new story line began to emerge.

One of the first biographers to look at the years 1907–1915 was Frances W. Saunders, who was writing a book about Wilson's first wife, Ellen Axson Wilson, who died during his first term. Poring through the papers in 1975, Saunders found intriguing letters. Curiously intimate letters. More than two hundred of them.

The letters.

"Woodrow Wilson was not," Saunders says today, "the old dried-up prune that people portray him to be."

The precise nature of the relationship between Wilson and Hulbert remains an enduring mystery, debated robustly by historians. Scholars have taken turns combing the same trove of lush correspondence, parsing it for revealing nuance or hidden metaphor. Both Wilson and Hulbert write with elegance and clarity, but the letters are very much a product of their time. Matters of the heart are discussed only obliquely, with Victorian propriety. Certain things must be understood by inference.

What these new documents made clear to Saunders and others is that the president and the society lady were, for a time at least, passionately in love. Also, that this relationship was liberating to Wilson at a critical time in his political life, and may even have affected the course of history.

What is not clear, to put it bluntly, is whether they ever had sex.

"I go back and forth on it," says David Wayne Hirst, Princeton historian and senior associate editor of the Wilson Papers. "So did Arthur." He means Arthur Link, who died last year, certain about most things related to Wilson, but uncertain of this.

Hulbert and Wilson met in 1907 in midwinter on the island of Bermuda. She was forty-four and temporarily alone, on her yearly escape from a loveless marriage in Massachusetts. Wilson was fifty, then president of Princeton University, also vacationing alone, decompressing from a grueling fight with university trustees and a popular dean over the disposition of private endowments to the graduate school. Wilson's wife, Ellen, was back in New Jersey, ailing, beset by a depression that strained their marriage. In Bermuda, the bougainvillea was in bloom.

"The setting for an affair," says Saunders, "was perfect."

Hulbert owned Shoreby, a huge, windswept estate on the island. She entertained governors and captains of industry and luminaries like Mark Twain. She was vivacious, free of spirit, fun-loving—everything the high-buttoned Princeton president was not. One day, Wilson noticed her hurrying across a hotel lobby, a trim, elegant woman aflutter in silken shawls. He wangled an invitation for dinner, and a friendship developed.

Side by side, he and she walked the beaches and country lanes of Bermuda. They discussed literature and politics; Hulbert was well read and well spoken, unsparing in her opinions, and Wilson appreciated strong, intelligent women. He counseled her on her marriage, advising her to seek a separation. He shared with her his professional frustrations, and she offered her advice.

For the next eight years, through much of his presidency, the two would exchange letters nearly weekly.

All of this was known. Wilson never denied their correspondence or the depth of their friendship. When he was president, his letters to Hulbert arrived on White House stationery. Her servants saw them. Rumors were inevitable, but they were steadfastly denied. In a fact frequently cited by early Wilson historians as proof of the innocence of the relationship, Wilson himself had introduced Mary to Ellen Wilson. The two women were friends. They had shopped together.

Hulbert was descended on more than once by men with agendas, politicians wishing to prove a romance. She always denied it.

The story of the alleged hotel room bribe appeared in a 1925 series of memoirs Hulbert wrote for *Liberty* magazine, a year after Wilson's death. When it was published, there was a one-day furor in Congress.

Representative Frank Reid, an Illinois Democrat, introduced a resolution demanding an investigation. If Hulbert was right, he said, there had been a heinous effort to smear an innocent man and subvert the Constitution for political gain. On January 4, 1925, this story was reported on page 1 of the *Washington Post*.

Congress at the time was heavily Republican. No one was about to investigate ten-year-old allegations of an attempted bribe engineered by the GOP. House records show the resolution was referred to committee, where it unceremoniously died.

As did Mary Hulbert, in 1939. The story of her alleged love affair, more or less, died with her. The Wilson Papers brought it back.

"Dearest friend" is how the married Woodrow Wilson addresses his most ardent letters to Hulbert. "With infinite tenderness" is how he signs them. He was smitten.

In one sequence of letters, Wilson is in Bermuda and Hulbert is not. He tells her he misses her, and says, "God was very good to me to send me such a friend, so perfectly satisfying and delightful, so delectable."

She responds: "Does the bougainvillea fling itself over the cottage as of old? Why, why can I not be there—to fling myself where I would!"

Once, Wilson writes her that he cannot walk the streets of the island without thinking of her. "Why have you taken such complete possession of Bermuda?" He was lonely without her, he said: "You really must come down to relieve me."

And then there is this, perhaps as close to a smoking gun as these elliptical and circumspect letters get. Among the letters of February 1, 1908, was a petition that Wilson had drafted and Mark Twain had signed, protesting a plan to bring automobiles to Bermuda. On the back was a scribble. Arthur Link recognized it as professional shorthand. Link knew Wilson better than any scholar alive. He knew Wilson knew shorthand. Link hunted up an expert.

The scribble was apparently the beginning of a draft of a letter. This is what it said: "My precious one, my beloved Mary . . ." Years later, Wilson would use "my precious one" as a salutation to another woman—Edith Bolling Galt, with whom he was in love, and would soon marry.

The most intriguing correspondence of all is a series of letters from September 1915 between Wilson and Galt. At the time, the two were secretly engaged, and they were planning to announce it to the public. Wilson's advisers were horrified. They thought it was too soon after Ellen Wilson's death from kidney disease in 1914.

So William G. McAdoo, Wilson's adviser and son-in-law, concocted a plan. He told the president he had heard that Mary Hulbert, incensed at rumors of the impending marriage, feeling jealous and misused, was showing his letters around. This was a wild stab in the dark, and a lie. Mary Hulbert was not, indeed, "that kind of a woman." But McAdoo hoped the threat alone would make Wilson reconsider his marriage plans.

Wilson, however, was no coward. When presented with a problem, he faced it down.

In the files is a letter from Wilson to Galt, dated September 18. It was dashed off hurriedly. It lacks Wilson's customary flourishes of both prose and penmanship. The letter cancels the couple's dinner at the White House that day, and begs Galt to accept a visit from him at her home to discuss "something personal about myself that I feel I must tell you about at once."

They spoke privately that night. No one alive knows what was said.

But in a subsequent letter, Galt tells Wilson that she was deeply troubled by his revelation but forgives him and trusts in his love. What follows is an embarrassing hemorrhage of correspondence from Wilson to Galt—wretched, writhing, abject letters declaring himself undeserving of her sweet and merciful forgiveness.

In one of these, dated September 21, he says of his confession: "I knew that it would give a tragically false impression of what I really have been and am, because it might make the contemptible error and madness of a few months seem a stain upon a whole life." In another letter, he cited "a folly long ago loathed and repented of," leaving him "stained and unworthy."

Clearly, Wilson had confessed something profound that day in September 1915. What was it? What was the "madness of a few months"?

Is it possible that Wilson was so stiff and proper, so straitlaced, that he might have been confessing no greater sin than lust in his heart—an unconsummated love affair that moved him to write intemperate letters? "It's entirely possible," says Hirst, the historian.

Is it possible that Wilson actually confessed to a torrid physical affair? "It's entirely possible," says Hirst.

The papers also reveal that Ellen Wilson herself knew of or deeply suspected a betrayal. Shortly before she died, she told White House physician Cary Grayson that Wilson's relationship with Mary Hulbert had been the only episode in their marriage in which Wilson had caused her pain. What she meant by that was never explained. (Whatever his relationship with Hulbert, Wilson deeply loved his wife, and was devastated by her death. At the time, he confided to an aide that he hoped to be assassinated.)

About Wilson and Hulbert, in short, there is ample room for suspicion. The rest is surmise and conjecture. "You can draw your own conclusions as to whether they were just dancing around the bougainvillea or not," Hirst laughs.

Actually, he suspects that's all it was: an infatuation that never resulted in a physical union. The late political historian August Heckscher looked at the same documents and reached a different conclusion. In his excellent 1991 biography of Wilson, he flatly declares it a love affair, and speculates that the "madness of a few months" took place between November 1909 and February 1910, when Hulbert was living in a New York apartment with her mother. Shortly before and during this period, Wilson's letters betray maximum ardor. And Wilson is known to have visited New York several times around then. Sometimes Ellen was with him. Sometimes she was not.

This is a fascinating time in Wilson's life, coinciding with a period of almost reckless political experimentation. During this time he would abandon his lifelong caution, initiating a series of moves that would lead to his resignation from Princeton. It was a major gamble: Wilson lost stature as an academic administrator but gained a national reputation as a fighter for intellectual freedom and an enemy of the monied elite. It launched a political career that would lead him first to the governorship of New Jersey and soon thereafter to one of the great presidencies in American history.

Is it possible that a romantic liaison had emboldened him? Consider this: In his June 1908 baccalaureate address, Wilson dourly told the young Princeton men: "I am not sure that it is of the first importance that you should be happy. Many an unhappy man has been of deep service to the world and to himself."

A year later, speaking before the next graduating class at a time when his letters indicate a growing passion for the company of Hulbert, Wilson changed his tone. He told the graduates that there are things one does for duty and things one does for joy "with the free spirit of the adventurer." These, he said, "are the inviting by-paths of life into which you go for discovery, to get off the dusty road of mere duty into cool meadows and shadowed glades where the scene is changed and the air seems full of the tonic of freedom."

Hulbert's correspondence at the time makes it clear that Wilson sought her opinion on his switch from academia to politics, and that she offered unambiguous advice: Go for it.

Did she also provide him a more explosive boost to his self-confidence?

———————

PERHAPS IT IS appropriate that the final words on this matter belong to Mary Hulbert herself.

After 1915, she stopped writing to Wilson, and he to her. Her fortunes had taken a downturn because of bad investments and the illness of her son. She remained indebted to the president; he purchased the mortgage on some of her real estate, and once lent her $600.

In her 1925 *Liberty* magazine articles, written "to silence whispering tongues," Hulbert is protective of Wilson's legacy and reticent about their relationship. She pronounces Wilson one of the giants of American history. Defiantly, she decries any efforts to sully his name: "Woodrow Wilson is dead; he will not be impeached in the court wherein God presides."

Yet this was not quite her final word. Years later, Hulbert would write of Wilson once again. In 1933, she authored *The Story of Mrs. Peck*, a book that was billed as a tell-all account. It did not make much of an impact. Americans scarcely remembered the story of Mrs. Peck, and those who did no longer much cared. It was 1933; the country had bigger things to worry about.

Even some Wilson historians don't know of, or fail to recall, this book. Frank Aucella, curator of the Woodrow Wilson House in Washington, hadn't heard of it.

There are perhaps a half-dozen copies of *The Story of Mrs. Peck* in existence. The Library of Congress has one. The pages are the color of buttermilk. They smell sturdy with age.

Perhaps, at last, we will get the lowdown on the sex.

Here, on p. 143, Woodrow Wilson makes his appearance.

He is called "Mr. Wilson."

He remains "Mr. Wilson" throughout the book.

Here he is, boyishly taking shorthand notes on his cuffs.

Here Mary gently rebukes him for leaving his teaspoon in the teacup. And another time for absentmindedly wearing his muffler in the house.

He cannot dance.

He has an excellent tenor.

He has sensitive digestion.

He doesn't much like dogs.

All his suits are made of the same gray cloth.

He is partial to chicken and rice, with corn and spinach.

Of romance, there is nothing. Mary does not deny it. She does not admit it. She simply does not address the question at all.

And that's all she wrote.

As the most tawdry presidential sex scandal in history unfolds in Congress, we are left to contemplate the lessons of the scandal that never was, the impeachment that never happened.

The fact is, we will never know the precise nature of the relationship between Woodrow Wilson and Mary Hulbert. Our curiosity will never be satiated.

In a sense, of course, it does not matter. A man and a woman loved and respected each other. They did not permit whatever passion they shared to destroy a marriage. What happened, happened. They took it to their graves.

Whatever degree of intimacy they enjoyed, the details shall remain—as one might argue these matters should remain—completely, eternally, gloriously private.

My Father's Vision,
Part II

*At my father's funeral, I'd planned to tell the story of
his final words. At the last moment I lost my nerve,
because I knew I'd break down. Instead, I held it for
nearly three years, until the perfect day.*

May 24, 2009

N O ONE ACCEPTED physical deterioration with greater
grace and humor than my father. Over the last two decades of his life, his eyesight clouded into a soup—at
first, a nice consommé, but eventually minestrone, and a hearty
one.

He was effectively blind but remarkably cheerful about it.
He read the *Washington Post* front to back every day, all day, on
a device that magnified each letter to the size of a fist; polysyl-
labic words required three screens' worth of letters and a nimble
short-term memory. My father understood the absurdity of it. He
said that using this machine to read was like putting on mittens
to tie your shoes.

At his assisted-living facility, my father dined with the same
man every day for years. They became good friends, sharing ob-

servations and the genteel sort of intimacies consistent with two gentlemen who addressed each other as "Mr. Williams" and "Mr. Weingarten."

One day my father told me that Mr. Williams had died. He was sad, but smiling. "I read his obituary in the paper today, and I learned something about him I never knew. Everyone else here knew it absolutely, but I didn't." He wanted me to guess.

"He was rich?"

"Nope!"

"He was famous?"

"Nope!"

"I give up, Pop."

"He was black!"

A widower for ten years, at eighty-five my father found a girlfriend. Jeanette was another resident at his complex; her age and the thermostat setting in her apartment were both in the mid-90s. I liked her, but could hardly bear to spend five minutes in her place. My father never seemed to mind at all.

Then one day, after a visit to Jeanette, he laughed and said, "It's like the woman lives on the surface of Mercury."

My father remained mentally sharp until two years before his death, when he fell under the thrall of a particularly insidious form of dementia.

His gaps in cognition were unpredictable; the fog came and went. Analytical as always, my father liked me to test his mind from time to time with questions for which he ought to know the answers. Sometimes, he was perfect, sometimes less so. Nothing was worse than the day I asked him the first name of my mother's only sister. He couldn't remember it.

We both knew I had to ask one more question. It was followed by a long, painful silence.

"Oboyoboy," was all he said. No, he could not remember my mother's first name, either.

The look on his face was as hopeless as I'd ever seen. Scouring the room for anything to change the subject, my eyes fell on the sports section. "Hey," I blurted, "the Yankees have picked up Al Leiter!"

My father brightened. "Oh, he's really good! Lefty, used to be with the Mets!"

He started laughing even before I did.

For the final few months of his life, as he sank into rambling incoherence, my father needed round-the-clock nursing. My visits became a little less frequent. My father was gone, and the babbling person in that bed did not know who I was, or even that I was there.

Not everything that happens in a writer's life is appropriate to publish, and you would not be reading this column except for one fact. When I came to visit my father one day in the summer of 2006, a few weeks before his death, the nurse had unexpected news: "He said something."

She meant he had said something that made sense. One sentence had fought its way through the swirling, toxic churn and came out intact.

My father was an uncomplicated man; in a way, that was his genius. He taught me that there are only a few things that are important in life, and that those things are the only things that matter at all. I never really got a chance to thank him for that.

My father's last coherent words were: "My granddaughter is going to be an animal doctor."

She graduates from veterinary school today, Pop.

The Fiddler in
the Subway

As I came up the Metro escalator one morning on the way to work, I heard music. At the top of the stairs was a man of middle age in a grimy trench coat, playing Beethoven skillfully on an electric keyboard.

Beside him was an open instrument case that held two singles and some change. People were scurrying past him as though he was some sort of annoyance. When I dropped in a buck, his look of gratitude was heartbreaking.

As I walked to my office, I thought: I bet if Yo-Yo Ma himself had been out there with his cello, dressed in rags, no one would have paid him any mind.

As soon as I got to my desk, I called Ma's agent. He was intrigued by the idea of carrying out a special stunt. We traded e-mails for a few months, but it never worked out.

The notion stayed with me, though. And when, a few years later, a colleague mentioned this young, talented, mischievous fellow named Joshua Bell . . .

April 8, 2007

H E EMERGED FROM the Metro at the L'Enfant Plaza
station and positioned himself against a wall beside a
trash basket. By most measures, he was nondescript: a
youngish white man in jeans, a long-sleeved T-shirt and a Washington Nationals baseball cap. From a small case, he removed a
violin. Placing the open case at his feet, he shrewdly threw in a
few dollars and pocket change as seed money, swiveled it to face
pedestrian traffic, and began to play.

It was 7:51 A.M. on Friday, January 12, the middle of the
morning rush hour. In the next forty-three minutes, as the violinist performed six classical pieces, 1,097 people passed by. Almost
all of them were on the way to work, which meant, for almost all
of them, a government job. L'Enfant Plaza is at the nucleus of
federal Washington, and these were mostly mid-level bureaucrats
with those indeterminate, oddly fungible titles: policy analyst,
project manager, budget officer, specialist, facilitator, consultant.

Each passerby had a quick choice to make, one familiar to
commuters in any urban area where the occasional street performer is part of the cityscape: Do you stop and listen? Do you
hurry past with a blend of guilt and irritation, aware of your cu-
pidity but annoyed by the unbidden demand on your time and
your wallet? Do you throw in a buck, just to be polite? Does
your decision change if he's really bad? What if he's really good?
Do you have time for beauty? Shouldn't you? What is the moral
mathematics of the moment?

On that Friday in January, those private questions would be
answered in an unusually public way. No one knew it, but the
fiddler standing against a bare wall outside the Metro in an indoor arcade at the top of the escalators was one of the finest
classical musicians in the world, playing some of the most elegant music ever written on one of the most valuable violins ever

made. His performance was arranged by the *Washington Post* as an experiment in context, perception, and priorities—as well as an unblinking assessment of public taste: In a banal setting at an inconvenient time, would beauty transcend?

The musician did not play popular tunes whose familiarity alone might have drawn interest. That was not the test. These were masterpieces that have endured for centuries on their brilliance alone, soaring music befitting the grandeur of cathedrals and concert halls.

The acoustics proved surprisingly kind. Though the arcade is of utilitarian design, a buffer between the Metro escalator and the outdoors, it somehow caught the sound and bounced it back, round and resonant. The violin is an instrument that is said to be much like the human voice, and in this musician's masterly hands, it sobbed and laughed and sang—ecstatic, sorrowful, importuning, adoring, flirtatious, castigating, playful, romancing, merry, triumphal, sumptuous.

So, what do you think happened?

HANG ON, WE'LL get you some expert help.

Leonard Slatkin, music director of the National Symphony Orchestra, was asked the same question. What did he think would occur, hypothetically, if one of the world's great violinists had performed incognito before a traveling rush-hour audience of 1,000-odd people?

"Let's assume," Slatkin said, "that he is not recognized and just taken for granted as a street musician . . . Still, I don't think that if he's really good, he's going to go unnoticed. He'd get a larger audience in Europe . . . but, okay, out of a thousand people, my guess is there might be thirty-five or forty who will recognize the quality for what it is. Maybe seventy-five to a hundred will stop and spend some time listening."

So, a crowd would gather?

"Oh, yes."

And how much will he make?

"About a hundred fifty dollars."

Thanks, Maestro. As it happens, this is not hypothetical. It really happened.

"How'd I do?"

We'll tell you in a minute.

"Well, who was the musician?"

Joshua Bell.

"NO!!!"

A ONETIME CHILD prodigy, at thirty-nine Joshua Bell has arrived as an internationally acclaimed virtuoso. Three days before he appeared at the Metro station, Bell had filled the house at Boston's stately Symphony Hall, where merely pretty good seats went for $100. Two weeks later, at the Music Center at Strathmore, in North Bethesda, Maryland, he would play to a standing-room-only audience so respectful of his artistry that they stifled their coughs until the silence between movements. But on that Friday in January, Joshua Bell was just another mendicant, competing for the attention of busy people on their way to work.

Bell was first pitched this idea shortly before Christmas, over coffee at a sandwich shop on Capitol Hill. A New Yorker, he was in town to perform at the Library of Congress and to visit the library's vaults to examine an unusual treasure: an eighteenth-century violin that once belonged to the great Austrian-born virtuoso and composer Fritz Kreisler. The curators invited Bell to play it; good sound, still.

"Here's what I'm thinking," Bell confided, as he sipped his coffee. "I'm thinking that I could do a tour where I'd play Kreisler's music . . ."

He smiled.

". . . on Kreisler's violin."

It was a snazzy, sequined idea—part inspiration and part gimmick—and it was typical of Bell, who has unapologetically embraced showmanship even as his concert career has become more and more august. He's soloed with the finest orchestras here and abroad, but he's also appeared on *Sesame Street*, done late-night talk TV, and performed in feature films. That was Bell playing the soundtrack on the 1998 movie *The Red Violin*. (He body-doubled, too, playing to a naked Greta Scacchi.) As composer John Corigliano accepted the Oscar for Best Original Dramatic Score, he credited Bell, who, he said, "plays like a god."

When Bell was asked if he'd be willing to don street clothes and perform at rush hour, he said, "Uh, a stunt?"

Well, yes. A stunt. Would he think it . . . unseemly?

Bell drained his cup.

"Sounds like fun," he said.

Bell's a heartthrob. Tall and handsome, he's got a Donny Osmond–like dose of the cutes, and, onstage, cute elides into hott. When he performs, he is usually the only man under the lights who is not in white tie and tails—he walks out to a standing O, looking like Zorro, in black pants and an untucked black dress shirt, shirttail dangling. That cute Beatles-style mop top is also a strategic asset: Because his technique is full of body—athletic and passionate—he's almost dancing with the instrument, and his hair flies.

He's single and straight, a fact not lost on some of his fans. In Boston, as he performed Max Bruch's dour Violin Concerto in G Minor, the few young women in the audience nearly disappeared in the deep sea of silver heads. But seemingly every single one of them—a distillate of the young and pretty—coalesced at the stage door after the performance, seeking an autograph. It's like that always, with Bell.

Bell's been accepting over-the-top accolades since puberty: *Interview* magazine once said his playing "does nothing less than tell human beings why they bother to live." He's learned to field these things graciously, with a bashful duck of the head and a modified "pshaw."

Bell had only one condition for participating in this incognito performance. The event had been described to him as a test of whether, in an incongruous context, ordinary people would recognize genius. His condition: "I'm not comfortable if you call this genius."

"Genius" is an overused word, he said: It can be applied to some of the composers whose work he plays, but not to him. His skills are largely interpretive, he said, and to imply otherwise would be unseemly and inaccurate.

It was an interesting request, and under the circumstances, one that will be honored. The word will not again appear in this article.

It would be breaking no rules, however, to note that the term in question, particularly as applied in the field of music, refers to a congenital brilliance—an elite, innate, preternatural ability that manifests itself early, and often in dramatic fashion. One biographically intriguing fact about Bell is that he got his first music lessons when he was a four-year-old in Bloomington, Indiana. His parents, both psychologists, decided formal training might be a good idea after they saw that their son had strung rubber bands across his dresser drawers and was replicating classical tunes by ear, plucking the strings and moving the drawers in and out to vary the pitch.

To GET TO the Metro from his hotel, a distance of three blocks, Bell took a taxi. He's neither lame nor lazy: He did it for his violin.

Bell always performs on the same instrument, and he ruled

out using another for this gig. Called the Gibson ex-Huberman, it was handcrafted in 1713 by Antonio Stradivari during the Italian master's "golden period," toward the end of his career, when he had access to the finest spruce, maple, and willow, and when his technique had been refined to perfection.

"Our knowledge of acoustics is still incomplete," Bell said, "but he, he just . . . *knew*."

Bell doesn't mention Stradivari by name. Just "he." When the violinist shows his Strad to people, he holds the instrument gingerly by its neck, resting it on a knee. "He made this to perfect thickness at all parts," Bell says, pivoting it. "If you shaved off a millimeter of wood at any point, it would totally imbalance the sound." No violins sound as wonderful as Strads from the 1710s, still.

The front of Bell's violin is in nearly perfect condition, with a deep, rich grain and luster. The back is a mess, its dark reddish finish bleeding away into a flatter, lighter shade and finally, in one section, to bare wood.

"This has never been refinished," Bell said. "That's his original varnish. People attribute aspects of the sound to the varnish. Each maker had his own secret formula." Stradivari is thought to have made his from an ingeniously balanced cocktail of honey, egg whites, and gum arabic from sub-Saharan trees.

Like the instrument in *The Red Violin*, this one has a past filled with mystery and malice. Twice, it was stolen from its illustrious prior owner, the Polish virtuoso Bronislaw Huberman. The first time, in 1919, it disappeared from Huberman's hotel room in Vienna but was quickly returned. The second time, nearly twenty years later, it was pinched from his dressing room in Carnegie Hall. He never got it back. It was not until 1985 that the thief— a minor New York violinist—made a deathbed confession to his wife and produced the instrument.

Bell bought it a few years ago. He had to sell his own Strad and borrow much of the rest. The price tag was reported to be about $3.5 million.

All of which is a long explanation for why, in the early morning chill of a day in January, Josh Bell took a three-block cab ride to the Orange Line, and rode one stop to L'Enfant.

As METRO STATIONS go, L'Enfant Plaza is more plebeian than most. Even before you arrive, it gets no respect. Metro conductors never seem to get it right: "Leh-fahn." "Layfont." "El'phant."

At the top of the escalators are a shoeshine stand and a busy kiosk that sells newspapers, lottery tickets, and a wall full of magazines with titles such as *Mammazons* and *Girls of Barely Legal*. The skin mags move, but it's that lottery ticket dispenser that stays the busiest, with customers queuing up for Daily 6 lotto and Powerball and the ultimate suckers' bait, those pamphlets that sell random number combinations purporting to be "hot." They sell briskly. There's also a quick-check machine to slide in your lotto ticket, post-drawing, to see if you've won. Beneath it is a forlorn pile of crumpled slips.

On Friday, January 12, the people waiting in the lottery line looking for a long shot would get a lucky break—a free, close-up ticket to a concert by one of the world's most famous classical musicians—but only if they were of a mind to take note.

Bell decided to begin with the Chaconne from Johann Sebastian Bach's Partita No. 2 in D Minor. Bell calls it "not just one of the greatest pieces of music ever written, but one of the greatest achievements of any man in history. It's a spiritually powerful piece, emotionally powerful, structurally perfect. Plus, it was written for a solo violin, so I won't be cheating with some half-assed version."

Bell didn't say it, but Bach's Chaconne is also considered one of the most difficult violin pieces to master. Many try; few succeed. It's exhaustingly long—fourteen minutes—and consists entirely of a single, succinct musical progression repeated in dozens of variations to create a dauntingly complex architecture of sound. Composed around 1720, on the eve of the European Enlightenment, it is said to be a celebration of the breadth of human possibility.

If Bell's encomium to the Chaconne seems overly effusive, consider this from the nineteenth-century composer Johannes Brahms, in a letter to Clara Schumann: "On one stave, for a small instrument, the man writes a whole world of the deepest thoughts and most powerful feelings. If I imagined that I could have created, even conceived the piece, I am quite certain that the excess of excitement and earth-shattering experience would have driven me out of my mind."

So, that's the piece Bell started with.

He'd clearly meant it when he promised not to cheap out this performance: He played with acrobatic enthusiasm, his body leaning into the music and arching on tiptoes at the high notes. The sound was nearly symphonic, carrying to all parts of the homely arcade as the pedestrian traffic filed past.

Three minutes went by before anything happened. Sixty-three people had already passed when, finally, there was a breakthrough of sorts. A middle-age man altered his gait for a split second, turning his head to notice that there seemed to be some guy playing music. Yes, the man kept walking, but it was something.

A half-minute later, Bell got his first donation. A woman threw in a buck and scooted off. It was not until six minutes into the performance that someone actually stood against a wall and listened.

Things never got much better. In the three-quarters of an hour that Joshua Bell played, seven people stopped what they were doing to hang around and take in the performance, at least for a minute. Twenty-seven gave money, most of them on the run—for a total of $32 and change. That leaves the 1,070 people who hurried by, oblivious, many only 3 feet away, few even turning to look.

No, Mr. Slatkin, there was never a crowd, not even for a second.

It was all videotaped by a hidden camera. You can play the recording once or fifteen times, and it never gets any easier to watch. Try speeding it up, and it becomes one of those herky-jerky World War I–era silent newsreels. The people scurry by in comical little hops and starts, cups of coffee in their hands, cell phones at their ears, ID tags slapping at their bellies, a grim *danse macabre* to indifference, inertia, and the dingy, gray rush of modernity.

Even at this accelerated pace, though, the fiddler's movements remain fluid and graceful; he seems so apart from his audience—unseen, unheard, otherworldly—that you find yourself thinking that he's not really there. A ghost.

Only then do you see it: He is the one who is real. They are the ghosts.

———

IF A GREAT musician plays great music but no one hears . . . was he really any good?

It's an old epistemological debate, older, actually, than the koan about the tree in the forest. Plato weighed in on it, and philosophers for two millennia afterward: What is beauty? Is it a measurable fact (Gottfried Leibniz), or merely an opinion (David Hume), or is it a little of each, colored by the immediate state of mind of the observer (Immanuel Kant)?

We'll go with Kant, because he's obviously right, and because he brings us pretty directly to Joshua Bell, sitting there in a hotel restaurant, picking at his breakfast, wryly trying to figure out what the hell had just happened back there at the Metro.

"At the beginning," Bell says, "I was just concentrating on playing the music. I wasn't really watching what was happening around me . . ."

Playing the violin looks all-consuming, mentally and physically, but Bell says that for him the mechanics of it are partly second nature, cemented by practice and muscle memory: It's like a juggler, he says, who can keep those balls in play while interacting with a crowd. What he's mostly thinking about as he plays, Bell says, is capturing emotion as a narrative: "When you play a violin piece, you are a storyteller, and you're telling a story."

With the Chaconne, the opening is filled with a building sense of awe. That kept him busy for a while. Eventually, though, he began to steal a sidelong glance.

"It was a strange feeling, that people were actually, ah . . ."

The word doesn't come easily.

". . . *ignoring* me."

Bell is laughing. It's at himself.

"At a music hall, I'll get upset if someone coughs or if someone's cell phone goes off. But here, my expectations quickly diminished. I started to appreciate any acknowledgment, even a slight glance up. I was oddly grateful when someone threw in a dollar instead of change." This is from a man whose talents can command $1,000 a minute.

Before he began, Bell hadn't known what to expect. What he does know is that, for some reason, he was nervous.

"It wasn't exactly stage fright, but there were butterflies," he says. "I was stressing a little."

Bell has played, literally, before crowned heads of Europe. Why the anxiety at the Washington Metro?

"When you play for ticket-holders," Bell explains, "you are already validated. I have no sense that I need to be accepted. I'm already accepted. Here, there was this thought: What if they don't like me? What if they resent my presence . . ."

He was, in short, art without a frame. Which, it turns out, may have a lot to do with what happened—or, more precisely, what didn't happen—on January 12.

MARK LEITHAUSER HAS held in his hands more great works of art than any king or pope or Medici ever did. A senior curator at the National Gallery, he oversees the framing of the paintings. Leithauser thinks he has some idea of what happened at that Metro station.

"Let's say I took one of our more abstract masterpieces, say an Ellsworth Kelly, and removed it from its frame, marched it down the fifty-two steps that people walk up to get to the National Gallery, past the giant columns, and brought it into a restaurant. It's a five-million-dollar painting. And it's one of those restaurants where there are pieces of original art for sale, by some industrious kids from the Corcoran School, and I hang that Kelly on the wall with a price tag of a hundred fifty dollars. No one is going to notice it. An art curator might look up and say: 'Hey, that looks a little like an Ellsworth Kelly. Please pass the salt.'"

Leithauser's point is that we shouldn't be too ready to label the Metro passersby unsophisticated boobs. Context matters.

Kant said the same thing. He took beauty seriously: In his *Critique of Aesthetic Judgment*, Kant argued that one's ability to appreciate beauty is related to one's ability to make moral judgments. But there was a caveat. Paul Guyer of the University of Pennsylvania, one of America's most prominent Kantian scholars, says the eighteenth-century German philosopher felt that to properly appreciate beauty, the viewing conditions must be optimal.

"Optimal," Guyer said, "doesn't mean heading to work, focusing on your report to the boss, maybe your shoes don't fit right."

So, if Kant had been at the Metro watching Joshua Bell play to a thousand unimpressed passersby?

"He would have inferred about them," Guyer said, "absolutely nothing."

And that's that.

Except it isn't. To really understand what happened, you have to rewind that video and play it back from the beginning, from the moment Bell's bow first touched the strings.

———————

WHITE GUY, KHAKIS, leather jacket, briefcase. Early thirties. John David Mortensen is on the final leg of his daily bus-to-Metro commute from Reston. He's heading up the escalator. It's a long ride—one minute and fifteen seconds if you don't walk. So, like most everyone who passes Bell this day, Mortensen gets a good earful of music before he has his first look at the musician. Like most of them, he notes that it sounds pretty good. But like very few of them, when he gets to the top, he doesn't race past as though Bell were some nuisance to be avoided. Mortensen is that first person to stop, that guy at the six-minute mark.

It's not that he has nothing else to do. He's a project manager for an international program at the Department of Energy; on this day, Mortensen has to participate in a monthly budget exercise, not the most exciting part of his job: "You review the past month's expenditures," he says, "forecast spending for the next month, if you have X dollars, where will it go, that sort of thing."

On the video, you can see Mortensen get off the escalator and look around. He locates the violinist, stops, walks away but then is drawn back. He checks the time on his cell phone—he's three minutes early for work—then settles against a wall to listen.

Mortensen doesn't know classical music at all; classic rock is as close as he comes. But there's something about what he's hearing that he really likes.

As it happens, he's arrived at the moment that Bell slides into the second section of the Chaconne. ("It's the point," Bell says, "where it moves from a darker, minor key into a major key. There's a religious, exalted feeling to it.") The violinist's bow begins to dance; the music becomes upbeat, playful, theatrical, big.

Mortensen doesn't know about major or minor keys: "Whatever it was," he says, "it made me feel at peace."

So, for the first time in his life, Mortensen lingers to listen to a street musician. He stays his allotted three minutes as ninety-four more people pass briskly by. When he leaves to help plan contingency budgets for the Department of Energy, there's another first. For the first time in his life, not quite knowing what had just happened but sensing it was special, John David Mortensen gives a street musician money.

———

THERE ARE SIX moments in the video that Bell finds particularly painful to relive: "The awkward times," he calls them. It's what happens right after each piece ends: nothing. The music stops. The same people who hadn't noticed him playing don't notice that he has finished. No applause, no acknowledgment. So Bell just saws out a small, nervous chord—the embarrassed musician's equivalent of, "Er, okay, moving right along . . ."—and begins the next piece.

After the Chaconne, it is Franz Schubert's "Ave Maria," which surprised some music critics when it debuted in 1825: Schubert seldom showed religious feeling in his compositions, yet "Ave Maria" is a breathtaking work of adoration of the Virgin Mary. What was with the sudden piety? Schubert dryly answered: "I think this is due to the fact that I never forced devotion in myself and never compose hymns or prayers of that kind unless it overcomes me unawares; but then it is usually the right and true devotion." This musical prayer became among the most familiar and enduring religious pieces in history.

A couple of minutes into it, something revealing happens.

A woman and her preschooler emerge from the escalator. The woman is walking briskly and, therefore, so is the child. She's got his hand.

"I had a time crunch," recalls Sheron Parker, an IT director for a federal agency. "I had an eight-thirty training class, and first I had to rush Evvie off to his teacher, then rush back to work, then to the training facility in the basement."

Evvie is her son, Evan. Evan is three.

You can see Evan clearly on the video. He's the cute black kid in the parka who keeps twisting around to look at Joshua Bell, as he is being propelled toward the door.

"There was a musician," Parker says, "and my son was intrigued. He wanted to pull over and listen, but I was rushed for time."

So Parker does what she has to do. She deftly moves her body between Evan's and Bell's, cutting off her son's line of sight. As they exit the arcade, Evan can still be seen craning to look. When Parker is told what she walked out on, she laughs.

"Evan is very smart!"

The poet Billy Collins once laughingly observed that all babies are born with a knowledge of poetry, because the lub-dub of the mother's heart is in iambic meter. Then, Collins said, life slowly starts to choke the poetry out of us. It may be true with music, too.

There was no ethnic or demographic pattern to distinguish the people who stayed to watch Bell, or the ones who gave money, from that vast majority who hurried on past, unheeding. Whites, blacks, and Asians, young and old, men and women, were represented in all three groups. But the behavior of one demographic remained absolutely consistent. Every single time a child walked past, he or she tried to stop and watch. And every single time, a parent scooted the kid away.

———

IF THERE WAS one person on that day who was too busy to pay attention to the violinist, it was George Tindley. Tindley wasn't hurrying to get to work. He was *at* work.

The glass doors through which most people exit the L'Enfant station lead into an indoor shopping mall, from which there are exits to the street and elevators to office buildings. The first store in the mall is an Au Bon Pain, the croissant and coffee shop where Tindley, in his forties, works in a white uniform busing the tables, restocking the salt and pepper packets, taking out the garbage. Tindley labors under the watchful eye of his bosses, and he's supposed to be hopping, and he was.

But every minute or so, as though drawn by something not entirely within his control, Tindley would walk to the very edge of the Au Bon Pain property, keeping his toes inside the line, still on the job. Then he'd lean forward, as far out into the hallway as he could, watching the fiddler on the other side of the glass doors. The foot traffic was steady, so the doors were usually open. The sound came through pretty well.

"You could tell in one second that this guy was good, that he was clearly a professional," Tindley says. He plays the guitar, loves the sound of strings, and has no respect for a certain kind of musician.

"Most people, they play music; they don't feel it," Tindley says. "Well, that man was *feeling* it. That man was moving. Moving into the sound."

A hundred feet away, across the arcade, was the lottery line, sometimes five or six people long. They had a much better view of Bell than Tindley did, if they had just turned around. But no one did. Not in the entire forty-three minutes. They just shuffled forward toward that machine spitting out numbers. Eyes on the prize.

J. T. Tillman was in that line. A computer specialist for the Department of Housing and Urban Development, he remembers every single number he played that day—ten of them, $2 apiece, for a total of $20. He doesn't recall what the violinist was playing, though. He says it sounded like generic classical music, the kind the ship's band was playing in *Titanic*, before the iceberg.

"I didn't think nothing of it," Tillman says, "just a guy trying to make a couple of bucks."

Tillman would have given him one or two, he said, but he spent all his cash on lotto. When he is told that he stiffed one of the best musicians in the world, he laughs.

"Is he ever going to play around here again?"

"Yeah, but you're going to have to pay a lot to hear him."

"Damn."

Tillman didn't win the lottery, either.

BELL ENDS "AVE MARIA" to another thunderous silence, plays Manuel Ponce's sentimental "Estrellita," then a piece by Jules Massenet, and then begins a Bach gavotte, a joyful, frolicsome, lyrical dance. It's got an Old World delicacy to it; you can imagine it entertaining bewigged dancers at a Versailles ball, or—in a lute, fiddle, and fife version—the boot-kicking peasants of a Pieter Bruegel painting.

Watching the video weeks later, Bell finds himself mystified by one thing only. He understands why he's not drawing a crowd, in the rush of a morning workday. But: "I'm surprised at the number of people who don't pay attention at all, as if I'm invisible. Because, you know what? I'm makin' a lot of noise!"

He is. You don't need to know music at all to appreciate the simple fact that there's a guy there, playing a violin that's throwing out a whole bucket of sound; at times, Bell's bowing is so intricate that you seem to be hearing two instruments playing in harmony. So those head-forward, quick-stepping passersby are a remarkable phenomenon.

Bell wonders whether their inattention may be deliberate:

If you don't take visible note of the musician, you don't have to feel guilty about not forking over money; you're not complicit in a rip-off.

It may be true, but no one gave that explanation. People just said they were busy, had other things on their mind. Some who were on cell phones spoke louder as they passed Bell, to compete with that infernal racket.

Calvin Myint works for the General Services Administration. He got to the top of the escalator, turned right, and headed out a door to the street. A few hours later, he had no memory that there had been a musician anywhere in sight.

"Where was he, in relation to me?"

"About four feet away."

"Oh."

There's nothing wrong with Myint's hearing. He had buds in his ear. He was listening to his iPod.

For many of us, the explosion in technology has perversely limited, not expanded, our exposure to new experiences. Increasingly, we get our news from sources that think as we already do. And with iPods, we hear what we already know; we program our own playlists.

The song that Calvin Myint was listening to was "Just Like Heaven," by the British rock band the Cure. It's a terrific song, actually. The meaning is a little opaque, and the Web is filled with earnest efforts to deconstruct it. Many are far-fetched, but some are right on point: It's about a tragic emotional disconnect. A man has found the woman of his dreams but can't express the depth of his feeling for her until she's gone. It's about failing to see the beauty of what's plainly in front of your eyes.

"YES, I SAW the violinist," Jackie Hessian says, "but nothing about him struck me as much of anything."

You couldn't tell that by watching her. Hessian was one of those people who gave Bell a long, hard look before walking on. It turns out that she wasn't noticing the music at all.

"I really didn't hear that much," she said. "I was just trying to figure out what he was doing there, how does this work for him, can he make much money, would it be better to start with some money in the case, or for it to be empty, so people feel sorry for you? I was analyzing it financially."

What do you do, Jackie?

"I'm a lawyer in labor relations with the United States Postal Service. I just negotiated a national contract."

THE BEST SEATS in the house were upholstered. In the balcony, more or less. On that day, for $5, you'd get a lot more than just a nice shine on your shoes.

Only one person occupied one of those seats when Bell played. Terence Holmes is a consultant for the Department of Transportation, and he liked the music just fine, but it was really about a shoeshine: "My father told me never to wear a suit with your shoes not cleaned and shined."

Holmes wears suits often, so he is up in that perch a lot, and he's got a good relationship with the shoeshine lady. Holmes is a good tipper and a good talker, which is a skill that came in handy that day. The shoeshine lady was upset about something, and the music got her more upset. She complained, Holmes said, that the violinist was too loud, and Holmes tried to calm her down.

Edna Souza is from Brazil. She's been shining shoes at L'Enfant Plaza for six years, and she's had her fill of street musicians there; when they play, she can't hear her customers, and that's bad for business. So she fights.

Souza points to the dividing line between the Metro property, at the top of the escalator, and the arcade, which is under control of the management company that runs the mall. Sometimes, Souza says, a musician will stand on the Metro side, sometimes on the mall side. Either way, she's got him. On her speed dial, she has phone numbers for both the mall cops and the Metro cops. The musicians seldom last long.

What about Joshua Bell?

He was too loud, too, Souza says. Then she looks down at her rag, sniffs. She hates to say anything positive about these damned musicians, but: "He was pretty good, that guy. It was the first time I didn't call the police."

Souza was surprised to learn he was a famous musician, but not that people rushed blindly by him. That, she said, was predictable. "If something like this happened in Brazil, everyone would stand around to see. Not here."

Souza nods sourly toward a spot near the top of the escalator: "Couple of years ago, a homeless guy died right there. He just lay down there and died. The police came, an ambulance came, and no one even stopped to see or slowed down to look.

"People walk up the escalator, they look straight ahead. Mind your own business, eyes forward. Everyone is stressed. Do you know what I mean?"

What is this life if, full of care,
We have no time to stand and stare.
—From "Leisure," by W. H. Davies

Let's say Kant is right. Let's accept that we can't look at what happened on January 12 and make any judgment whatever about people's sophistication or their ability to appreciate beauty. But what about their ability to appreciate life?

We're busy. Americans have been busy, as a people, since at least 1831, when a young French sociologist named Alexis de

Tocqueville visited the States and found himself impressed, bemused, and slightly dismayed at the degree to which people were
driven, to the exclusion of everything else, by hard work and the
accumulation of wealth.

Not much has changed. Pop in a DVD of *Koyaanisqatsi*, the
wordless, darkly brilliant, avant-garde 1982 film about the fre-
netic speed of modern life. Backed by the minimalist music of
Philip Glass, director Godfrey Reggio takes film clips of Americans going about their daily business, but speeds them up until
they resemble assembly-line machines, robots marching lockstep
to nowhere. Now look at the video from L'Enfant Plaza, in fast-
forward. The Philip Glass soundtrack fits it perfectly.

Koyaanisqatsi is a Hopi word. It means "life out of balance."

In his 2003 book, *Timeless Beauty: In the Arts and Everyday
Life*, British author John Lane writes about the loss of the ap-
preciation for beauty in the modern world. The experiment at
L'Enfant Plaza may be symptomatic of that, he said—not because people didn't have the capacity to understand beauty, but
because it was irrelevant to them. "This is about having the wrong
priorities," Lane said.

If we can't take the time out of our lives to stay a moment
and listen to one of the best musicians on Earth play some of the
best music ever written; if the surge of modern life so overpowers
us that we are deaf and blind to something like that—then what
else are we missing?

That's what the Welsh poet W. H. Davies meant in 1911
when he published those two lines that begin this section. They
made him famous. The thought was simple, even primitive, but
somehow no one had put it quite that way before.

Of course, Davies had an advantage—an advantage of perception. He wasn't a tradesman or a laborer or a bureaucrat or
a consultant or a policy analyst or a labor lawyer or a program
manager. He was a hobo.

THE CULTURAL HERO of the day arrived at L'Enfant Plaza pretty late, in the unprepossessing figure of one John Picarello, a small-ish man with a baldish head. Picarello hit the top of the escalator just after Bell began his final piece, a reprise of the Chaconne. In the video, you see Picarello stop dead in his tracks, locate the source of the music, and then retreat to the other end of the arcade. He takes up a position past the shoeshine stand, across from that lottery line, and he will not budge for the next nine minutes.

Like all the passersby interviewed for this article, Picarello was stopped by a reporter after he left the building and was asked for his phone number. Like everyone, he was told only that this was to be an article about commuting. When he was called later in the day, like everyone else, he was first asked if anything un-usual had happened to him on his trip into work. Of the more than forty people contacted, Picarello was the only one who im-mediately mentioned the violinist.

"There was a musician playing at the top of the escalator at L'Enfant Plaza."

Haven't you seen musicians there before?

"Not like this one."

What do you mean?

"This was a superb violinist. I've never heard anyone of that caliber. He was technically proficient, with very good phrasing. He had a good fiddle, too, with a big, lush sound. I walked a distance away, to hear him. I didn't want to be intrusive on his space."

Really?

"Really. It was that kind of experience. It was a treat, just a brilliant, incredible way to start the day."

Picarello knows classical music. He is a fan of Joshua Bell

but didn't recognize him; he hadn't seen a recent photo, and besides, for most of the time Picarello was pretty far away. But he knew this was not a run-of-the-mill guy out there performing. On the video, you can see Picarello look around him now and then, almost bewildered.

"Yeah, other people just were not getting it. It just wasn't registering. That was baffling to me."

When Picarello was growing up in New York, he studied violin seriously, intending to be a concert musician. But he gave it up at eighteen, when he decided he'd never be good enough to make it pay. Life does that to you sometimes. Sometimes, you have to do the prudent thing. So he went into another line of work. He's a supervisor at the U.S. Postal Service. Doesn't play the violin much anymore.

When he left, Picarello says, "I humbly threw in five dollars." It *was* humble: You can actually see that on the video. Picarello walks up, barely looking at Bell, and tosses in the money. Then, as if embarrassed, he quickly walks away from the man he once wanted to be.

BELL THINKS HE did his best work of the day in those final few minutes, in the second Chaconne. And that also was the only time that more than one person was staying to watch. As Picarello stood in the back, Janice Olu arrived and took up a position a few feet away from Bell. Olu, a public trust officer with HUD, also played the violin as a kid. She didn't know the name of the piece she was hearing, but she knew the man playing it has a gift.

Olu was on a coffee break and stayed as long as she dared. As she turned to go, she whispered to the stranger next to her, "I *really* don't want to leave." The stranger standing next to her happened to be working for the *Washington Post*.

In preparing for this event, editors at the *Post Magazine* discussed how to deal with likely outcomes. The most widely held assumption was that there could be a problem with crowd control: In a demographic as sophisticated as Washington, the thinking went, several people would surely recognize Bell. Nervous "what-if" scenarios abounded. As people gathered, what if others stopped just to see what the attraction was? Word would spread through the crowd. Cameras would flash. More people flock to the scene; rush-hour pedestrian traffic backs up; tempers flare; the National Guard is called; tear gas, rubber bullets, etc.

As it happens, exactly one person recognized Bell, and she didn't arrive until near the very end. For Stacy Furukawa, a demographer at the Commerce Department, there was no doubt. She doesn't know much about classical music, but she had been in the audience three weeks earlier, at Bell's free concert at the Library of Congress. And here he was, the international virtuoso, sawing away, begging for money. She had no idea what the heck was going on, but whatever it was, she wasn't about to miss it.

Furukawa positioned herself 10 feet away from Bell, front row, center. She had a huge grin on her face. The grin, and Furukawa, remained planted in that spot until the end.

"It was the most astonishing thing I've ever seen in Washington," Furukawa says. "Joshua Bell was standing there playing at rush hour, and people were not stopping, and not even looking, and some were flipping quarters at him! Quarters! I wouldn't do that to anybody. I was thinking, Omigosh, what kind of a city do I live in that this could happen?"

When it was over, Furukawa introduced herself to Bell and tossed in a twenty. Not counting that—it was tainted by recognition—the final haul for his forty-three minutes of playing was $32.17. Yes, some people gave pennies.

"Actually," Bell said with a laugh, "that's not so bad, considering. That's forty bucks an hour. I could make an okay living doing this, and I wouldn't have to pay an agent."

THESE DAYS, AT L'Enfant Plaza, lotto ticket sales remain brisk. Musicians still show up from time to time, and they still tick off Edna Souza. Joshua Bell's latest album, *The Voice of the Violin*, has received the usual critical acclaim. ("Delicate urgency." "Masterful intimacy." "Unfailingly exquisite." "A musical summit." ". . . will make your heart thump and weep at the same time.")

Bell headed off on a concert tour of European capitals. But he is back in the States this week. He has to be. On Tuesday, he will be accepting the Avery Fisher Prize, recognizing the Flop of L'Enfant Plaza as the finest classical musician in America.

About the Author

GENE WEINGARTEN IS an essayist, a feature writer, and the nationally syndicated humor columnist for *The Washington Post*. He has written three books: *The Hypochondriac's Guide to Life. And Death.* (Simon & Schuster, 1998); *I'm with Stupid* (with Gina Barreca, Simon & Schuster, 2004); and *Old Dogs* (with Michael S. Williamson, Simon & Schuster, 2008). His story about violinist Joshua Bell playing in the Washington, D.C., Metro won the 2008 Pulitzer Prize in Feature Writing. In 2010 Weingarten won a second Pulitzer Prize in Feature Writing for a story about parents who accidentally leave their infant children to die in cars.

Together with his son, Dan, and cartoonist David Clark, Weingarten has created a new daily comic strip, *Barney & Clyde,* which is scheduled for release by The Washington Post Writers Group in summer 2010.